# Constitutional Law

**Fifth Edition**

*2018 Supplement*

2018 Supplement

# Constitutional Law

**Fifth Edition**

**Erwin Chemerinsky**
*Dean and Jesse H. Choper Distinguished Professor of Law*
*University of California, Berkeley School of Law*

Wolters Kluwer

Published by Wolters Kluwer in New York.

Wolters Kluwer Legal & Regulatory U.S. serves customers worldwide with CCH, Aspen Publishers, and Kluwer Law International products. (www.WKLegaledu.com)

To contact Customer Service, e-mail customer.service@wolterskluwer.com, call 1-800-234-1660, fax 1-800-901-9075, or mail correspondence to:

>   Wolters Kluwer
>   Attn: Order Department
>   PO Box 990
>   Frederick, MD 21705

Printed in the United States of America.

1 2 3 4 5 6 7 8 9 0

ISBN 978-1-4548-9466-7

# About Wolters Kluwer Legal & Regulatory U.S.

Wolters Kluwer Legal & Regulatory U.S. delivers expert content and solutions in the areas of law, corporate compliance, health compliance, reimbursement, and legal education. Its practical solutions help customers successfully navigate the demands of a changing environment to drive their daily activities, enhance decision quality and inspire confident outcomes.

Serving customers worldwide, its legal and regulatory portfolio includes products under the Aspen Publishers, CCH Incorporated, Kluwer Law International, ftwilliam.com and MediRegs names. They are regarded as exceptional and trusted resources for general legal and practice-specific knowledge, compliance and risk management, dynamic workflow solutions, and expert commentary.

# Contents

# Preface

This Supplement presents the Supreme Court's decisions from October Terms 2016 and 2017.

October Term 2017 was filled with a number of exceptionally important cases. Many could be covered at different places in constitutional law courses. For example, the decision on President Trump's "travel ban"—*Trump v. Hawaii*—is presented in Chapter 3 on presidential power, but could be in Chapter 10 on religious freedom. *Gill v. Whitford*, on partisan gerrymandering, was decided on standing grounds, and is thus presented in Chapter 1, but could be covered in the discussion of voting in Chapter 8. *Masterpiece Cake Shop v. Colorado Civil Rights Commission* was decided based on free exercise of religion, and thus is presented in Chapter 10, but it also raises issues of freedom of speech (though they were not the basis for the decision).

Other major cases in the Supplement are:

Chapter 2—*Murphy v. NCAA* (2018)—concerning the Tenth Amendment

Chapter 3—*Lucia v. Securities and Exchange Commission* (2018)—on the distinction between officers of the United States and government employees

Chapter 4—*South Dakota v. Wayfair* (2018)—regarding the ability of states to require that businesses collect sales tax even if they do not have a physical presence in the state

Chapter 6—*Murr v. Wisconsin* (2017)—concerning the takings clause and how to determine what is the "property."

Chapter 7—*Bethune Hill v. Virginia State Board of Elections* (2017) and *Cooper v. Harris* (2017)—concerning the use of race in drawing election district lines. Also presented is *Pena-Rodriguez v. Colorado* (2017) on race and jury deliberations.

Chapter 8—*Pavan v. Smith* (2017)—regarding the constitutionality of denying a married same-sex couple the ability to list both parents on a child's birth certificate.

Chapter 9—four free speech cases are presented: *Matal v. Tam* (2017), *NIFLA v. Becerra* (2018), *Packingham v. North Carolina* (2017), and *Expressions Hair Design v. Schneiderman* (2017).

Chapter 10—*Trinity Lutheran, Columbia, Missouri v. Pauley* (2017), involved whether the denial of aid to a religious institution infringed free exercise of religion.

I will continue to prepare a Supplement each summer and a new edition every four years. I welcome comments and suggestions from users of the casebook and the supplement.

Erwin Chemerinsky
Berkeley, California
July 2018

# Constitutional Law

**Fifth Edition**

*2018 Supplement*

# Chapter 1

# The Federal Judicial Power

## B. Limits on the Federal Judicial Power

## 3. Justiciability Limits

### b. Standing (casebook p. 45)

In *Gill v Whitford*, the Court considered whether federal courts can hear challenges to partisan gerrymandering, the practice where the political party controlling the legislature draws election districts to maximize safe seats for their party. In *Vieth v. Jubelirer* (casebook p. 96), the Court held that such challenges pose a non-justiciable political question. In *Gill*, the Court dismissed the case for lack of standing. But notice Justice Kagan's concurring opinion expresses the view (for four justices) as to how standing can be established and why partisan gerrymandering violates the Constitution.

GILL v. WHITFORD
138 S. Ct. 1916 (2018)

Chief Justice ROBERTS delivered the opinion of the Court.

The State of Wisconsin, like most other States, entrusts to its legislature the periodic task of redrawing the boundaries of the State's legislative districts. A group of Wisconsin Democratic voters filed a complaint in the District Court, alleging that the legislature carried out this task with an eye to diminishing the ability of Wisconsin Democrats to convert Democratic votes into Democratic seats in the legislature. The plaintiffs asserted that, in so doing, the legislature had infringed their rights under the First and Fourteenth Amendments.

But a plaintiff seeking relief in federal court must first demonstrate that he has standing to do so, including that he has "a personal stake in the outcome," distinct from a "generally available grievance about government." That threshold requirement "ensures that we act *as judges*, and do not engage in policymaking properly left to elected representatives." Certain of the plaintiffs before us alleged that they had such a personal stake in this case, but never followed up with the requisite proof. The District Court and this Court therefore lack the power to resolve their claims. We vacate the judgment and remand the case for further proceedings, in the course of which those plaintiffs may attempt to demonstrate standing in accord with the analysis in this opinion.

## I

Wisconsin's Legislature consists of a State Assembly and a State Senate. The 99 members of the Assembly are chosen from single districts that must "consist of contiguous territory and be in as compact form as practicable." State senators are likewise chosen from single-member districts, which are laid on top of the State Assembly districts so that three Assembly districts form one Senate district.

The Wisconsin Constitution gives the legislature the responsibility to "apportion and district anew the members of the senate and assembly" at the first session following each census. In recent decades, however, that responsibility has just as often been taken up by federal courts. Following the census in 1980, 1990, and 2000, federal courts drew the State's legislative districts when the Legislature and the Governor—split on party lines—were unable to agree on new districting plans. The Legislature has broken the logjam just twice in the last 40 years. In 1983, a Democratic Legislature passed, and a Democratic Governor signed, a new districting plan that remained in effect until the 1990 census. In 2011, a Republican Legislature passed, and a Republican Governor signed, the districting plan at issue here, known as Act 43. Following the passage of Act 43, Republicans won majorities in the State Assembly in the 2012 and 2014 elections. In 2012, Republicans won 60 Assembly seats with 48.6% of the two-party statewide vote for Assembly candidates. In 2014, Republicans won 63 Assembly seats with 52% of the statewide vote.

In July 2015, twelve Wisconsin voters filed a complaint in the Western District of Wisconsin challenging Act 43. The plaintiffs identified themselves as "supporters of the public policies espoused by the Democratic Party and of Democratic Party candidates." They alleged that Act 43 is a partisan gerrymander that "unfairly favor[s] Republican voters and candidates," and that it does so by "cracking" and "packing" Democratic voters around Wisconsin. As they explained:

Cracking means dividing a party's supporters among multiple districts so that they fall short of a majority in each one. Packing means concentrating one party's backers in a few districts that they win by overwhelming margins.

Four of the plaintiffs—Mary Lynne Donohue, Wendy Sue Johnson, Janet Mitchell, and Jerome Wallace—alleged that they lived in State Assembly districts where Democrats have been cracked or packed. All of the plaintiffs also alleged that, regardless of "whether they themselves reside in a district that has been packed or cracked," they have been "harmed by the manipulation of district boundaries" because Democrats statewide "do not have the same opportunity provided to Republicans to elect representatives of their choice to the Assembly."

The plaintiffs argued that, on a statewide level, the degree to which packing and cracking has favored one party over another can be measured by a single calculation: an "efficiency gap" that compares each party's respective "wasted" votes across all legislative districts. "Wasted" votes are those cast for a losing candidate or for a winning candidate in excess of what that candidate needs to win. The plaintiffs alleged that Act 43 resulted in an unusually large efficiency gap that favored Republicans. They also submitted a "Demonstration Plan" that, they asserted, met all of the legal criteria for apportionment, but was at the same time "almost perfectly balanced in its partisan consequences." They argued that because Act 43 generated a large and unnecessary efficiency gap in favor of Republicans, it violated the First Amendment right of association of Wisconsin Democratic voters and their Fourteenth Amendment right to equal protection. The plaintiffs named several members of the state election commission as defendants in the action.

At the close of evidence [at a trial], the District Court concluded—over the dissent of Judge Griesbach—that the plaintiffs had proved a violation of the First and Fourteenth Amendments. The court set out a three-part test for identifying unconstitutional gerrymanders: A redistricting map violates the First Amendment and the Equal Protection Clause of the Fourteenth Amendment if it "(1) is intended to place a severe impediment on the effectiveness of the votes of individual citizens on the basis of their political affiliation, (2) has that effect, and (3) cannot be justified on other, legitimate legislative grounds."

The court went on to find, based on evidence concerning the manner in which Act 43 had been adopted, that "one of the purposes of Act 43 was to secure Republican control of the Assembly under any likely future electoral scenario for the remainder of the decade." It also found that the "more efficient distribution of Republican voters has allowed the Republican

Party to translate its votes into seats with significantly greater ease and to achieve—and preserve—control of the Wisconsin legislature." As to the third prong of its test, the District Court concluded that the burdens the Act 43 map imposed on Democrats could not be explained by "legitimate state prerogatives [or] neutral factors." The court recognized that "Wisconsin's political geography, particularly the high concentration of Democratic voters in urban centers like Milwaukee and Madison, affords the Republican Party a natural, but modest, advantage in the districting process," but found that this inherent geographic disparity did not account for the magnitude of the Republican advantage.

Regarding standing, the court held that the plaintiffs had a "cognizable equal protection right against state-imposed barriers on [their] ability to vote effectively for the party of [their] choice." It concluded that Act 43 "prevent[ed] Wisconsin Democrats from being able to translate their votes into seats as effectively as Wisconsin Republicans," and that "Wisconsin Democrats, therefore, have suffered a personal injury to their Equal Protection rights." The court turned away the defendants' argument that the plaintiffs' injury was not sufficiently particularized by finding that "[t]he harm that the plaintiffs have experienced . . . is one shared by Democratic voters in the State of Wisconsin. The dilution of their votes is both personal and acute."

The District Court enjoined the defendants from using the Act 43 map in future elections and ordered them to have a remedial districting plan in place no later than November 1, 2017.

## II

### A

Over the past five decades this Court has been repeatedly asked to decide what judicially enforceable limits, if any, the Constitution sets on the gerrymandering of voters along partisan lines. Our previous attempts at an answer have left few clear landmarks for addressing the question. What our precedents have to say on the topic is, however, instructive as to the myriad competing considerations that partisan gerrymandering claims involve. Our efforts to sort through those considerations have generated conflicting views both of how to conceive of the injury arising from partisan gerrymandering and of the appropriate role for the Federal Judiciary in remedying that injury.

At argument on appeal in this case, counsel for the plaintiffs argued that this Court *can* address the problem of partisan gerrymandering because it *must*: The Court should exercise its power here because it is the "only institution in the United States" capable of "solv[ing] this problem." Such invitations must be answered with care. "Failure of political will does not justify unconstitutional remedies." Our power as judges to "say what the law is," *Marbury v. Madison* (1803), rests not on the default of politically accountable officers, but is instead grounded in and limited by the necessity of resolving, according to legal principles, a plaintiff's particular claim of legal right.

Our considerable efforts in [earlier cases about partisan gerrymandering] leave unresolved whether such claims may be brought in cases involving allegations of partisan gerrymandering. In particular, two threshold questions remain: what is necessary to show standing in a case of this sort, and whether those claims are justiciable. Here we do not decide the latter question because the plaintiffs in this case have not shown standing under the theory upon which they based their claims for relief.

To ensure that the Federal Judiciary respects "the proper—and properly limited—role of the courts in a democratic society," a plaintiff may not invoke federal-court jurisdiction unless he can show "a personal stake in the outcome of the controversy." A federal court is not "a forum for generalized grievances," and the requirement of such a personal stake "ensures that courts exercise power that is judicial in nature." We enforce that requirement by insisting that a plaintiff satisfy the familiar three-part test for Article III standing: that he "(1) suffered an injury in fact, (2) that is fairly traceable to the challenged conduct of the defendant, and (3) that is likely to be redressed by a favorable judicial decision." Foremost among these requirements is injury in fact—a plaintiff's pleading and proof that he has suffered the "invasion of a legally protected interest" that is "concrete and particularized," *i.e.*, which "affect [s] the plaintiff in a personal and individual way."

We have long recognized that a person's right to vote is "individual and personal in nature." Thus, "voters who allege facts showing disadvantage to themselves as individuals have standing to sue" to remedy that disadvantage. The plaintiffs in this case alleged that they suffered such injury from partisan gerrymandering, which works through "packing" and "cracking" voters of one party to disadvantage those voters. That is, the plaintiffs claim a constitutional right not to be placed in legislative districts deliberately designed to "waste" their votes in elections where their chosen candidates will win in landslides (packing) or are destined to lose by closer margins (cracking).

To the extent the plaintiffs' alleged harm is the dilution of their votes, that injury is district specific. An individual voter in Wisconsin is placed in a single district. He votes for a single representative. The boundaries of the district, and the composition of its voters, determine whether and to what extent a particular voter is packed or cracked. This "disadvantage to [the voter] as [an] individual[ ]," therefore results from the boundaries of the particular district in which he resides. And a plaintiff's remedy must be "limited to the inadequacy that produced [his] injury in fact." In this case the remedy that is proper and sufficient lies in the revision of the boundaries of the individual's own district.

For similar reasons, we have held that a plaintiff who alleges that he is the object of a racial gerrymander—a drawing of district lines on the basis of race—has standing to assert only that his own district has been so gerrymandered. A plaintiff who complains of gerrymandering, but who does not live in a gerrymandered district, "assert[s] only a generalized grievance against governmental conduct of which he or she does not approve." Plaintiffs who complain of racial gerrymandering in their State cannot sue to invalidate the whole State's legislative districting map; such complaints must proceed "district-by-district."

The plaintiffs argue that their claim of statewide injury is analogous to the claims presented in *Baker* and *Reynolds*, which they assert were "statewide in nature" because they rested on allegations that "districts *throughout a state* [had] been malapportioned." But, as we have already noted, the holdings in *Baker* and *Reynolds* were expressly premised on the understanding that the injuries giving rise to those claims were "individual and personal in nature," because the claims were brought by voters who alleged "facts showing disadvantage to themselves as individuals."

The plaintiffs' mistaken insistence that the claims in *Baker* and *Reynolds* were "statewide in nature" rests on a failure to distinguish injury from remedy. In those malapportionment cases, the only way to vindicate an individual plaintiff's right to an equally weighted vote was through a wholesale "restructuring of the geographical distribution of seats in a state legislature." Here, the plaintiffs' partisan gerrymandering claims turn on allegations that their votes have been diluted. That harm arises from the particular composition of the voter's own district, which causes his vote—having been packed or cracked—to carry less weight than it would carry in another, hypothetical district. Remedying the individual voter's harm, therefore, does not necessarily require restructuring all of the State's legislative districts. It requires revising only such districts as are necessary to reshape the voter's district—so that the voter may be unpacked or uncracked, as the case may be. This fits the rule that a "remedy must of course be limited to the inadequacy that produced the injury in fact that the plaintiff has established."

The plaintiffs argue that their legal injury is not limited to the injury that they have suffered as individual voters, but extends also to the statewide harm to their interest "in their collective representation in the legislature," and in influencing the legislature's overall "composition and policymaking." But our cases to date have not found that this presents an individual and personal injury of the kind required for Article III standing. On the facts of this case, the plaintiffs may not rely on "the kind of undifferentiated, generalized grievance about the conduct of government that we have refused to countenance in the past." A citizen's interest in the overall composition of the legislature is embodied in his right to vote for his representative. And the citizen's abstract interest in policies adopted by the legislature on the facts here is a nonjusticiable "general interest common to all members of the public."

Four of the plaintiffs in this case—Mary Lynne Donohue, Wendy Sue Johnson, Janet Mitchell, and Jerome Wallace—pleaded a particularized burden along such lines. They alleged that Act 43 had "dilut[ed] the influence" of their votes as a result of packing or cracking in their legislative districts. The facts necessary to establish standing, however, must not only be alleged at the pleading stage, but also proved at trial. As the proceedings in the District Court progressed to trial, the plaintiffs failed to meaningfully pursue their allegations of individual harm. The plaintiffs did not seek to show such requisite harm since, on this record, it appears that not a single plaintiff sought to prove that he or she lives in a cracked or packed district. They instead rested their case at trial—and their arguments before this Court—on their theory of statewide injury to Wisconsin Democrats.

## III

In cases where a plaintiff fails to demonstrate Article III standing, we usually direct the dismissal of the plaintiff's claims. This is not the usual case. It concerns an unsettled kind of claim this Court has not agreed upon, the contours and justiciability of which are unresolved. Under the circumstances, and in light of the plaintiffs' allegations that Donohue, Johnson, Mitchell, and Wallace live in districts where Democrats like them have been packed or cracked, we decline to direct dismissal.

We therefore remand the case to the District Court so that the plaintiffs may have an opportunity to prove concrete and particularized injuries using evidence—unlike the bulk of the evidence presented thus far—that would tend to demonstrate a burden on their individual votes. We express no view on the merits of the plaintiffs' case. We caution, however, that "standing is not dispensed in gross": A plaintiff's remedy must be tailored to redress the plaintiff's particular injury.

Justice KAGAN, with whom Justice GINSBURG, Justice BREYER, and Justice SOTOMAYOR join, concurring.

The Court holds today that a plaintiff asserting a partisan gerrymandering claim based on a theory of vote dilution must prove that she lives in a packed or cracked district in order to establish standing. The Court also holds that none of the plaintiffs here have yet made that required showing.

I agree with both conclusions, and with the Court's decision to remand this case to allow the plaintiffs to prove that they live in packed or cracked districts. I write to address in more detail what kind of evidence the present plaintiffs (or any additional ones) must offer to support that allegation. And I write to make some observations about what would happen if they succeed in proving standing—that is, about how their vote dilution case could then proceed on the merits. The key point is that the case could go forward in much the same way it did below: Given the charges of statewide packing and cracking, affecting a slew of districts and residents, the challengers could make use of statewide evidence and seek a statewide remedy.

I also write separately because I think the plaintiffs may have wanted to do more than present a vote dilution theory. Partisan gerrymandering no doubt burdens individual votes, but it also causes other harms. And at some points in this litigation, the plaintiffs complained of a different injury—an infringement of their First Amendment right of association. The Court rightly does not address that alternative argument: The plaintiffs did not advance it with sufficient clarity or concreteness to make it a real part of the case. But because on remand they may well develop the associational theory, I address the standing requirement that would then apply. As I'll explain, a plaintiff presenting such a theory would not need to show that her particular voting district was packed or cracked for standing purposes because that fact would bear no connection to her substantive claim. Indeed, everything about the litigation of that claim—from standing on down to remedy—would be statewide in nature.

Partisan gerrymandering, as this Court has recognized, is "incompatible with democratic principles." More effectively every day, that practice enables politicians to entrench themselves in power against the people's will. And only the courts can do anything to remedy the problem, because gerrymanders benefit those who control the political branches. None of those facts gives judges any excuse to disregard Article III's demands. The Court is right to say they were not met here. But partisan gerrymandering injures enough individuals and organizations in enough concrete ways to ensure that standing requirements, properly applied, will not often or long prevent courts from reaching the merits of cases like this one. Or from insisting, when they do, that partisan officials stop degrading the nation's democracy.

## I

As the Court explains, the plaintiffs' theory in this case focuses on vote dilution. That is, the plaintiffs assert that Wisconsin's State Assembly Map has caused their votes "to carry less weight than [they] would carry in another, hypothetical district." And the mechanism used to wreak that harm is "packing" and "cracking." In a relatively few districts, the mapmakers packed supermajorities of Democratic voters—well beyond the number needed for a Democratic candidate to prevail. And in many more districts, dispersed throughout the State, the mapmakers cracked Democratic voters—spreading them sufficiently thin to prevent them from electing their preferred candidates. The result of both practices is to "waste" Democrats' votes.

The harm of vote dilution, as this Court has long stated, is "individual and personal in nature." It arises when an election practice—most commonly, the drawing of district lines—devalues one citizen's vote as compared to others. Of course, such practices invariably affect more than one citizen at a time. For example, our original one-person, one-vote cases considered how malapportioned maps "contract[ed] the value" of urban citizens' votes while "expand[ing]" the value of rural citizens' votes. But we understood the injury as giving diminished weight to each particular vote, even if millions were so touched. In such cases, a voter living in an overpopulated district suffered "disadvantage to [herself] as [an] individual [ ]": Her vote counted for less than the votes of other citizens in her State. And that kind of disadvantage is what a plaintiff asserting a vote dilution claim—in the one-person, one-vote context or any other—always alleges.

To have standing to bring a partisan gerrymandering claim based on vote dilution, then, a plaintiff must prove that the value of her own vote has been "contract[ed]." And that entails showing, as the Court holds, that she lives in a district that has been either packed or cracked. For packing and cracking are the ways in which a partisan gerrymander dilutes votes. Consider the perfect form of each variety. When a voter resides in a packed district, her preferred candidate will win no matter what; when a voter lives in a cracked district, her chosen candidate stands no chance of prevailing. But either way, such a citizen's vote carries less weight—has less consequence—than it would under a neutrally drawn map. So when she shows that her district has been packed or cracked, she proves, as she must to establish standing, that she is "among the injured."

In many partisan gerrymandering cases, that threshold showing will not be hard to make. Among other ways of proving packing or cracking, a plaintiff could produce an alternative map (or set of alternative maps)—comparably consistent with traditional districting principles—under which her vote would carry more weight. For example, a Democratic plaintiff living in a 75%-Democratic district could prove she was packed by presenting a different map, drawn without a focus on partisan advantage, that would place her in a 60%-Democratic district. Or conversely, a Democratic plaintiff residing in a 35%-Democratic district could prove she was cracked by offering an alternative, neutrally drawn map putting her in a 50-50 district. The precise numbers are of no import. The point is that the plaintiff can show, through drawing alternative district lines, that partisan-based packing or cracking diluted her vote.

[T]he government allegedly packed and cracked Democrats throughout the State, not just in a particular district or region. Assuming that is true, the plaintiffs should have a mass of packing and cracking proof, which they can now also present in district-by-district form to support their standing. In other words, a plaintiff residing in each affected district can show, through an alternative map or other evidence, that packing or cracking indeed occurred there. And if (or to the extent) that test is met, the court can proceed to decide all distinctive merits issues and award appropriate remedies.

When the court addresses those merits questions, it can consider statewide (as well as local) evidence. But assume that the plaintiffs must prove illicit partisan intent—a purpose to dilute Democrats' votes in drawing district lines. The plaintiffs could then offer evidence about the mapmakers' goals in formulating the entire statewide map (which would predictably carry down to individual districting decisions). So, for example, the plaintiffs here introduced proof that the mapmakers looked to partisan voting data when drawing districts throughout the State—and that they graded draft maps according to the amount of advantage those maps conferred on Republicans. This Court has explicitly recognized the relevance of such statewide evidence in addressing racial gerrymandering claims of a district-specific nature. "Voters," we held, "of course[ ] can present statewide *evidence* in order to prove racial gerrymandering in a particular district." And in particular, "[s]uch evidence is perfectly relevant" to showing that mapmakers had an invidious "motive" in drawing the lines of "multiple districts in the State." The same should be true for partisan gerrymandering.

## II

Everything said so far relates only to suits alleging that a partisan gerrymander dilutes individual votes. That is the way the Court sees this litigation. And as I'll discuss, that is the most reasonable view. But partisan gerrymanders inflict other kinds of constitutional harm as well. Among those injuries, partisan gerrymanders may infringe the First Amendment rights of association held by parties, other political organizations, and their members. The plaintiffs here have sometimes pointed to that kind of harm. To the extent they meant to do so, and choose to do so on remand, their associational claim would occasion a different standing inquiry than the one in the Court's opinion.

Justice Kennedy explained the First Amendment associational injury deriving from a partisan gerrymander in his concurring opinion in *Vieth* [v. *Jubelirer*]. "Representative democracy," Justice Kennedy pointed out, is today "unimaginable without the ability of citizens to band together" to advance their political beliefs. That means significant "First Amendment concerns arise" when a State purposely "subject[s] a group of voters or their party to disfavored treatment." Such action "burden[s] a group of voters' representational rights." And it does so because of their "political association," "participation in the electoral process," "voting history," or "expression of political views."

As so formulated, the associational harm of a partisan gerrymander is distinct from vote dilution. Consider an active member of the Democratic Party in Wisconsin who resides in a district that a partisan gerrymander has left untouched (neither packed nor cracked). His individual vote carries no less weight than it did before. But if the gerrymander ravaged the party he works to support, then he indeed suffers harm, as do all other involved members of that party. This is the kind of "burden" to "a group of voters' representational rights" Justice Kennedy spoke of. Members of the "disfavored party" in the State, deprived of their natural political strength by a partisan gerrymander, may face difficulties fundraising, registering voters, attracting volunteers, generating support from independents, and recruiting candidates to run for office (not to mention eventually accomplishing their policy objectives). By placing a state party at an enduring electoral disadvantage, the gerrymander weakens its capacity to perform all its functions.

III

Partisan gerrymandering jeopardizes "[t]he ordered working of our Republic, and of the democratic process." It enables a party that happens to be in power at the right time to entrench itself there for a decade or more, no matter what the voters would prefer. At its most extreme, the practice amounts to "rigging elections." It thus violates the most fundamental of all democratic principles — that "the voters should choose their representatives, not the other way around."

And our history offers little comfort. Yes, partisan gerrymandering goes back to the Republic's earliest days; and yes, American democracy has survived. But technology makes today's gerrymandering altogether different from the crude linedrawing of the past. New redistricting software enables pinpoint precision in designing districts. With such tools, mapmakers can capture every last bit of partisan advantage, while still meeting traditional districting requirements (compactness, contiguity, and the like). Gerrymanders have thus become ever more extreme and durable, insulating officeholders against all but the most titanic shifts in the political tides. The 2010 redistricting cycle produced some of the worst partisan gerrymanders on record. The technology will only get better, so the 2020 cycle will only get worse.

Courts have a critical role to play in curbing partisan gerrymandering. Over fifty years ago, we committed to providing judicial review in the redistricting arena, because we understood that "a denial of constitutionally protected rights demands judicial protection." Indeed, the need for judicial review is at its most urgent in these cases. For here, politicians' incentives conflict with voters' interests, leaving citizens without any political remedy for their constitutional harms. Of course, their dire need provides no warrant for courts to disregard Article III. Because of the way this suit was litigated, I agree that the plaintiffs have so far failed to establish their standing to sue, and I fully concur in the Court's opinion. But of one thing we may unfortunately be sure. Courts — and in particular this Court — will again be called on to redress extreme partisan gerrymanders. I am hopeful we will then step up to our responsibility to vindicate the Constitution against a contrary law.

Justice THOMAS, with whom Justice GORSUCH joins, concurring in part and concurring in the judgment.

I join Parts I and II of the Court's opinion because I agree that the plaintiffs have failed to prove Article III standing. I do not join Part III, which gives the plaintiffs another chance to prove their standing on remand.

When a plaintiff lacks standing, our ordinary practice is to remand the case with instructions to dismiss for lack of jurisdiction. The Court departs from our usual practice because this is supposedly "not the usual case." But there is nothing unusual about it. As the Court explains, the plaintiffs' lack of standing follows from long-established principles of law. After a year and a half of litigation in the District Court, including a 4-day trial, the plaintiffs had a more-than-ample opportunity to prove their standing under these principles. They failed to do so. Accordingly, I would have remanded this case with instructions to dismiss.

# Chapter 2

# The Federal Legislative Power

## C.  The Commerce Power

### 4.  1990s-???: Narrowing of the Commerce Power and Revival of the Tenth Amendment as a Limit on Congress

#### b.  *Does the Tenth Amendment Limit Congress's Authority?* (casebook p. 217)

In *New York v. United States* (casebook p. 217) and *Printz v. United States* (casebook p. 227), the Court held that Congress cannot "commandeer" state and local governments by forcing them to adopt laws or enforce federal mandates. The Court applied this in *Murphy v. NCAA.*

MURPHY v. NATIONAL COLLEGIATE ATHLETIC ASSOCIATION
138 S. Ct. 1461 (2018)

Justice ALITO delivered the opinion of the Court.

The State of New Jersey wants to legalize sports gambling at casinos and horseracing tracks, but a federal law, the Professional and Amateur Sports Protection Act, generally makes it unlawful for a State to "authorize" sports gambling schemes. We must decide whether this provision is compatible with the system of "dual sovereignty" embodied in the Constitution.

I

Americans have never been of one mind about gambling, and attitudes have swung back and forth. By the end of the 19th century, gambling was largely banned throughout the country, but beginning in the 1920s and 1930s, laws prohibiting gambling were gradually loosened.

New Jersey's experience is illustrative. In 1897, New Jersey adopted a constitutional amendment that barred all gambling in the State. But during the Depression, the State permitted parimutuel betting on horse races as a way of increasing state revenue, and in 1953, churches and other nonprofit organizations were allowed to host bingo games. In 1970, New Jersey became the third State to run a state lottery, and within five years, 10 other States followed suit.

By the 1960s, Atlantic City, "once the most fashionable resort of the Atlantic Coast," had fallen on hard times, and casino gambling came to be seen as a way to revitalize the city. In 1974, a referendum on state-wide legalization failed, but two years later, voters approved a narrower measure allowing casino gambling in Atlantic City alone. At that time, Nevada was the only other State with legal casinos, and thus for a while the Atlantic City casinos had an east coast monopoly. "With 60 million people living within a one-tank car trip away," Atlantic City became "the most popular tourist destination in the United States." But that favorable situation eventually came to an end.

With the enactment of the Indian Gaming Regulatory Act in 1988, casinos opened on Indian land throughout the country. Some were located within driving distance of Atlantic City, and nearby States (and many others) legalized casino gambling. But Nevada remained the only state venue for legal sports gambling in casinos, and sports gambling is immensely popular.

Sports gambling, however, has long had strong opposition. Opponents argue that it is particularly addictive and especially attractive to young people with a strong interest in sports, and in the past gamblers corrupted and seriously damaged the reputation of professional and amateur sports. Apprehensive about the potential effects of sports gambling, professional sports leagues and the National Collegiate Athletic Association (NCAA) long opposed legalization.

By the 1990s, there were signs that the trend that had brought about the legalization of many other forms of gambling might extend to sports gambling, and this sparked federal efforts to stem the tide. Opponents of sports gambling turned to the legislation now before us, the Professional and Amateur Sports Protection Act (PASPA). PASPA's proponents argued that it would protect young people, and one of the bill's sponsors, Senator Bill Bradley of New Jersey, a former college and professional basketball star, stressed that the law was needed to safeguard the integrity of sports.

PASPA's most important provision, part of which is directly at issue in these cases, makes it "unlawful" for a State or any of its subdivisions "to sponsor, operate, advertise, promote, license, or authorize by law or compact . . . a lottery, sweepstakes, or other betting, gambling, or wagering scheme based . . . on" competitive sporting events. § 3702(1). In parallel, § 3702(2) makes it "unlawful" for "a person to sponsor, operate, advertise, or promote" those same gambling schemes—but only if this is done "pursuant to the law or compact of a governmental entity." PASPA does not make sports gambling a federal crime (and thus was not anticipated to impose a significant law enforcement burden on the Federal Government). Instead, PASPA allows the Attorney General, as well as professional and amateur sports organizations, to bring civil actions to enjoin violations.

At the time of PASPA's adoption, a few jurisdictions allowed some form of sports gambling. In Nevada, sports gambling was legal in casinos, and three States hosted sports lotteries or allowed sports pools. PASPA contains "grandfather" provisions allowing these activities to continue. Another provision gave New Jersey the option of legalizing sports gambling in Atlantic City—provided that it did so within one year of the law's effective date.

New Jersey did not take advantage of this special option, but by 2011, with Atlantic City facing stiff competition, the State had a change of heart. New Jersey voters approved an amendment to the State Constitution making it lawful for the legislature to authorize sports gambling, and in 2012 the legislature enacted a law doing just that.

The 2012 Act quickly came under attack. The major professional sports leagues and the NCAA brought an action in federal court against the New Jersey Governor and other state officials (hereinafter New Jersey), seeking to enjoin the new law on the ground that it violated PASPA. [The New Jersey law was struck down].

[T]he New Jersey Legislature enacted the law now before us. The 2014 Act declares that it is not to be interpreted as causing the State to authorize, license, sponsor, operate, advertise, or promote sports gambling. Instead, it is framed as a repealer. Specifically, it repeals the provisions of state law prohibiting sports gambling insofar as they concerned the "placement and acceptance of wagers" on sporting events by persons 21 years of age or older at a horseracing track or a casino or gambling house in Atlantic City. The new law also specified that the repeal was effective only as to wagers on sporting events not involving a New Jersey college team or a collegiate event taking place in the State.

Predictably, the same plaintiffs promptly commenced a new action in federal court. They won in the District Court, and the case was eventually heard by the Third Circuit sitting en banc. The en banc court affirmed, finding that the new law, no less than the old one, violated PASPA by "author[izing]" sports gambling.

II

Before considering the constitutionality of the PASPA provision prohibiting States from "author[izing]" sports gambling, we first examine its
meaning. The parties advance dueling interpretations, and this dispute
has an important bearing on the constitutional issue that we must decide.
Neither respondents nor the United States, appearing as an *amicus* in support of respondents, contends that the provision at issue would be constitutional if petitioners' interpretation is correct. Indeed, the United States
expressly concedes that the provision is unconstitutional if it means what
petitioners claim.

Petitioners argue that the anti-authorization provision requires States to
maintain their existing laws against sports gambling without alteration.
One of the accepted meanings of the term "authorize," they point out, is
"permit." They therefore contend that any state law that has the effect of
permitting sports gambling, including a law totally or partially repealing a
prior prohibition, amounts to an authorization.

Respondents interpret the provision more narrowly. They claim that the
*primary* definition of "authorize" requires affirmative action. To authorize,
they maintain, means "'[t]o empower; to give a right or authority to act; to
endow with authority.'" And this, they say, is precisely what the 2014 Act
does: It empowers a defined group of entities, and it endows them with the
authority to conduct sports gambling operations. Respondents do not take
the position that PASPA bans all modifications of old laws against sports
gambling, but just how far they think a modification could go is not clear.

In our view, petitioners' interpretation is correct: When a State completely or partially repeals old laws banning sports gambling, it "authorize[s]" that activity. This is clear when the state-law landscape at the time
of PASPA's enactment is taken into account. At that time, all forms of
sports gambling were illegal in the great majority of States, and in that
context, the competing definitions offered by the parties lead to the same
conclusion. The repeal of a state law banning sports gambling not only
"permits" sports gambling (petitioners' favored definition); it also gives
those now free to conduct a sports betting operation the "right or authority to act"; it "empowers" them (respondents' and the United States's
definition).

The concept of state "authorization" makes sense only against a backdrop of prohibition or regulation. A State is not regarded as authorizing
everything that it does not prohibit or regulate. No one would use the
term in that way. For example, no one would say that a State "authorizes" its residents to brush their teeth or eat apples or sing in the shower.

We commonly speak of state authorization only if the activity in question would otherwise be restricted.

## III

The anticommandeering doctrine may sound arcane, but it is simply the expression of a fundamental structural decision incorporated into the Constitution, *i.e.*, the decision to withhold from Congress the power to issue orders directly to the States. When the original States declared their independence, they claimed the powers inherent in sovereignty—in the words of the Declaration of Independence, the authority "to do all . . . Acts and Things which Independent States may of right do." The Constitution limited but did not abolish the sovereign powers of the States, which retained "a residuary and inviolable sovereignty." Thus, both the Federal Government and the States wield sovereign powers, and that is why our system of government is said to be one of "dual sovereignty."

The legislative powers granted to Congress are sizable, but they are not unlimited. The Constitution confers on Congress not plenary legislative power but only certain enumerated powers. Therefore, all other legislative power is reserved for the States, as the Tenth Amendment confirms. And conspicuously absent from the list of powers given to Congress is the power to issue direct orders to the governments of the States. The anticommandeering doctrine simply represents the recognition of this limit on congressional authority.

Although the anticommandeering principle is simple and basic, it did not emerge in our cases until relatively recently, when Congress attempted in a few isolated instances to extend its authority in unprecedented ways.

Our opinions in *New York* and *Printz* explained why adherence to the anticommandeering principle is important. Without attempting a complete survey, we mention several reasons that are significant here. First, the rule serves as "one of the Constitution's structural protections of liberty." "The Constitution does not protect the sovereignty of States for the benefit of the States or state governments as abstract political entities." "To the contrary, the Constitution divides authority between federal and state governments for the protection of individuals." "'[A] healthy balance of power between the States and the Federal Government [reduces] the risk of tyranny and abuse from either front.'"

Second, the anticommandeering rule promotes political accountability. When Congress itself regulates, the responsibility for the benefits and burdens of the regulation is apparent. Voters who like or dislike the effects of the regulation know who to credit or blame. By contrast, if a State imposes regulations only because it has been commanded to do so by Congress, responsibility is blurred.

Third, the anticommandeering principle prevents Congress from shifting the costs of regulation to the States. If Congress enacts a law and requires enforcement by the Executive Branch, it must appropriate the funds needed to administer the program. It is pressured to weigh the expected benefits of the program against its costs. But if Congress can compel the States to enact and enforce its program, Congress need not engage in any such analysis.

## IV

The PASPA provision at issue here—prohibiting state authorization of sports gambling—violates the anticommandeering rule. That provision unequivocally dictates what a state legislature may and may not do. And this is true under either our interpretation or that advocated by respondents and the United States. In either event, state legislatures are put under the direct control of Congress. It is as if federal officers were installed in state legislative chambers and were armed with the authority to stop legislators from voting on any offending proposals. A more direct affront to state sovereignty is not easy to imagine.

Neither respondents nor the United States contends that Congress can compel a State to enact legislation, but they say that prohibiting a State from enacting new laws is another matter.

This distinction is empty. It was a matter of happenstance that the laws challenged in *New York* and *Printz* commanded "affirmative" action as opposed to imposing a prohibition. The basic principle—that Congress cannot issue direct orders to state legislatures—applies in either event.

Here is an illustration. PASPA includes an exemption for States that permitted sports betting at the time of enactment, § 3704, but suppose Congress did not adopt such an exemption. Suppose Congress ordered States with legalized sports betting to take the affirmative step of criminalizing that activity and ordered the remaining States to retain their laws prohibiting sports betting. There is no good reason why the former would intrude more deeply on state sovereignty than the latter.

## V

Respondents and the United States defend the anti-authorization prohibition on the ground that it constitutes a valid preemption provision, but it is no such thing. Preemption is based on the Supremacy Clause, and that Clause is not an independent grant of legislative power to Congress. Instead, it simply provides "a rule of decision." It specifies that federal law is supreme in case of a conflict with state law. Therefore, in order for the PASPA provision to preempt state law, it must satisfy two requirements. First, it must represent the exercise of a power conferred on Congress by the Constitution; pointing to the Supremacy Clause will not do. Second, since the Constitution "confers upon Congress the power to regulate individuals, not States," the PASPA provision at issue must be best read as one that regulates private actors.

In sum, regardless of the language sometimes used by Congress and this Court, every form of preemption is based on a federal law that regulates the conduct of private actors, not the States. Once this is understood, it is clear that the PASPA provision prohibiting state authorization of sports gambling is not a preemption provision because there is no way in which this provision can be understood as a regulation of private actors. It certainly does not confer any federal rights on private actors interested in conducting sports gambling operations. (It does not give them a federal right to engage in sports gambling.) Nor does it impose any federal restrictions on private actors. If a private citizen or company started a sports gambling operation, either with or without state authorization, § 3702(1) would not be violated and would not provide any ground for a civil action by the Attorney General or any other party. Thus, there is simply no way to understand the provision prohibiting state authorization as anything other than a direct command to the States. And that is exactly what the anticommandeering rule does not allow.

[The Court then turned to whether other provisions of the Act should be upheld. The Court concluded:] "We hold that no provision of PASPA is severable from the provision directly at issue in these cases."

The legalization of sports gambling is a controversial subject. Supporters argue that legalization will produce revenue for the States and critically weaken illegal sports betting operations, which are often run by organized crime. Opponents contend that legalizing sports gambling will hook the young on gambling, encourage people of modest means to squander their savings and earnings, and corrupt professional and college sports.

The legalization of sports gambling requires an important policy choice, but the choice is not ours to make. Congress can regulate sports gambling directly, but if it elects not to do so, each State is free to act on its own. Our job is to interpret the law Congress has enacted and decide whether it is consistent with the Constitution. PASPA is not. PASPA "regulate[s] state governments' regulation" of their citizens. The Constitution gives Congress no such power.

[The other opinions focused entirely on the question of severability. Justice Thomas questioned the severability doctrine as developed by the Supreme Court. Justice Breyer concurred and dissented in part, and said that the provisions should be regarded as severable. He stated:]

I agree with Justice Ginsburg that 28 U.S.C. § 3702(2) is severable from the challenged portion of § 3702(1). The challenged part of subsection (1) prohibits a State from "author[izing]" or "licens[ing]" sports gambling schemes; subsection (2) prohibits individuals from "sponsor[ing], operat[ing], advertis[ing], or promot[ing]" sports gambling schemes "pursuant to the law . . . of a governmental entity." As Justice Ginsburg makes clear, the latter section can live comfortably on its own without the first. Why would Congress enact both these provisions? The obvious answer is that Congress wanted to "keep sports gambling from spreading."

[Justice Ginsburg wrote a dissent, joined by Justice Sotomayor, and in part by Justice Breyer. It focused entirely on the severability question and said the rest of the statute, which does not commandeer the states, should be upheld. She concluded:]

In PASPA, shorn of the prohibition on modifying or repealing state law, Congress permissibly exercised its authority to regulate commerce by instructing States and private parties to refrain from operating sports-gambling schemes. On no rational ground can it be concluded that Congress would have preferred no statute at all if it could not prohibit States from authorizing or licensing such schemes. Deleting the alleged "commandeering" directions would free the statute to accomplish just what Congress legitimately sought to achieve: stopping sports-gambling regimes while making it clear that the stoppage is attributable to federal, not state, action. I therefore dissent from the Court's determination to destroy PASPA rather than salvage the statute.

# Chapter 3

# The Federal Executive Power

## A. Inherent Presidential Power (casebook p. 321)

In considering the constitutionality of President Trump's travel ban, the Supreme Court expressed the view that the President has broad powers as to immigration and that only a rational basis test is to be used for restrictions on immigration. Under rational basis review, a court asks only whether there is a conceivable permissible purpose for the government's action; its actual purpose is irrelevant. The Court found national security to be a conceivable permissible purpose, whereas the dissent focused on what it saw as the actual purpose: a ban on Muslims entering the United States.

### TRUMP v. HAWAII
138 S. Ct. 2392 (2018)

Chief Justice ROBERTS delivered the opinion of the Court.

Under the Immigration and Nationality Act, foreign nationals seeking entry into the United States undergo a vetting process to ensure that they satisfy the numerous requirements for admission. The Act also vests the President with authority to restrict the entry of aliens whenever he finds that their entry "would be detrimental to the interests of the United States." Relying on that delegation, the President concluded that it was necessary to impose entry restrictions on nationals of countries that do not share adequate information for an informed entry determination, or that otherwise present national security risks. The plaintiffs in this litigation, respondents here, challenged the application of those entry restrictions to certain aliens abroad. We now decide whether the President had authority under the Act to issue the Proclamation, and whether the entry policy violates the Establishment Clause of the First Amendment.

I

Shortly after taking office, President Trump signed Executive Order No. 13769, Protecting the Nation From Foreign Terrorist Entry Into the United States. EO-1 directed the Secretary of Homeland Security to conduct a review to examine the adequacy of information provided by foreign governments about their nationals seeking to enter the United States. Pending that review, the order suspended for 90 days the entry of foreign nationals from seven countries—Iran, Iraq, Libya, Somalia, Sudan, Syria, and Yemen—that had been previously identified by Congress or prior administrations as posing heightened terrorism risks. The District Court for the Western District of Washington entered a temporary restraining order blocking the entry restrictions, and the Court of Appeals for the Ninth Circuit denied the Government's request to stay that order.

In response, the President revoked EO-1, replacing it with Executive Order No. 13780, which again directed a worldwide review. Citing investigative burdens on agencies and the need to diminish the risk that dangerous individuals would enter without adequate vetting, EO-2 also temporarily restricted the entry (with case-by-case waivers) of foreign nationals from six of the countries covered by EO-1: Iran, Libya, Somalia, Sudan, Syria, and Yemen. The order explained that those countries had been selected because each "is a state sponsor of terrorism, has been significantly compromised by terrorist organizations, or contains active conflict zones." The entry restriction was to stay in effect for 90 days, pending completion of the worldwide review.

These interim measures were immediately challenged in court. The District Courts for the Districts of Maryland and Hawaii entered nationwide preliminary injunctions barring enforcement of the entry suspension, and the respective Courts of Appeals upheld those injunctions, albeit on different grounds. The temporary restrictions in EO-2 expired before this Court took any action, and we vacated the lower court decisions as moot.

On September 24, 2017, after completion of the worldwide review, the President issued the Proclamation before us—Proclamation No. 9645, Enhancing Vetting Capabilities and Processes for Detecting Attempted Entry Into the United States by Terrorists or Other Public-Safety Threats. The Proclamation (as its title indicates) sought to improve vetting procedures by identifying ongoing deficiencies in the information needed to assess whether nationals of particular countries present "public safety threats." To further that purpose, the Proclamation placed entry restrictions on the nationals of eight foreign states whose systems for managing and sharing information about their nationals the President deemed inadequate.

Following the 50-day period, the Acting Secretary of Homeland Security concluded that eight countries—Chad, Iran, Iraq, Libya, North Korea, Syria, Venezuela, and Yemen—remained deficient in terms of their risk profile and willingness to provide requested information. The Proclamation further directs DHS to assess on a continuing basis whether entry restrictions should be modified or continued, and to report to the President every 180 days. § 4. Upon completion of the first such review period, the President, on the recommendation of the Secretary of Homeland Security, determined that Chad had sufficiently improved its practices, and he accordingly lifted restrictions on its nationals. Presidential Proclamation No. 9723, 83 Fed. Reg. 15937 (2018).

[II]

The text of [8 U.S.C.] § 1182(f) states:

> Whenever the President finds that the entry of any aliens or of any class of aliens into the United States would be detrimental to the interests of the United States, he may by proclamation, and for such period as he shall deem necessary, suspend the entry of all aliens or any class of aliens as immigrants or nonimmigrants, or impose on the entry of aliens any restrictions he may deem to be appropriate.

By its terms, § 1182(f) exudes deference to the President in every clause. It entrusts to the President the decisions whether and when to suspend entry ("[w]henever [he] finds that the entry" of aliens "would be detrimental" to the national interest); whose entry to suspend ("all aliens or any class of aliens"); for how long ("for such period as he shall deem necessary"); and on what conditions ("any restrictions he may deem to be appropriate").

The Proclamation falls well within this comprehensive delegation. The sole prerequisite set forth in § 1182(f) is that the President "find[ ]" that the entry of the covered aliens "would be detrimental to the interests of the United States." The President has undoubtedly fulfilled that requirement here.

Plaintiffs' final statutory argument is that the President's entry suspension violates § 1152(a)(1)(A), which provides that "no person shall . . . be discriminated against in the issuance of an immigrant visa because of the person's race, sex, nationality, place of birth, or place of residence." In any event, we reject plaintiffs' interpretation because it ignores the basic distinction between admissibility determinations and visa issuance that runs throughout the INA.

The distinction between admissibility—to which § 1152(a)(1)(A) does not apply—and visa issuance—to which it does—is apparent from the text of the provision, which specifies only that its protections apply to the "issuance" of "immigrant visa[s]," without mentioning admissibility or entry. Had Congress instead intended in § 1152(a)(1)(A) to constrain the President's power to determine who may enter the country, it could easily have chosen language directed to that end.

Common sense and historical practice confirm as much. Section 1152(a)(1)(A) has never been treated as a constraint on the criteria for admissibility in § 1182. Presidents have repeatedly exercised their authority to suspend entry on the basis of nationality.

## IV

We now turn to plaintiffs' claim that the Proclamation was issued for the unconstitutional purpose of excluding Muslims.

Our cases recognize that "[t]he clearest command of the Establishment Clause is that one religious denomination cannot be officially preferred over another." Plaintiffs believe that the Proclamation violates this prohibition by singling out Muslims for disfavored treatment. The entry suspension, they contend, operates as a "religious gerrymander," in part because most of the countries covered by the Proclamation have Muslim-majority populations. Relying on Establishment Clause precedents concerning laws and policies applied domestically, plaintiffs allege that the primary purpose of the Proclamation was religious animus and that the President's stated concerns about vetting protocols and national security were but pretexts for discriminating against Muslims.

At the heart of plaintiffs' case is a series of statements by the President and his advisers casting doubt on the official objective of the Proclamation. For example, while a candidate on the campaign trail, the President published a "Statement on Preventing Muslim Immigration" that called for a "total and complete shutdown of Muslims entering the United States until our country's representatives can figure out what is going on." Then-candidate Trump also stated that "Islam hates us" and asserted that the United States was "having problems with Muslims coming into the country." Shortly after being elected, when asked whether violence in Europe had affected his plans to "ban Muslim immigration," the President replied, "You know my plans. All along, I've been proven to be right."

One week after his inauguration, the President issued EO-1. In a television interview, one of the President's campaign advisers explained that when the President "first announced it, he said, 'Muslim ban.' He called me up. He said, 'Put a commission together. Show me the right way to do it legally.'" The adviser said he assembled a group of Members of Congress and lawyers that "focused on, instead of religion, danger. . . . [The order] is based on places where there [is] substantial evidence that people are sending terrorists into our country."

Plaintiffs also note that after issuing EO-2 to replace EO-1, the President expressed regret that his prior order had been "watered down" and called for a "much tougher version" of his "Travel Ban." Shortly before the release of the Proclamation, he stated that the "travel ban . . . should be far larger, tougher, and more specific," but "stupidly that would not be politically correct." More recently, on November 29, 2017, the President retweeted links to three anti-Muslim propaganda videos. In response to questions about those videos, the President's deputy press secretary denied that the President thinks Muslims are a threat to the United States, explaining that "the President has been talking about these security issues for years now, from the campaign trail to the White House" and "has addressed these issues with the travel order that he issued earlier this year and the companion proclamation."

The President of the United States possesses an extraordinary power to speak to his fellow citizens and on their behalf. Our Presidents have frequently used that power to espouse the principles of religious freedom and tolerance on which this Nation was founded.

Plaintiffs argue that this President's words strike at fundamental standards of respect and tolerance, in violation of our constitutional tradition. But the issue before us is not whether to denounce the statements. It is instead the significance of those statements in reviewing a Presidential directive, neutral on its face, addressing a matter within the core of executive responsibility. In doing so, we must consider not only the statements of a particular President, but also the authority of the Presidency itself.

The case before us differs in numerous respects from the conventional Establishment Clause claim. Unlike the typical suit involving religious displays or school prayer, plaintiffs seek to invalidate a national security directive regulating the entry of aliens abroad. Their claim accordingly raises a number of delicate issues regarding the scope of the constitutional right and the manner of proof. The Proclamation, moreover, is facially neutral toward religion. Plaintiffs therefore ask the Court to probe the sincerity of the stated justifications for the policy by reference to extrinsic statements—many of which were made before the President took the oath of office. These various aspects of plaintiffs' challenge inform our standard of review.

For more than a century, this Court has recognized that the admission and exclusion of foreign nationals is a "fundamental sovereign attribute exercised by the Government's political departments largely immune from judicial control." Because decisions in these matters may implicate "relations with foreign powers," or involve "classifications defined in the light of changing political and economic circumstances," such judgments "are frequently of a character more appropriate to either the Legislature or the Executive."

Nonetheless, although foreign nationals seeking admission have no constitutional right to entry, this Court has engaged in a circumscribed judicial inquiry when the denial of a visa allegedly burdens the constitutional rights of a U.S. citizen.

"[J]udicial inquiry into the national-security realm raises concerns for the separation of powers" by intruding on the President's constitutional responsibilities in the area of foreign affairs. For another, "when it comes to collecting evidence and drawing inferences" on questions of national security, "the lack of competence on the part of the courts is marked."

The upshot of our cases in this context is clear: "Any rule of constitutional law that would inhibit the flexibility" of the President "to respond to changing world conditions should be adopted only with the greatest caution," and our inquiry into matters of entry and national security is highly constrained. For our purposes today, we assume that we may look behind the face of the Proclamation to the extent of applying rational basis review. That standard of review considers whether the entry policy is plausibly related to the Government's stated objective to protect the country and improve vetting processes. As a result, we may consider plaintiffs' extrinsic evidence, but will uphold the policy so long as it can reasonably be understood to result from a justification independent of unconstitutional grounds.

Given the standard of review, it should come as no surprise that the Court hardly ever strikes down a policy as illegitimate under rational basis scrutiny. On the few occasions where we have done so, a common thread has been that the laws at issue lack any purpose other than a "bare . . . desire to harm a politically unpopular group."

The Proclamation does not fit this pattern. It cannot be said that it is impossible to "discern a relationship to legitimate state interests" or that the policy is "inexplicable by anything but animus." Indeed, the dissent can only attempt to argue otherwise by refusing to apply anything resembling rational basis review. But because there is persuasive evidence that the entry suspension has a legitimate grounding in national security concerns, quite apart from any religious hostility, we must accept that independent justification.

The Proclamation is expressly premised on legitimate purposes: preventing entry of nationals who cannot be adequately vetted and inducing other nations to improve their practices. The text says nothing about religion. Plaintiffs and the dissent nonetheless emphasize that five of the seven nations currently included in the Proclamation have Muslim-majority populations. Yet that fact alone does not support an inference of religious hostility, given that the policy covers just 8% of the world's Muslim population and is limited to countries that were previously designated by Congress or prior administrations as posing national security risks.

The Proclamation, moreover, reflects the results of a worldwide review process undertaken by multiple Cabinet officials and their agencies.

Finally, the dissent invokes *Korematsu v. United States* (1944). Whatever rhetorical advantage the dissent may see in doing so, *Korematsu* has nothing to do with this case. The forcible relocation of U.S. citizens to concentration camps, solely and explicitly on the basis of race, is objectively unlawful and outside the scope of Presidential authority. But it is wholly inapt to liken that morally repugnant order to a facially neutral policy denying certain foreign nationals the privilege of admission. The entry suspension is an act that is well within executive authority and could have been taken by any other President—the only question is evaluating the actions of this particular President in promulgating an otherwise valid Proclamation.

The dissent's reference to *Korematsu*, however, affords this Court the opportunity to make express what is already obvious: *Korematsu* was gravely wrong the day it was decided, has been overruled in the court of history, and—to be clear—"has no place in law under the Constitution."

Under these circumstances, the Government has set forth a sufficient national security justification to survive rational basis review. We express no view on the soundness of the policy. We simply hold today that plaintiffs have not demonstrated a likelihood of success on the merits of their constitutional claim. Because plaintiffs have not shown that they are likely to succeed on the merits of their claims, we reverse the grant of the preliminary injunction as an abuse of discretion.

Justice KENNEDY, concurring.

I join the Court's opinion in full. In all events, it is appropriate to make this further observation. There are numerous instances in which the statements and actions of Government officials are not subject to judicial scrutiny or intervention. That does not mean those officials are free to disregard the Constitution and the rights it proclaims and protects. The oath that all officials take to adhere to the Constitution is not confined to those spheres in which the Judiciary can correct or even comment upon what those officials say or do. Indeed, the very fact that an official may have broad discretion, discretion free from judicial scrutiny, makes it all the more imperative for him or her to adhere to the Constitution and to its meaning and its promise.

The First Amendment prohibits the establishment of religion and promises the free exercise of religion. From these safeguards, and from the guarantee of freedom of speech, it follows there is freedom of belief and expression. It is an urgent necessity that officials adhere to these constitutional guarantees and mandates in all their actions, even in the sphere of foreign affairs. An anxious world must know that our Government remains committed always to the liberties the Constitution seeks to preserve and protect, so that freedom extends outward, and lasts.

Justice BRYER, with whom Justice KAGAN joins, dissenting.

The question before us is whether Proclamation No. 9645 is lawful. If its promulgation or content was significantly affected by religious animus against Muslims, it would violate the relevant statute or the First Amendment itself. If, however, its sole *ratio decidendi* was one of national security, then it would be unlikely to violate either the statute or the Constitution. Which is it? Members of the Court principally disagree about the answer to this question, *i.e.*, about whether or the extent to which religious animus played a significant role in the Proclamation's promulgation or content.

In my view, the Proclamation's elaborate system of exemptions and waivers can and should help us answer this question. That system provides for case-by-case consideration of persons who may qualify for visas despite the Proclamation's general ban. Those persons include lawful permanent residents, asylum seekers, refugees, students, children, and numerous others. There are likely many such persons, perhaps in the thousands. And I believe it appropriate to take account of their Proclamation-granted status when considering the Proclamation's lawfulness.

Further, since the case-by-case exemptions and waivers apply without regard to the individual's religion, application of that system would help make clear that the Proclamation does not deny visas to numerous Muslim individuals (from those countries) who do not pose a security threat. And that fact would help to rebut the First Amendment claim that the Proclamation rests upon anti-Muslim bias rather than security need. Finally, of course, the very fact that Muslims from those countries would enter the United States (under Proclamation-provided exemptions and waivers) would help to show the same thing.

On the other hand, if the Government is *not* applying the system of exemptions and waivers that the Proclamation contains, then its argument for the Proclamation's lawfulness becomes significantly weaker. And, perhaps most importantly, if the Government is not applying the Proclamation's exemption and waiver system, the claim that the Proclamation is a "Muslim ban," rather than a "security-based" ban, becomes much stronger. How could the Government successfully claim that the Proclamation rests on security needs if it is excluding Muslims who satisfy the Proclamation's own terms? At the same time, denying visas to Muslims who meet the Proclamation's own security terms would support the view that the Government excludes them for reasons based upon their religion.

Unfortunately there is evidence that supports the second possibility, *i.e.*, that the Government is not applying the Proclamation as written. An examination of publicly available statistics also provides cause for concern. The State Department reported that during the Proclamation's first month, two waivers were approved out of 6,555 eligible applicants. In its reply brief, the Government claims that number increased from 2 to 430 during the first four months of implementation. That number, 430, however, when compared with the number of pre-Proclamation visitors, accounts for a miniscule percentage of those likely eligible for visas, in such categories as persons requiring medical treatment, academic visitors, students, family members, and others belonging to groups that, when considered as a group (rather than case by case), would not seem to pose security threats.

*Amici* have suggested that there are numerous applicants who could meet the waiver criteria. Other data suggest the same. The Proclamation does not apply to asylum seekers or refugees. Yet few refugees have been admitted since the Proclamation took effect. While more than 15,000 Syrian refugees arrived in the United States in 2016, only 13 have arrived since January 2018.

Declarations, anecdotal evidence, facts, and numbers taken from *amicus* briefs are not judicial factfindings. The Government has not had an opportunity to respond, and a court has not had an opportunity to decide. But, given the importance of the decision in this case, the need for assurance that the Proclamation does not rest upon a "Muslim ban," and the assistance in deciding the issue that answers to the "exemption and waiver" questions may provide, I would send this case back to the District Court for further proceedings. And, I would leave the injunction in effect while the matter is litigated. Regardless, the Court's decision today leaves the District Court free to explore these issues on remand.

Justice SOTOMAYOR, with whom Justice GINSBURG joins, dissenting.

The United States of America is a Nation built upon the promise of religious liberty. Our Founders honored that core promise by embedding the principle of religious neutrality in the First Amendment. The Court's decision today fails to safeguard that fundamental principle. It leaves undisturbed a policy first advertised openly and unequivocally as a "total and complete shutdown of Muslims entering the United States" because the policy now masquerades behind a facade of national-security concerns. But this repackaging does little to cleanse Presidential Proclamation No. 9645 of the appearance of discrimination that the President's words have created. Based on the evidence in the record, a reasonable observer would conclude that the Proclamation was motivated by anti-Muslim animus. That alone suffices to show that plaintiffs are likely to succeed on the merits of their Establishment Clause claim. The majority holds otherwise by ignoring the facts, misconstruing our legal precedent, and turning a blind eye to the pain and suffering the Proclamation inflicts upon countless families and individuals, many of whom are United States citizens. Because that troubling result runs contrary to the Constitution and our precedent, I dissent.

I

Whatever the merits of plaintiffs' complex statutory claims, the Proclamation must be enjoined for a more fundamental reason: It runs afoul of the Establishment Clause's guarantee of religious neutrality.

The Establishment Clause forbids government policies "respecting an establishment of religion." The "clearest command" of the Establishment Clause is that the Government cannot favor or disfavor one religion over another. "When the government acts with the ostensible and predominant purpose" of disfavoring a particular religion, "it violates that central Establishment Clause value of official religious neutrality, there being no neutrality when the government's ostensible object is to take sides." To determine whether plaintiffs have proved an Establishment Clause violation, the Court asks whether a reasonable observer would view the government action as enacted for the purpose of disfavoring a religion.

In answering that question, this Court has generally considered the text of the government policy, its operation, and any available evidence regarding "the historical background of the decision under challenge, the specific series of events leading to the enactment or official policy in question, and the legislative or administrative history, including contemporaneous statements made by" the decisionmaker.

Although the majority briefly recounts a few of the statements and background events that form the basis of plaintiffs' constitutional challenge, that highly abridged account does not tell even half of the story. The full record paints a far more harrowing picture, from which a reasonable observer would readily conclude that the Proclamation was motivated by hostility and animus toward the Muslim faith.

During his Presidential campaign, then-candidate Donald Trump pledged that, if elected, he would ban Muslims from entering the United States. Specifically, on December 7, 2015, he issued a formal statement "calling for a total and complete shutdown of Muslims entering the United States." That statement remained on his campaign website until May 2017 (several months into his Presidency).

On December 8, 2015, Trump justified his proposal during a television interview by noting that President Franklin D. Roosevelt "did the same thing" with respect to the internment of Japanese Americans during World War II. . In January 2016, during a Republican primary debate, Trump was asked whether he wanted to "rethink [his] position" on "banning Muslims from entering the country." He answered, "No." A month later, at a rally in South Carolina, Trump told an apocryphal story about United States General John J. Pershing killing a large group of Muslim insurgents in the Philippines with bullets dipped in pigs' blood in the early 1900's. . In March 2016, he expressed his belief that "Islam hates us. . . . [W]e can't allow people coming into this country who have this hatred of the United States . . . [a]nd of people that are not Muslim." That same month, Trump asserted that "[w]e're having problems with the Muslims, and we're having problems with Muslims coming into the country." He therefore called for surveillance of mosques in the United States, blaming terrorist attacks on Muslims' lack of "assimilation" and their commitment to "sharia law." A day later, he opined that Muslims "do not respect us at all" and "don't respect a lot of the things that are happening throughout not only our country, but they don't respect other things."

As Trump's presidential campaign progressed, he began to describe his policy proposal in slightly different terms. In June 2016, for instance, he characterized the policy proposal as a suspension of immigration from countries "where there's a proven history of terrorism." He also described the proposal as rooted in the need to stop "importing radical Islamic terrorism to the West through a failed immigration system." Asked in July 2016 whether he was "pull[ing] back from" his pledged Muslim ban, Trump responded, "I actually don't think it's a rollback. In fact, you could say it's an expansion." He then explained that he used different terminology because "[p]eople were so upset when [he] used the word Muslim."

A month before the 2016 election, Trump reiterated that his proposed "Muslim ban" had "morphed into a[n] extreme vetting from certain areas of the world." Then, on December 21, 2016, President-elect Trump was asked whether he would "rethink" his previous "plans to create a Muslim registry or ban Muslim immigration." He replied: "You know my plans. All along, I've proven to be right."

On January 27, 2017, one week after taking office, President Trump signed entitled "Protecting the Nation From Foreign Terrorist Entry Into the United States." As he signed it, President Trump read the title, looked up, and said "We all know what that means." That same day, President Trump explained to the media that, under EO-1, Christians would be given priority for entry as refugees into the United States. The following day, one of President Trump's key advisers candidly drew the connection between EO-1 and the "Muslim ban" that the President had pledged to implement if elected. According to that adviser, "[W]hen [Donald Trump] first announced it, he said, 'Muslim ban.' He called me up. He said, 'Put a commission together. Show me the right way to do it legally.'"

While litigation over EO-2 was ongoing, President Trump repeatedly made statements alluding to a desire to keep Muslims out of the country. For instance, he said at a rally of his supporters that EO-2 was just a "watered down version of the first one" and had been "tailor[ed]" at the behest of "the lawyers." He further added that he would prefer "to go back to the first [executive order] and go all the way" and reiterated his belief that it was "very hard" for Muslims to assimilate into Western culture. Then, on August 17, 2017, President Trump issued yet another tweet about Islam, once more referencing the story about General Pershing's massacre of Muslims in the Philippines: "Study what General Pershing . . . did to terrorists when caught. There was no more Radical Islamic Terror for 35 years!"

In September 2017, President Trump tweeted that "[t]he travel ban into the United States should be far larger, tougher and more specific—but stupidly, that would not be politically correct!" On November 29, 2017, President Trump "retweeted" three anti-Muslim videos, entitled "Muslim Destroys a Statue of Virgin Mary!", "Islamist mob pushes teenage boy off roof and beats him to death!", and "Muslim migrant beats up Dutch boy on crutches!"

As the majority correctly notes, "the issue before us is not whether to denounce" these offensive statements. Rather, the dispositive and narrow question here is whether a reasonable observer, presented with all "openly available data," the text and "historical context" of the Proclamation, and the "specific sequence of events" leading to it, would conclude that the primary purpose of the Proclamation is to disfavor Islam and its adherents by excluding them from the country. The answer is unquestionably yes.

Taking all the relevant evidence together, a reasonable observer would conclude that the Proclamation was driven primarily by anti-Muslim animus, rather than by the Government's asserted national-security justifications. Moreover, despite several opportunities to do so, President Trump has never disavowed any of his prior statements about Islam. Instead, he has continued to make remarks that a reasonable observer would view as an unrelenting attack on the Muslim religion and its followers. Given President Trump's failure to correct the reasonable perception of his apparent hostility toward the Islamic faith, it is unsurprising that the President's lawyers have, at every step in the lower courts, failed in their attempts to launder the Proclamation of its discriminatory taint.

Ultimately, what began as a policy explicitly "calling for a total and complete shutdown of Muslims entering the United States" has since morphed into a "Proclamation" putatively based on national-security concerns. But this new window dressing cannot conceal an unassailable fact: the words of the President and his advisers create the strong perception that the Proclamation is contaminated by impermissible discriminatory animus against Islam and its followers.


## II

Rather than defend the President's problematic statements, the Government urges this Court to set them aside and defer to the President on issues related to immigration and national security. The majority accepts that invitation and incorrectly applies a watered-down legal standard in an effort to short circuit plaintiffs' Establishment Clause claim.

But even under rational-basis review, the Proclamation must fall. That is so because the Proclamation is "'divorced from any factual context from which we could discern a relationship to legitimate state interests,' and 'its sheer breadth [is] so discontinuous with the reasons offered for it'" that the policy is "'inexplicable by anything but animus.'"

In sum, none of the features of the Proclamation highlighted by the majority supports the Government's claim that the Proclamation is genuinely and primarily rooted in a legitimate national-security interest. What the unrebutted evidence actually shows is that a reasonable observer would conclude, quite easily, that the primary purpose and function of the Proclamation is to disfavor Islam by banning Muslims from entering our country.

[III]

The First Amendment stands as a bulwark against official religious prejudice and embodies our Nation's deep commitment to religious plurality and tolerance. That constitutional promise is why, "[f]or centuries now, people have come to this country from every corner of the world to share in the blessing of religious freedom." Instead of vindicating those principles, today's decision tosses them aside. In holding that the First Amendment gives way to an executive policy that a reasonable observer would view as motivated by animus against Muslims, the majority opinion upends this Court's precedent, repeats tragic mistakes of the past, and denies countless individuals the fundamental right of religious liberty.

Just weeks ago, the Court rendered its decision in which applied the bedrock principles of religious neutrality and tolerance in considering a First Amendment challenge to government action. Those principles should apply equally here. In both instances, the question is whether a government actor exhibited tolerance and neutrality in reaching a decision that affects individuals' fundamental religious freedom. But unlike in *Masterpiece*, where a state civil rights commission was found to have acted without "the neutrality that the Free Exercise Clause requires," the government actors in this case will not be held accountable for breaching the First Amendment's guarantee of religious neutrality and tolerance. Unlike in *Masterpiece*, where the majority considered the state commissioners' statements about religion to be persuasive evidence of unconstitutional government action, the majority here completely sets aside the President's charged statements about Muslims as irrelevant. That holding erodes the foundational principles of religious tolerance that the Court elsewhere has so emphatically protected, and it tells members of minority religions in our country "'that they are outsiders, not full members of the political community.'"

Today's holding is all the more troubling given the stark parallels between the reasoning of this case and that of *Korematsu v. United States* (1944). In *Korematsu*, the Court gave "a pass [to] an odious, gravely injurious racial classification" authorized by an executive order. As here, the Government invoked an ill-defined national-security threat to justify an exclusionary policy of sweeping proportion. As here, the exclusion order was rooted in dangerous stereotypes about, *inter alia*, a particular group's supposed inability to assimilate and desire to harm the United States. As here, the Government was unwilling to reveal its own intelligence agencies' views of the alleged security concerns to the very citizens it purported to protect. And as here, there was strong evidence that impermissible hostility and animus motivated the Government's policy.

Today, the Court takes the important step of finally overruling *Korematsu*, denouncing it as "gravely wrong the day it was decided." This formal repudiation of a shameful precedent is laudable and long overdue. But it does not make the majority's decision here acceptable or right. By blindly accepting the Government's misguided invitation to sanction a discriminatory policy motivated by animosity toward a disfavored group, all in the name of a superficial claim of national security, the Court redeploys the same dangerous logic underlying *Korematsu* and merely replaces one "gravely wrong" decision with another.

Our Constitution demands, and our country deserves, a Judiciary willing to hold the coordinate branches to account when they defy our most sacred legal commitments. Because the Court's decision today has failed in that respect, with profound regret, I dissent.

## C.  Constitutional Problems of the Administrative State

## 3.  Checking Administrative Power (casebook p. 378)

In *Lucia v. Securities and Exchange Commission*, the Court considered when a person should be regarded as an "officer"—who must be appointed by the President, the heads of departments or the lower federal courts—as opposed to a government employee.

LUCIA v. SECURITIES AND EXCHANGE COMMISSION
138 S. Ct. 2044 (2018)

Justice KAGAN delivered the opinion of the Court.

The Appointments Clause of the Constitution lays out the permissible methods of appointing "Officers of the United States," a class of government officials distinct from mere employees. This case requires us to decide whether administrative law judges (ALJs) of the Securities and Exchange Commission (SEC or Commission) qualify as such "Officers." In keeping with *Freytag v. Commissioner* (1991), we hold that they do.

I

The SEC has statutory authority to enforce the nation's securities laws. One way it can do so is by instituting an administrative proceeding against an alleged wrongdoer. By law, the Commission may itself preside over such a proceeding. But the Commission also may, and typically does, delegate that task to an ALJ. The SEC currently has five ALJs. Other staff members, rather than the Commission proper, selected them all.

An ALJ assigned to hear an SEC enforcement action has extensive powers — the "authority to do all things necessary and appropriate to discharge his or her duties" and ensure a "fair and orderly" adversarial proceeding. Those powers "include, but are not limited to," supervising discovery; issuing, revoking, or modifying subpoenas; deciding motions; ruling on the admissibility of evidence; administering oaths; hearing and examining witnesses; generally "[r]egulating the course of" the proceeding and the "conduct of the parties and their counsel"; and imposing sanctions for "[c]ontemptuous conduct" or violations of procedural requirements. As that list suggests, an SEC ALJ exercises authority "comparable to" that of a federal district judge conducting a bench trial.

After a hearing ends, the ALJ issues an "initial decision." That decision must set out "findings and conclusions" about all "material issues of fact [and] law"; it also must include the "appropriate order, sanction, relief, or denial thereof." The Commission can then review the ALJ's decision, either upon request or *sua sponte*. But if it opts against review, the Commission "issue[s] an order that the [ALJ's] decision has become final." At that point, the initial decision is "deemed the action of the Commission."

This case began when the SEC instituted an administrative proceeding against petitioner Raymond Lucia and his investment company. Lucia marketed a retirement savings strategy called "Buckets of Money." In the SEC's view, Lucia used misleading slideshow presentations to deceive prospective clients. The SEC charged Lucia under the Investment Advisers Act, and assigned ALJ Cameron Elliot to adjudicate the case. After nine days of testimony and argument, Judge Elliot issued an initial decision concluding that Lucia had violated the Act and imposing sanctions, including civil penalties of $300,000 and a lifetime bar from the investment industry. In his decision, Judge Elliot made factual findings about only one of the four ways the SEC thought Lucia's slideshow misled investors. The Commission thus remanded for factfinding on the other three claims, explaining that an ALJ's "personal experience with the witnesses" places him "in the best position to make findings of fact" and "resolve any conflicts in the evidence." Judge Elliot then made additional findings of deception and issued a revised initial decision, with the same sanctions.

On appeal to the SEC, Lucia argued that the administrative proceeding was invalid because Judge Elliot had not been constitutionally appointed.

According to Lucia, the Commission's ALJs are "Officers of the United States" and thus subject to the Appointments Clause. Under that Clause, Lucia noted, only the President, "Courts of Law," or "Heads of Departments" can appoint "Officers." And none of those actors had made Judge Elliot an ALJ. To be sure, the Commission itself counts as a "Head[ ] of Department[ ]." But the Commission had left the task of appointing ALJs, including Judge Elliot, to SEC staff members. As a result, Lucia contended, Judge Elliot lacked constitutional authority to do his job.

The Commission rejected Lucia's argument. It held that the SEC's ALJs are not "Officers of the United States." Instead, they are "mere employees"—officials with lesser responsibilities who fall outside the Appointments Clause's ambit. Lucia's claim fared no better in the Court of Appeals for the D.C. Circuit. A panel of that court seconded the Commission's view that SEC ALJs are employees rather than officers, and so are not subject to the Appointments Clause.

## II

The sole question here is whether the Commission's ALJs are "Officers of the United States" or simply employees of the Federal Government. The Appointments Clause prescribes the exclusive means of appointing "Officers." Only the President, a court of law, or a head of department can do so.[3] And as all parties agree, none of those actors appointed Judge Elliot before he heard Lucia's case; instead, SEC staff members gave him an ALJ slot. So if the Commission's ALJs are constitutional officers, Lucia raises a valid Appointments Clause claim. The only way to defeat his position is to show that those ALJs are not officers at all, but instead non-officer employees—part of the broad swath of "lesser functionaries" in the Government's workforce. For if that is true, the Appointments Clause cares not a whit about who named them.

[I]n *Freytag v. Commissioner* (1991), we applied the unadorned "significant authority" test to adjudicative officials who are near-carbon copies of the Commission's ALJs. As we now explain, our analysis there (sans any more detailed legal criteria) necessarily decides this case.

---

3. That statement elides a distinction, not at issue here, between "principal" and "inferior" officers. Only the President, with the advice and consent of the Senate, can appoint a principal officer; but Congress (instead of relying on that method) may authorize the President alone, a court, or a department head to appoint an inferior officer. Both the Government and Lucia view the SEC's ALJs as inferior officers and acknowledge that the Commission, as a head of department, can constitutionally appoint them. [Footnote by the Court.]

The officials at issue in *Freytag* were the "special trial judges" (STJs) of the United States Tax Court. The authority of those judges depended on the significance of the tax dispute before them. In "comparatively narrow and minor matters," they could both hear and definitively resolve a case for the Tax Court. In more major matters, they could preside over the hearing, but could not issue the final decision; instead, they were to "prepare proposed findings and an opinion" for a regular Tax Court judge to consider. This Court held that the Tax Court's STJs are officers, not mere employees.

Still more, the Commission's ALJs exercise the same "significant discretion" when carrying out the same "important functions" as STJs do. Both sets of officials have all the authority needed to ensure fair and orderly adversarial hearings—indeed, nearly all the tools of federal trial judges. Consider in order the four specific (if overlapping) powers *Freytag* mentioned. First, the Commission's ALJs (like the Tax Court's STJs) "take testimony." More precisely, they "[r]eceiv[e] evidence" and "[e]xamine witnesses" at hearings, and may also take pre-hearing depositions. Second, the ALJs (like STJs) "conduct trials." As detailed earlier, they administer oaths, rule on motions, and generally "regulat[e] the course of" a hearing, as well as the conduct of parties and counsel. Third, the ALJs (like STJs) "rule on the admissibility of evidence." They thus critically shape the administrative record (as they also do when issuing document subpoenas). And fourth, the ALJs (like STJs) "have the power to enforce compliance with discovery orders." In particular, they may punish all "[c]ontemptuous conduct," including violations of those orders, by means as severe as excluding the offender from the hearing. So point for point—straight from *Freytag*'s list—the Commission's ALJs have equivalent duties and powers as STJs in conducting adversarial inquiries.

And at the close of those proceedings, ALJs issue decisions much like that in *Freytag*—except with potentially more independent effect. As the *Freytag* Court recounted, STJs "prepare proposed findings and an opinion" adjudicating charges and assessing tax liabilities. Similarly, the Commission's ALJs issue decisions containing factual findings, legal conclusions, and appropriate remedies. And what happens next reveals that the ALJ can play the more autonomous role. In a major case like *Freytag*, a regular Tax Court judge must always review an STJ's opinion. And that opinion counts for nothing unless the regular judge adopts it as his own. By contrast, the SEC can decide against reviewing an ALJ decision at all. And when the SEC declines review (and issues an order saying so), the ALJ's decision itself "becomes final" and is "deemed the action of the Commission." That last-word capacity makes this an *a fortiori* case: If the Tax Court's STJs are officers, as *Freytag* held, then the Commission's ALJs must be too.

For all the reasons we have given, and all those *Freytag* gave before, the Commission's ALJs are "Officers of the United States," subject to the Appointments Clause. And as noted earlier, Judge Elliot heard and decided Lucia's case without the kind of appointment the Clause requires. This Court has held that "one who makes a timely challenge to the constitutional validity of the appointment of an officer who adjudicates his case" is entitled to relief. Lucia made just such a timely challenge: He contested the validity of Judge Elliot's appointment before the Commission, and continued pressing that claim in the Court of Appeals and this Court. So what relief follows? This Court has also held that the "appropriate" remedy for an adjudication tainted with an appointments violation is a new "hearing before a properly appointed" official. And we add today one thing more. That official cannot be Judge Elliot, even if he has by now received (or receives sometime in the future) a constitutional appointment. Judge Elliot has already both heard Lucia's case and issued an initial decision on the merits. He cannot be expected to consider the matter as though he had not adjudicated it before. To cure the constitutional error, another ALJ (or the Commission itself) must hold the new hearing to which Lucia is entitled.

Justice THOMAS, with whom Justice GORSUCH joins, concurring.

I agree with the Court that this case is indistinguishable from *Freytag v. Commissioner* (1991). If the special trial judges in *Freytag* were "Officers of the United States," Art. II, § 2, cl. 2, then so are the administrative law judges of the Securities and Exchange Commission. The Appointments Clause provides the exclusive process for appointing "Officers of the United States." While principal officers must be nominated by the President and confirmed by the Senate, Congress can authorize the appointment of "inferior Officers" by "the President alone," "the Courts of Law," or "the Heads of Departments."

This alternative process for appointing inferior officers strikes a balance between efficiency and accountability. Given the sheer number of inferior officers, it would be too burdensome to require each of them to run the gauntlet of Senate confirmation. But, by specifying only a limited number of actors who can appoint inferior officers without Senate confirmation, the Appointments Clause maintains clear lines of accountability — encouraging good appointments and giving the public someone to blame for bad ones.

The Founders likely understood the term "Officers of the United States" to encompass all federal civil officials who perform an ongoing, statutory duty—no matter how important or significant the duty. "Officers of the United States" was probably not a term of art that the Constitution used to signify some special type of official. Based on how the Founders used it and similar terms, the phrase "of the United States" was merely a synonym for "federal," and the word "Office[r]" carried its ordinary meaning. The ordinary meaning of "officer" was anyone who performed a continuous public duty. The Founders considered individuals to be officers even if they performed only ministerial statutory duties—including record-keepers, clerks, and tidewaiters (individuals who watched goods land at a customhouse). Early congressional practice reflected this understanding. With exceptions not relevant here, Congress required all federal officials with ongoing statutory duties to be appointed in compliance with the Appointments Clause.

Applying the original meaning here, the administrative law judges of the Securities and Exchange Commission easily qualify as "Officers of the United States." These judges exercise many of the agency's statutory duties, including issuing initial decisions in adversarial proceedings. As explained, the importance or significance of these statutory duties is irrelevant. All that matters is that the judges are continuously responsible for performing them.

Justice BREYER, with whom Justice GINSBURG and Justice SOTOMAYOR join as to Part III, concurring in the judgment in part and dissenting in part.

I agree with the Court that the Securities and Exchange Commission did not properly appoint the Administrative Law Judge who presided over petitioner Lucia's hearing. But I disagree with the majority in respect to two matters. First, I would rest our conclusion upon statutory, not constitutional, grounds. I believe it important to do so because I cannot answer the constitutional question that the majority answers without knowing the answer to a different, embedded constitutional question, which the Solicitor General urged us to answer in this case: the constitutionality of the statutory "for cause" removal protections that Congress provided for administrative law judges. Second, I disagree with the Court in respect to the proper remedy.

I

The relevant statute here is the Administrative Procedure Act. That Act governs the appointment of administrative law judges.

I do not believe that the Administrative Procedure Act permits the Commission to delegate its power to appoint its administrative law judges to its staff. We have held that, for purposes of the Constitution's Appointments Clause, the Commission itself is a "'Hea[d]'" of a "'Departmen[t].'" Thus, reading the statute as referring to the Commission itself, and not to its staff, avoids a difficult constitutional question, namely, the very question that the Court answers today: whether the Commission's administrative law judges are constitutional "inferior Officers" whose appointment Congress may vest only in the President, the "Courts of Law," or the "Heads of Departments."

I have found no other statutory provision that would permit the Commission to delegate the power to appoint its administrative law judges to its staff. Regardless, the same constitutional-avoidance reasons that should inform our construction of the Administrative Procedure Act should also lead us to interpret the Commission's general delegation authority as excluding the power to delegate to staff the authority to appoint its administrative law judges, so as to avoid the constitutional question the Court reaches in this case.

The upshot, in my view, is that for statutory, not constitutional, reasons, the Commission did not lawfully appoint the Administrative Law Judge here at issue. And this Court should decide no more than that.

## II

The Administrative Procedure Act thus allows administrative law judges to be removed only "for good cause" found by the Merit Systems Protection Board. And the President may, in turn, remove members of the Merit Systems Protection Board only for "inefficiency, neglect of duty, or malfeasance in office." Thus, Congress seems to have provided administrative law judges with two levels of protection from removal without cause — just what *Free Enterprise Fund* interpreted the Constitution to forbid in the case of the Board members.

The substantial independence that the Administrative Procedure Act's removal protections provide to administrative law judges is a central part of the Act's overall scheme. Before the Administrative Procedure Act, hearing examiners "were in a dependent status" to their employing agency, with their classification, compensation, and promotion all dependent on how the agency they worked for rated them. As a result of that dependence, "[m]any complaints were voiced against the actions of the hearing examiners, it being charged that they were mere tools of the agency concerned and subservient to the agency heads in making their proposed findings of fact and recommendations." The Administrative Procedure Act responded to those complaints by giving administrative law judges "independence and tenure within the existing Civil Service system."

*If* the *Free Enterprise Fund* [*v. Bennett*]'s Court's holding applies equally to the administrative law judges—and I stress the "if"—then to hold that the administrative law judges are "Officers of the United States" is, *perhaps*, to hold that their removal protections are unconstitutional. This would risk transforming administrative law judges from independent adjudicators into *dependent* decisionmakers, serving at the pleasure of the Commission. Similarly, to apply *Free Enterprise Fund*'s holding to high-level civil servants threatens to change the nature of our merit-based civil service as it has existed from the time of President Chester Alan Arthur.

I have stressed the words "if" and "perhaps" in the previous paragraph because *Free Enterprise Fund*'s holding may not invalidate the removal protections applicable to the Commission's administrative law judges even if the judges are inferior "officers of the United States" for purposes of the Appointments Clause.

How is the Court to decide whether Congress intended that the holder of a particular Government position count as an "Office[r] of the United States"? Congress might, of course, write explicitly into the statute that the employee "is an officer of the United States under the Appointments Clause," but an explicit phrase of this kind is unlikely to appear. If it does not, then I would approach the question like any other difficult question of statutory interpretation. Several considerations, among others, are likely to be relevant. First, as the Court said in *Freytag v. Commissioner* (1991) and repeats today, where Congress grants an appointee "'significant authority pursuant to the laws to the United States,'" that supports the view that (but should not determinatively decide that) Congress made that appointee an "Office[r] of the United States." The means of appointment that Congress chooses is also instructive. Where Congress provides a method of appointment that mimics a method the Appointments Clause allows for "Officers," that fact too supports the view that (but does not determinatively decide that) Congress viewed the position as one to be held by an "Officer," and vice versa. And the Court's decision in *Free Enterprise Fund* suggests a third indication of "Officer" status—did Congress provide the position with removal protections that would be unconstitutional if provided for an "That fact would support (but again not be determinative of) the opposite view—that Congress did not intend to confer "inferior Officer" status on the position.

As I said, these statutory features, while highly relevant, need not always prove determinative. The vast number of different civil service positions, with different tasks, different needs, and different requirements for independence, mean that this is not the place to lay down bright-line rules. Rather, as this Court has said, "[t]he versatility of circumstances often mocks a natural desire for definitiveness" in this area.

No case from this Court holds that Congress lacks this sort of constitutional leeway in determining whether a particular Government position will be filled by an "Office[r] of the United States."

The Court's decision to address the Appointments Clause question separately from the constitutional removal question is problematic. By considering each question in isolation, the Court risks (should the Court later extend *Free Enterprise Fund*) unraveling, step-by-step, the foundations of the Federal Government's administrative adjudication system as it has existed for decades, and perhaps of the merit-based civil-service system in general. And the Court risks doing so without considering that potential consequence. For these reasons, I concur in the judgment in part and, with respect, I dissent in part.

Justice SOTOMAYOR, with whom Justice GINSBURG joins, dissenting.

The Court today and scholars acknowledge that this Court's Appointments Clause jurisprudence offers little guidance on who qualifies as an "Officer of the United States." The lack of guidance is not without consequence. "[Q]uestions about the Clause continue to arise regularly both in the operation of the Executive Branch and in proposed legislation." This confusion can undermine the reliability and finality of proceedings and result in wasted resources.

As the majority notes, this Court's decisions currently set forth at least two prerequisites to officer status: (1) an individual must hold a "continuing" office established by law, and (2) an individual must wield "significant authority." The first requirement is relatively easy to grasp; the second, less so. To be sure, to exercise "significant authority," the person must wield considerable powers in comparison to the average person who works for the Federal Government. As this Court has noted, the vast majority of those who work for the Federal Government are not "Officers of the United States." But this Court's decisions have yet to articulate the types of powers that will be deemed significant enough to constitute "significant authority."

To provide guidance to Congress and the Executive Branch, I would hold that one requisite component of "significant authority" is the ability to make final, binding decisions on behalf of the Government. Accordingly, a person who merely advises and provides recommendations to an officer would not herself qualify as an officer.

There is some historical support for such a requirement. Confirming that final decisionmaking authority is a prerequisite to officer status would go a long way to aiding Congress and the Executive Branch in sorting out who is an officer and who is a mere employee. At the threshold, Congress and the Executive Branch could rule out as an officer any person who investigates, advises, or recommends, but who has no power to issue binding policies, execute the laws, or finally resolve adjudicatory questions.

Turning to the question presented here, it is true that the administrative law judges (ALJs) of the Securities and Exchange Commission wield "extensive powers." Nevertheless, I would hold that Commission ALJs are not officers because they lack final decisionmaking authority. As the Commission explained below, the Commission retains "'plenary authority over the course of [its] administrative proceedings and the rulings of [its] law judges.'" In other words, Commission ALJs do not exercise significant authority because they do not, and cannot, enter final, binding decisions against the Government or third parties.

Because I would conclude that Commission ALJs are not officers for purposes of the Appointments Clause, it is not necessary to reach the constitutionality of their removal protections.

# Chapter 4

# Limits on State Regulatory and Taxing Power

## B.  *The Dormant Commerce Clause* (casebook p. 476)

One application of the dormant commerce clause is as a limit on state taxation of interstate commerce. Previously the Supreme Court had ruled that a state could not require businesses to collect sales tax unless the business had a physical presence in the state. In *South Dakota v. Wayfair*, the Court overruled the earlier decisions and clarifies the ability of a state to impose taxes on interstate commerce.

## SOUTH DAKOTA v. WAYFAIR, INC.
### 138 S. Ct. 2080 (2018)

Justice KENNEDY delivered the opinion of the Court.

When a consumer purchases goods or services, the consumer's State often imposes a sales tax. This case requires the Court to determine when an out-of-state seller can be required to collect and remit that tax. All concede that taxing the sales in question here is lawful. The question is whether the out-of-state seller can be held responsible for its payment, and this turns on a proper interpretation of the Commerce Clause.

In two earlier cases the Court held that an out-of-state seller's liability to collect and remit the tax to the consumer's State depended on whether the seller had a physical presence in that State, but that mere shipment of goods into the consumer's State, following an order from a catalog, did not satisfy the physical presence requirement. *National Bellas Hess, Inc. v. Department of Revenue of Ill.* (1967); *Quill Corp. v. North Dakota* (1992).

I

Like most States, South Dakota has a sales tax. It taxes the retail sales of goods and services in the State. Sellers are generally required to collect and remit this tax to the Department of Revenue. If for some reason the sales tax is not remitted by the seller, then in-state consumers are separately responsible for paying a use tax at the same rate. Many States employ this kind of complementary sales and use tax regime.

Under this Court's decisions in *Bellas Hess* and *Quill*, South Dakota may not require a business to collect its sales tax if the business lacks a physical presence in the State. Without that physical presence, South Dakota instead must rely on its residents to pay the use tax owed on their purchases from out-of-state sellers. "[T]he impracticability of [this] collection from the multitude of individual purchasers is obvious." And consumer compliance rates are notoriously low. It is estimated that *Bellas Hess* and *Quill* cause the States to lose between $8 and $33 billion every year. In South Dakota alone, the Department of Revenue estimates revenue loss at $48 to $58 million annually. Particularly because South Dakota has no state income tax, it must put substantial reliance on its sales and use taxes for the revenue necessary to fund essential services. Those taxes account for over 60 percent of its general fund.

In 2016, South Dakota confronted the serious inequity *Quill* imposes by enacting S. 106—"An Act to provide for the collection of sales taxes from certain remote sellers, to establish certain Legislative findings, and to declare an emergency." The legislature found that the inability to collect sales tax from remote sellers was "seriously eroding the sales tax base" and "causing revenue losses and imminent harm . . . through the loss of critical funding for state and local services." The legislature also declared an emergency: "Whereas, this Act is necessary for the support of the state government and its existing public institutions, an emergency is hereby declared to exist." Fearing further erosion of the tax base, the legislature expressed its intention to "apply South Dakota's sales and use tax obligations to the limit of federal and state constitutional doctrines" and noted the urgent need for this Court to reconsider its precedents.

To that end, the Act requires out-of-state sellers to collect and remit sales tax "as if the seller had a physical presence in the state." The Act applies only to sellers that, on an annual basis, deliver more than $100,000 of goods or services into the State or engage in 200 or more separate transactions for the delivery of goods or services into the State. The Act also forecloses the retroactive application of this requirement and provides means for the Act to be appropriately stayed until the constitutionality of the law has been clearly established.

Respondents Wayfair, Inc., Overstock.com, Inc., and Newegg, Inc., are merchants with no employees or real estate in South Dakota. Wayfair, Inc., is a leading online retailer of home goods and furniture and had net revenues of over $4.7 billion last year. Overstock.com, Inc., is one of the top online retailers in the United States, selling a wide variety of products from home goods and furniture to clothing and jewelry; and it had net revenues of over $1.7 billion last year. Newegg, Inc., is a major online retailer of consumer electronics in the United States. Each of these three companies ships its goods directly to purchasers throughout the United States, including South Dakota. Each easily meets the minimum sales or transactions requirement of the Act, but none collects South Dakota sales tax.

## II

From early in its history, a central function of this Court has been to adjudicate disputes that require interpretation of the Commerce Clause in order to determine its meaning, its reach, and the extent to which it limits state regulations of commerce. Modern precedents rest upon two primary principles that mark the boundaries of a State's authority to regulate interstate commerce. First, state regulations may not discriminate against interstate commerce; and second, States may not impose undue burdens on interstate commerce. State laws that discriminate against interstate commerce face "a virtually *per se* rule of invalidity." State laws that "regulat[e] even-handedly to effectuate a legitimate local public interest . . . will be upheld unless the burden imposed on such commerce is clearly excessive in relation to the putative local benefits." Although subject to exceptions and variations, these two principles guide the courts in adjudicating cases challenging state laws under the Commerce Clause.

These principles also animate the Court's Commerce Clause precedents addressing the validity of state taxes. The Court explained the now-accepted framework for state taxation in *Complete Auto Transit, Inc. v. Brady* (1977). The Court held that a State "may tax exclusively interstate commerce so long as the tax does not create any effect forbidden by the Commerce Clause." After all, "interstate commerce may be required to pay its fair share of state taxes." The Court will sustain a tax so long as it (1) applies to an activity with a substantial nexus with the taxing State, (2) is fairly apportioned, (3) does not discriminate against interstate commerce, and (4) is fairly related to the services the State provides.

Before *Complete Auto*, the Court had addressed a challenge to an Illinois tax that required out-of-state retailers to collect and remit taxes on sales made to consumers who purchased goods for use within Illinois. The Court held that a mail-order company "whose only connection with customers in the State is by common carrier or the United States mail" lacked the requisite minimum contacts with the State required by both the Due

Process Clause and the Commerce Clause. Unless the retailer maintained a physical presence such as "retail outlets, solicitors, or property within a State," the State lacked the power to require that retailer to collect a local use tax.

In 1992, the Court reexamined the physical presence rule in *Quill*. That case presented a challenge to North Dakota's "attempt to require an out-of-state mail-order house that has neither outlets nor sales representatives in the State to collect and pay a use tax on goods purchased for use within the State." Despite the fact that *Bellas Hess* linked due process and the Commerce Clause together, the Court in *Quill* overruled the due process holding, but not the Commerce Clause holding; and it thus reaffirmed the physical presence rule.

## III

The physical presence rule has "been the target of criticism over many years from many quarters." *Quill*, it has been said, was "premised on assumptions that are unfounded" and "riddled with internal inconsistencies." *Quill* created an inefficient "online sales tax loophole" that gives out-of-state businesses an advantage. And "while nexus rules are clearly necessary," the Court "should focus on rules that are appropriate to the twenty-first century, not the nineteenth." Each year, the physical presence rule becomes further removed from economic reality and results in significant revenue losses to the States. These critiques underscore that the physical presence rule, both as first formulated and as applied today, is an incorrect interpretation of the Commerce Clause.

*Quill* is flawed on its own terms. First, the physical presence rule is not a necessary interpretation of the requirement that a state tax must be "applied to an activity with a substantial nexus with the taxing State." Second, *Quill* creates rather than resolves market distortions. And third, *Quill* imposes the sort of arbitrary, formalistic distinction that the Court's modern Commerce Clause precedents disavow.

All agree that South Dakota has the authority to tax these transactions. S.B. 106 applies to sales of "tangible personal property, products transferred electronically, or services *for delivery into South Dakota*." "It has long been settled" that the sale of goods or services "has a sufficient nexus to the State in which the sale is consummated to be treated as a local transaction taxable by that State."

The central dispute is whether South Dakota may require remote sellers to collect and remit the tax without some additional connection to the State. The Court has previously stated that "[t]he imposition on the seller of the duty to insure collection of the tax from the purchaser does not violate the [C]ommerce [C]lause." There just must be "a substantial nexus with the taxing State." This nexus requirement is "closely related" to the due process requirement that there be "some definite link, some minimum connection, between a state and the person, property or transaction it seeks to tax."

The Court has consistently explained that the Commerce Clause was designed to prevent States from engaging in economic discrimination so they would not divide into isolated, separable units. But it is "not the purpose of the [C]ommerce [C]lause to relieve those engaged in interstate commerce from their just share of state tax burden." And it is certainly not the purpose of the Commerce Clause to permit the Judiciary to create market distortions. "If the Commerce Clause was intended to put businesses on an even playing field, the [physical presence] rule is hardly a way to achieve that goal."

*Quill* puts both local businesses and many interstate businesses with physical presence at a competitive disadvantage relative to remote sellers. Remote sellers can avoid the regulatory burdens of tax collection and can offer *de facto* lower prices caused by the widespread failure of consumers to pay the tax on their own. This "guarantees a competitive benefit to certain firms simply because of the organizational form they choose" while the rest of the Court's jurisprudence "is all about preventing discrimination between firms." In effect, *Quill* has come to serve as a judicially created tax shelter for businesses that decide to limit their physical presence and still sell their goods and services to a State's consumers—something that has become easier and more prevalent as technology has advanced.

Worse still, the rule produces an incentive to avoid physical presence in multiple States. Distortions caused by the desire of businesses to avoid tax collection mean that the market may currently lack storefronts, distribution points, and employment centers that otherwise would be efficient or desirable. The Commerce Clause must not prefer interstate commerce only to the point where a merchant physically crosses state borders. Rejecting the physical presence rule is necessary to ensure that artificial competitive advantages are not created by this Court's precedents. This Court should not prevent States from collecting lawful taxes through a physical presence rule that can be satisfied only if there is an employee or a building in the State.

The Court's Commerce Clause jurisprudence has "eschewed formalism for a sensitive, case-by-case analysis of purposes and effects." *Quill*, in contrast, treats economically identical actors differently, and for arbitrary reasons.

The *Quill* Court itself acknowledged that the physical presence rule is "artificial at its edges." That was an understatement when *Quill* was decided; and when the day-to-day functions of marketing and distribution in the modern economy are considered, it is all the more evident that the physical presence rule is artificial in its entirety.

Modern e-commerce does not align analytically with a test that relies on the sort of physical presence defined in *Quill*. In a footnote, *Quill* rejected the argument that "title to 'a few floppy diskettes' present in a State" was sufficient to constitute a "substantial nexus." But it is not clear why a single employee or a single warehouse should create a substantial nexus while "physical" aspects of pervasive modern technology should not. For example, a company with a website accessible in South Dakota may be said to have a physical presence in the State via the customers' computers. A website may leave cookies saved to the customers' hard drives, or customers may download the company's app onto their phones. Or a company may lease data storage that is permanently, or even occasionally, located in South Dakota. What may have seemed like a "clear," "bright-line tes[t]" when *Quill* was written now threatens to compound the arbitrary consequences that should have been apparent from the outset.

The "dramatic technological and social changes" of our "increasingly interconnected economy" mean that buyers are "closer to most major retailers" than ever before—"regardless of how close or far the nearest storefront." Between targeted advertising and instant access to most consumers via any internet-enabled device, "a business may be present in a State in a meaningful way without" that presence "being physical in the traditional sense of the term." A virtual showroom can show far more inventory, in far more detail, and with greater opportunities for consumer and seller interaction than might be possible for local stores. Yet the continuous and pervasive virtual presence of retailers today is, under *Quill*, simply irrelevant. This Court should not maintain a rule that ignores these substantial virtual connections to the State.

The physical presence rule as defined and enforced in *Bellas Hess* and *Quill* is not just a technical legal problem—it is an extraordinary imposition by the Judiciary on States' authority to collect taxes and perform critical public functions. Forty-one States, two Territories, and the District of Columbia now ask this Court to reject the test formulated in *Quill*. *Quill*'s physical presence rule intrudes on States' reasonable choices in enacting their tax systems. And that it allows remote sellers to escape an obligation to remit a lawful state tax is unfair and unjust. It is unfair and unjust to those competitors, both local and out of State, who must remit the tax; to the consumers who pay the tax; and to the States that seek fair enforcement of the sales tax, a tax many States for many years have considered an indispensable source for raising revenue.

In essence, respondents ask this Court to retain a rule that allows their customers to escape payment of sales taxes—taxes that are essential to create and secure the active market they supply with goods and services.

It is essential to public confidence in the tax system that the Court avoid creating inequitable exceptions. This is also essential to the confidence placed in this Court's Commerce Clause decisions. Yet the physical presence rule undermines that necessary confidence by giving some online retailers an arbitrary advantage over their competitors who collect state sales taxes.

In the name of federalism and free markets, *Quill* does harm to both. The physical presence rule it defines has limited States' ability to seek long-term prosperity and has prevented market participants from competing on an even playing field.

"Although we approach the reconsideration of our decisions with the utmost caution, *stare decisis* is not an inexorable command." Here, *stare decisis* can no longer support the Court's prohibition of a valid exercise of the States' sovereign power.

If it becomes apparent that the Court's Commerce Clause decisions prohibit the States from exercising their lawful sovereign powers in our federal system, the Court should be vigilant in correcting the error. While it can be conceded that Congress has the authority to change the physical presence rule, Congress cannot change the constitutional default rule. It is inconsistent with the Court's proper role to ask Congress to address a false constitutional premise of this Court's own creation. Courts have acted as the front line of review in this limited sphere; and hence it is important that their principles be accurate and logical, whether or not Congress can or will act in response. It is currently the Court, and not Congress, that is limiting the lawful prerogatives of the States.

Further, the real world implementation of Commerce Clause doctrines now makes it manifest that the physical presence rule as defined by *Quill* must give way to the "far-reaching systemic and structural changes in the economy" and "many other societal dimensions" caused by the Cyber Age. Though *Quill* was wrong on its own terms when it was decided in 1992, since then the Internet revolution has made its earlier error all the more egregious and harmful.

This expansion has also increased the revenue shortfall faced by States seeking to collect their sales and use taxes. In 1992, it was estimated that the States were losing between $694 million and $3 billion per year in sales tax revenues as a result of the physical presence rule. Now estimates range from $8 to $33 billion. The South Dakota Legislature has declared an emergency, S.B. 106, § 9, which again demonstrates urgency of over-turning the physical presence rule.

The argument, moreover, that the physical presence rule is clear and easy to apply is unsound. Attempts to apply the physical presence rule to online retail sales are proving unworkable. States are already confronting the complexities of defining physical presence in the Cyber Age.

Respondents argue that "the physical presence rule has permitted start-ups and small businesses to use the Internet as a means to grow their companies and access a national market, without exposing them to the daunting complexity and business-development obstacles of nationwide sales tax collection." These burdens may pose legitimate concerns in some instances, particularly for small businesses that make a small volume of sales to customers in many States. State taxes differ, not only in the rate imposed but also in the categories of goods that are taxed and, some-times, the relevant date of purchase. Eventually, software that is available at a reasonable cost may make it easier for small businesses to cope with these problems. Indeed, as the physical presence rule no longer controls, those systems may well become available in a short period of time, either from private providers or from state taxing agencies themselves. And in all events, Congress may legislate to address these problems if it deems it necessary and fit to do so.

For these reasons, the Court concludes that the physical presence rule of *Quill* is unsound and incorrect. The Court's decisions in *Quill Corp. v. North Dakota*, (1992), and *National Bellas Hess, Inc. v. Department of Revenue of Ill.*, (1967), should be, and now are, overruled.

V

In the absence of *Quill* and *Bellas Hess*, the first prong of the *Complete Auto* test simply asks whether the tax applies to an activity with a substan-tial nexus with the taxing State. "[S]uch a nexus is established when the taxpayer [or collector] 'avails itself of the substantial privilege of carrying on business' in that jurisdiction."

Here, the nexus is clearly sufficient based on both the economic and vir-tual contacts respondents have with the State. The Act applies only to sell-ers that deliver more than $100,000 of goods or services into South Dakota or engage in 200 or more separate transactions for the delivery of goods and services into the State on an annual basis. This quantity of business could not have occurred unless the seller availed itself of the substantial privilege of carrying on business in South Dakota. And respondents are large, national companies that undoubtedly maintain an extensive virtual presence. Thus, the substantial nexus requirement of *Complete Auto* is satisfied in this case.

Chief Justice ROBERTS, with whom Justice BREYER, Justice SOTOMAYOR, and Justice KAGAN join, dissenting.

I agree that *Bellas Hess* was wrongly decided, for many of the reasons given by the Court. The Court argues in favor of overturning that decision because the "Internet's prevalence and power have changed the dynamics of the national economy." But that is the very reason I oppose discarding the physical-presence rule. E-commerce has grown into a significant and vibrant part of our national economy against the backdrop of established rules, including the physical-presence rule. Any alteration to those rules with the potential to disrupt the development of such a critical segment of the economy should be undertaken by Congress. The Court should not act on this important question of current economic policy, solely to expiate a mistake it made over 50 years ago.

## I

This Court "does not overturn its precedents lightly." Departing from the doctrine of *stare decisis* is an "exceptional action" demanding "special justification." The bar is even higher in fields in which Congress "exercises primary authority" and can, if it wishes, override this Court's decisions with contrary legislation. In such cases, we have said that "the burden borne by the party advocating the abandonment of an established precedent" is "greater" than usual. That is so "even where the error is a matter of serious concern, provided correction can be had by legislation."

We have applied this heightened form of *stare decisis* in the dormant Commerce Clause context. Under our dormant Commerce Clause precedents, when Congress has not yet legislated on a matter of interstate commerce, it is the province of "the courts to formulate the rules." But because Congress "has plenary power to regulate commerce among the States," it may at any time replace such judicial rules with legislation of its own. The Court thus left it to Congress "to decide whether, when, and to what extent the States may burden interstate mail-order concerns with a duty to collect use taxes."

## II

This is neither the first, nor the second, but the third time this Court has been asked whether a State may obligate sellers with no physical presence within its borders to collect tax on sales to residents. Whatever salience the adage "third time's a charm" has in daily life, it is a poor guide to Supreme Court decisionmaking. If *stare decisis* applied with special force in *Quill*, it should be an even greater impediment to overruling precedent now, particularly since this Court in *Quill* "tossed [the ball] into Congress's court, for acceptance or not as that branch elects."

Congress has in fact been considering whether to alter the rule established in *Bellas Hess* for some time. Nothing in today's decision precludes Congress from continuing to seek a legislative solution. But by suddenly changing the ground rules, the Court may have waylaid Congress's consideration of the issue. Armed with today's decision, state officials can be expected to redirect their attention from working with Congress on a national solution, to securing new tax revenue from remote retailers.

The Court, for example, breezily disregards the costs that its decision will impose on retailers. Correctly calculating and remitting sales taxes on all e-commerce sales will likely prove baffling for many retailers. Over 10,000 jurisdictions levy sales taxes, each with "different tax rates, different rules governing tax-exempt goods and services, different product category definitions, and different standards for determining whether an out-of-state seller has a substantial presence" in the jurisdiction.

The burden will fall disproportionately on small businesses. One vitalizing effect of the Internet has been connecting small, even "micro" businesses to potential buyers across the Nation. People starting a business selling their embroidered pillowcases or carved decoys can offer their wares throughout the country—but probably not if they have to figure out the tax due on every sale. And the software said to facilitate compliance is still in its infancy, and its capabilities and expense are subject to debate. The Court's decision today will surely have the effect of dampening opportunities for commerce in a broad range of new markets.

A good reason to leave these matters to Congress is that legislators may more directly consider the competing interests at stake. Unlike this Court, Congress has the flexibility to address these questions in a wide variety of ways. As we have said in other dormant Commerce Clause cases, Congress "has the capacity to investigate and analyze facts beyond anything the Judiciary could match."

Here, after investigation, Congress could reasonably decide that current trends might sufficiently expand tax revenues, obviating the need for an abrupt policy shift with potentially adverse consequences for e-commerce. Or Congress might decide that the benefits of allowing States to secure additional tax revenue outweigh any foreseeable harm to e-commerce. Or Congress might elect to accommodate these competing interests, by, for example, allowing States to tax Internet sales by remote retailers only if revenue from such sales exceeds some set amount per year. In any event, Congress can focus directly on current policy concerns rather than past legal mistakes. Congress can also provide a nuanced answer to the troubling question whether any change will have retroactive effect.

An erroneous decision from this Court may well have been an unintended factor contributing to the growth of e-commerce. The Court is of course correct that the Nation's economy has changed dramatically since the time that *Bellas Hess* and *Quill* roamed the earth. I fear the Court today is compounding its past error by trying to fix it in a totally different era. The Constitution gives Congress the power "[t]o regulate Commerce . . . among the several States." I would let Congress decide whether to depart from the physical-presence rule that has governed this area for half a century.

# Chapter 6

# *Economic Liberties*

## D. *The Takings Clause*

## 2. Is There a Taking? (casebook p. 671)

With regard to regulatory takings, the issue often arises as to how to determine what is the "property." That is the issue in *Murr v. Wisconsin.*

### MURR v. WISCONSIN
### 137 S. Ct. 1933 (2017)

Justice KENNEDY delivered the opinion of the Court.

The classic example of a property taking by the government is when the property has been occupied or otherwise seized. In the case now before the Court, petitioners contend that governmental entities took their real property—an undeveloped residential lot—not by some physical occupation but instead by enacting burdensome regulations that forbid its improvement or separate sale because it is classified as substandard in size. The relevant governmental entities are the respondents.

Against the background justifications for the challenged restrictions, respondents contend there is no regulatory taking because petitioners own an adjacent lot. The regulations, in effecting a merger of the property, permit the continued residential use of the property including for a single improvement to extend over both lots. This retained right of the landowner, respondents urge, is of sufficient offsetting value that the regulation is not severe enough to be a regulatory taking. To resolve the issue whether the landowners can insist on confining the analysis just to the lot in question, without regard to their ownership of the adjacent lot, it is necessary to discuss the background principles that define regulatory takings.

I

The St. Croix River originates in northwest Wisconsin and flows approximately 170 miles until it joins the Mississippi River, forming the boundary between Minnesota and Wisconsin for much of its length. The lower portion of the river slows and widens to create a natural water area known as Lake St. Croix. Tourists and residents of the region have long extolled the picturesque grandeur of the river and surrounding area.

Under the Wild and Scenic Rivers Act, the river was designated, by 1972, for federal protection. The law required the States of Wisconsin and Minnesota to develop "a management and development program" for the river area. In compliance, Wisconsin authorized the State Department of Natural Resources to promulgate rules limiting development in order to "guarantee the protection of the wild, scenic and recreational qualities of the river for present and future generations."

Petitioners are two sisters and two brothers in the Murr family. Petitioners' parents arranged for them to receive ownership of two lots the family used for recreation along the Lower St. Croix River in the town of Troy, Wisconsin. The lots are adjacent, but the parents purchased them separately, put the title of one in the name of the family business, and later arranged for transfer of the two lots, on different dates, to petitioners. The lots, which are referred to in this litigation as Lots E and F, are described in more detail below.

For the area where petitioners' property is located, the Wisconsin rules prevent the use of lots as separate building sites unless they have at least one acre of land suitable for development. A grandfather clause relaxes this restriction for substandard lots which were "in separate ownership from abutting lands" on January 1, 1976, the effective date of the regulation. The clause permits the use of qualifying lots as separate building sites. The rules also include a merger provision, however, which provides that adjacent lots under common ownership may not be "sold or developed as separate lots" if they do not meet the size requirement. The Wisconsin rules require localities to adopt parallel provisions, so the St. Croix County zoning ordinance contains identical restrictions. The Wisconsin rules also authorize the local zoning authority to grant variances from the regulations where enforcement would create "unnecessary hardship."

B

Petitioners' parents purchased Lot F in 1960 and built a small recreational cabin on it. In 1961, they transferred title to Lot F to the family plumbing company. In 1963, they purchased neighboring Lot E, which they held in their own names.

The lots have the same topography. A steep bluff cuts through the middle of each, with level land suitable for development above the bluff and next to the water below it. The line dividing Lot E from Lot F runs from the riverfront to the far end of the property, crossing the blufftop along the way. Lot E has approximately 60 feet of river frontage, and Lot F has approximately 100 feet. Though each lot is approximately 1.25 acres in size, because of the waterline and the steep bank they each have less than one acre of land suitable for development. Even when combined, the lots' buildable land area is only 0.98 acres due to the steep terrain.

The lots remained under separate ownership, with Lot F owned by the plumbing company and Lot E owned by petitioners' parents, until transfers to petitioners. Lot F was conveyed to them in 1994, and Lot E was conveyed to them in 1995.

A decade later, petitioners became interested in moving the cabin on Lot F to a different portion of the lot and selling Lot E to fund the project. The unification of the lots under common ownership, however, had implicated the state and local rules barring their separate sale or development. Petitioners then sought variances from the St. Croix County Board of Adjustment to enable their building and improvement plan, including a variance to allow the separate sale or use of the lots. The Board denied the requests, and the state courts affirmed in relevant part. In particular, the Wisconsin Court of Appeals agreed with the Board's interpretation that the local ordinance "effectively merged" Lots E and F, so petitioners "could only sell or build on the single larger lot."

The Circuit Court of St. Croix County granted summary judgment to the State, explaining that petitioners retained "several available options for the use and enjoyment of their property." For example, they could preserve the existing cabin, relocate the cabin, or eliminate the cabin and build a new residence on Lot E, on Lot F, or across both lots. The court also found petitioners had not been deprived of all economic value of their property. Considering the valuation of the property as a single lot versus two separate lots, the court found the market value of the property was not significantly affected by the regulations because the decrease in value was less than 10 percent.

The Wisconsin Court of Appeals affirmed. . . . The Supreme Court of Wisconsin denied discretionary review. This Court granted certiorari . . . .

II

A central dynamic of the Court's regulatory takings jurisprudence is its flexibility. This has been and remains a means to reconcile two competing objectives central to regulatory takings doctrine. One is the individual's right to retain the interests and exercise the freedoms at the core of private property ownership. Property rights are necessary to preserve freedom, for property ownership empowers persons to shape and to plan their own destiny in a world where governments are always eager to do so for them. The other persisting interest is the government's well-established power to "adjus[t] rights for the public good." As Justice Holmes declared, "Government hardly could go on if to some extent values incident to property could not be diminished without paying for every such change in the general law." In adjudicating regulatory takings cases a proper balancing of these principles requires a careful inquiry informed by the specifics of the case. In all instances, the analysis must be driven "by the purpose of the Takings Clause, which is to prevent the government from'forcing some people alone to bear public burdens which, in all fairness and justice, should be borne by the public as a whole.'"

This case presents a question that is linked to the ultimate determination whether a regulatory taking has occurred: What is the proper unit of property against which to assess the effect of the challenged governmental action? Put another way, "[b]ecause our test for regulatory taking requires us to compare the value that has been taken from the property with the value that remains in the property, one of the critical questions is determining how to define the unit of property 'whose value is to furnish the denominator of the fraction.'" As commentators have noted, the answer to this question may be outcome determinative. This Court, too, has explained that the question is important to the regulatory takings inquiry. "To the extent that any portion of property is taken, that portion is always taken in its entirety; the relevant question, however, is whether the property taken is all, or only a portion of, the parcel in question."

Defining the property at the outset, however, should not necessarily preordain the outcome in every case. In some, though not all, cases the effect of the challenged regulation must be assessed and understood by the effect on the entire property held by the owner, rather than just some part of the property that, considered just on its own, has been diminished in value. This demonstrates the contrast between regulatory takings, where the goal is usually to determine how the challenged regulation affects the property's value to the owner, and physical takings, where the impact of physical appropriation or occupation of the property will be evident.

While the Court has not set forth specific guidance on how to identify the relevant parcel for the regulatory taking inquiry, there are two concepts which the Court has indicated can be unduly narrow.

First, the Court has declined to limit the parcel in an artificial manner to the portion of property targeted by the challenged regulation. The second concept about which the Court has expressed caution is the view that property rights under the Takings Clause should be coextensive with those under state law. By the same measure, defining the parcel by reference to state law could defeat a challenge even to a state enactment that alters permitted uses of property in ways inconsistent with reasonable investment-backed expectations. For example, a State might enact a law that consolidates nonadjacent property owned by a single person or entity in different parts of the State and then imposes development limits on the aggregate set. If a court defined the parcel according to the state law requiring consolidation, this improperly would fortify the state law against a takings claim, because the court would look to the retained value in the property as a whole rather than considering whether individual holdings had lost all value.

## III

As the foregoing discussion makes clear, no single consideration can supply the exclusive test for determining the denominator. Instead, courts must consider a number of factors. These include the treatment of the land under state and local law; the physical characteristics of the land; and the prospective value of the regulated land. The endeavor should determine whether reasonable expectations about property ownership would lead a landowner to anticipate that his holdings would be treated as one parcel, or, instead, as separate tracts. The inquiry is objective, and the reasonable expectations at issue derive from background customs and the whole of our legal tradition.

First, courts should give substantial weight to the treatment of the land, in particular how it is bounded or divided, under state and local law. The reasonable expectations of an acquirer of land must acknowledge legitimate restrictions affecting his or her subsequent use and dispensation of the property.

Second, courts must look to the physical characteristics of the landowner's property. These include the physical relationship of any distinguishable tracts, the parcel's topography, and the surrounding human and ecological environment. In particular, it may be relevant that the property is located in an area that is subject to, or likely to become subject to, environmental or other regulation.

Third, courts should assess the value of the property under the challenged regulation, with special attention to the effect of burdened land on the value of other holdings. Though a use restriction may decrease the market value of the property, the effect may be tempered if the regulated land adds value to the remaining property, such as by increasing privacy, expanding recreational space, or preserving surrounding natural beauty. A law that limits use of a landowner's small lot in one part of the city by reason of the landowner's nonadjacent holdings elsewhere may decrease the market value of the small lot in an unmitigated fashion. The absence of a special relationship between the holdings may counsel against consideration of all the holdings as a single parcel, making the restrictive law susceptible to a takings challenge. On the other hand, if the landowner's other property is adjacent to the small lot, the market value of the properties may well increase if their combination enables the expansion of a structure, or if development restraints for one part of the parcel protect the unobstructed skyline views of another part. That, in turn, may counsel in favor of treatment as a single parcel and may reveal the weakness of a regulatory takings challenge to the law.

State and federal courts have considerable experience in adjudicating regulatory takings claims that depart from these examples in various ways. The Court anticipates that in applying the test above they will continue to exercise care in this complex area.

IV

Under the appropriate multifactor standard, it follows that for purposes of determining whether a regulatory taking has occurred here, petitioners' property should be evaluated as a single parcel consisting of Lots E and F together.

First, the treatment of the property under state and local law indicates petitioners' property should be treated as one when considering the effects of the restrictions. As the Wisconsin courts held, the state and local regulations merged Lots E and F. The decision to adopt the merger provision at issue here was for a specific and legitimate purpose, consistent with the widespread understanding that lot lines are not dominant or controlling in every case. Petitioners' land was subject to this regulatory burden, moreover, only because of voluntary conduct in bringing the lots under common ownership after the regulations were enacted. As a result, the valid merger of the lots under state law informs the reasonable expectation they will be treated as a single property.

Second, the physical characteristics of the property support its treatment as a unified parcel. The lots are contiguous along their longest edge. Their rough terrain and narrow shape make it reasonable to expect their range of potential uses might be limited. The land's location along the river is also significant. Petitioners could have anticipated public regulation might affect their enjoyment of their property, as the Lower St. Croix was a regulated area under federal, state, and local law long before petitioners possessed the land.

Third, the prospective value that Lot E brings to Lot F supports considering the two as one parcel for purposes of determining if there is a regulatory taking. Petitioners are prohibited from selling Lots E and F separately or from building separate residential structures on each. Yet this restriction is mitigated by the benefits of using the property as an integrated whole, allowing increased privacy and recreational space, plus the optimal location of any improvements.

The special relationship of the lots is further shown by their combined valuation. Were Lot E separately saleable but still subject to the development restriction, petitioners' appraiser would value the property at only $40,000. We express no opinion on the validity of this figure. We also note the number is not particularly helpful for understanding petitioners' retained value in the properties because Lot E, under the regulations, cannot be sold without Lot F. The point that is useful for these purposes is that the combined lots are valued at $698,300, which is far greater than the summed value of the separate regulated lots (Lot F with its cabin at $373,000, according to respondents' appraiser, and Lot E as an undevelopable plot at $40,000, according to petitioners' appraiser). The value added by the lots' combination shows their complementarity and supports their treatment as one parcel.

Considering petitioners' property as a whole, the state court was correct to conclude that petitioners cannot establish a compensable taking in these circumstances. Petitioners have not suffered a taking under *Lucas*, as they have not been deprived of all economically beneficial use of their property. They can use the property for residential purposes, including an enhanced, larger residential improvement. The property has not lost all economic value, as its value has decreased by less than 10 percent.

Petitioners furthermore have not suffered a taking under the more general test of *Penn Central*. The expert appraisal relied upon by the state courts refutes any claim that the economic impact of the regulation is severe. Petitioners cannot claim that they reasonably expected to sell or develop their lots separately given the regulations which predated their acquisition of both lots. Finally, the governmental action was a reasonable land-use regulation, enacted as part of a coordinated federal, state, and local effort to preserve the river and surrounding land.

Like the ultimate question whether a regulation has gone too far, the question of the proper parcel in regulatory takings cases cannot be solved by any simple test. Courts must instead define the parcel in a manner that reflects reasonable expectations about the property. Courts must strive for consistency with the central purpose of the Takings Clause: to "bar Government from forcing some people alone to bear public burdens which, in all fairness and justice, should be borne by the public as a whole." Treating the lot in question as a single parcel is legitimate for purposes of this takings inquiry, and this supports the conclusion that no regulatory taking occurred here.

Chief Justice ROBERTS, with whom Justice THOMAS and Justice ALITO join, dissenting.

Where the majority goes astray is in concluding that the definition of the "private property" at issue in a case such as this turns on an elaborate test looking not only to state and local law, but also to (1) "the physical characteristics of the land," (2) "the prospective value of the regulated land," (3) the "reasonable expectations" of the owner, and (4) "background customs and the whole of our legal tradition." Our decisions have, time and again, declared that the Takings Clause protects private property rights as state law creates and defines them. By securing such *established* property rights, the Takings Clause protects individuals from being forced to bear the full weight of actions that should be borne by the public at large. The majority's new, malleable definition of "private property" — adopted solely "for purposes of th[e] takings inquiry," undermines that protection.

I would stick with our traditional approach: State law defines the boundaries of distinct parcels of land, and those boundaries should determine the "private property" at issue in regulatory takings cases. Whether a regulation effects a taking of that property is a separate question, one in which common ownership of adjacent property may be taken into account. Because the majority departs from these settled principles, I respectfully dissent.

Because a regulation amounts to a taking if it completely destroys a property's productive use, there is an incentive for owners to define the relevant "private property" narrowly. This incentive threatens the careful balance between property rights and government authority that our regulatory takings doctrine strikes: Put in terms of the familiar "bundle" analogy, each "strand" in the bundle of rights that comes along with owning real property is a distinct property interest. If owners could define the relevant "private property" at issue as the specific "strand" that the challenged regulation affects, they could convert nearly all regulations into *per se* takings.

And so we do not allow it. In *Penn Central Transportation Co. v. New York City*, we held that property owners may not "establish a 'taking' simply by showing that they have been denied the ability to exploit a property interest." In that case, the owner of Grand Central Terminal in New York City argued that a restriction on the owner's ability to add an office building atop the station amounted to a taking of its air rights. We rejected that narrow definition of the "property" at issue, concluding that the correct unit of analysis was the owner's "rights in the parcel as a whole." "[W]here an owner possesses a full 'bundle' of property rights, the destruction of one strand of the bundle is not a taking, because the aggregate must be viewed in its entirety."

The question presented in today's case concerns the "parcel as a whole" language from *Penn Central*. This enigmatic phrase has created confusion about how to identify the relevant property in a regulatory takings case when the claimant owns more than one plot of land. Should the impact of the regulation be evaluated with respect to each individual plot, or with respect to adjacent plots grouped together as one unit? According to the majority, a court should answer this question by considering a number of facts about the land and the regulation at issue. The end result turns on whether those factors "would lead a landowner to anticipate that his holdings would be treated as one parcel, or, instead, as separate tracts."

I think the answer is far more straightforward: State laws define the boundaries of distinct units of land, and those boundaries should, in all but the most exceptional circumstances, determine the parcel at issue. Even in regulatory takings cases, the first step of the Takings Clause analysis is still to identify the relevant "private property." States create property rights with respect to particular "things." And in the context of real property, those "things" are horizontally bounded plots of land. States may define those plots differently—some using metes and bounds, others using government surveys, recorded plats, or subdivision maps. But the definition of property draws the basic line between, as P.G. Wodehouse would put it, *meum* and *tuum*. The question of who owns what is pretty important: The rules must provide a readily ascertainable definition of the land to which a particular bundle of rights attaches that does not vary depending upon the purpose at issue.

Following state property lines is also entirely consistent with *Penn Central*. Requiring consideration of the "parcel as a whole" is a response to the risk that owners will strategically pluck one strand from their bundle of property rights—such as the air rights at issue in *Penn Central*—and claim a complete taking based on that strand alone. That risk of strategic unbundling is not present when a legally distinct parcel is the basis of the regulatory takings claim. State law defines all of the interests that come along with owning a particular parcel, and both property owners and the government must take those rights as they find them.

The majority envisions that relying on state law will create other opportunities for "gamesmanship" by landowners and States: The former, it contends, "might seek to alter [lot] lines in anticipation of regulation," while the latter might pass a law that "consolidates . . . property" to avoid a successful takings claim. But such obvious attempts to alter the legal landscape in anticipation of a lawsuit are unlikely and not particularly difficult to detect and disarm. We rejected the strategic splitting of property rights in *Penn Central*, and courts could do the same if faced with an attempt to create a takings-specific definition of "private property."

Once the relevant property is identified, the real work begins. To decide whether the regulation at issue amounts to a "taking," courts should focus on the effect of the regulation on the "private property" at issue. Adjacent land under common ownership may be relevant to that inquiry. The owner's possession of such a nearby lot could, for instance, shed light on how the owner reasonably expected to use the parcel at issue before the regulation. If the court concludes that the government's action amounts to a taking, principles of "just compensation" may also allow the owner to recover damages "with regard to a separate parcel" that is contiguous and used in conjunction with the parcel at issue.

In sum, the "parcel as a whole" requirement prevents a property owner from identifying a single "strand" in his bundle of property rights and claiming that interest has been taken. Allowing that strategic approach to defining "private property" would undermine the balance struck by our regulatory takings cases. Instead, state law creates distinct parcels of land and defines the rights that come along with owning those parcels. Those established bundles of rights should define the "private property" in regulatory takings cases. While ownership of contiguous properties may bear on whether a person's plot has been "taken," *Penn Central* provides no basis for disregarding state property lines when identifying the "parcel as a whole."

## II

The lesson that the majority draws from *Penn Central* is that defining "the proper parcel in regulatory takings cases cannot be solved by any simple test." Following through on that stand against simplicity, the majority lists a complex set of factors theoretically designed to reveal whether a hypothetical landowner might expect that his property "would be treated as one parcel, or, instead, as separate tracts." Those factors, says the majority, show that Lots E and F of the Murrs' property constitute a single parcel and that the local ordinance requiring the Murrs to develop and sell those lots as a pair does not constitute a taking.

In deciding that Lots E and F are a single parcel, the majority focuses on the importance of the ordinance at issue and the extent to which the Murrs may have been especially surprised, or unduly harmed, by the application of that ordinance to their property. But these issues should be considered when deciding if a regulation constitutes a "taking." Cramming them into the definition of "private property" undermines the effectiveness of the Takings Clause as a check on the government's power to shift the cost of public life onto private individuals.

In departing from state property principles, the majority authorizes governments to do precisely what we rejected in *Penn Central*: create a litigation-specific definition of "property" designed for a claim under the Takings Clause. Whenever possible, governments in regulatory takings cases will ask courts to aggregate legally distinct properties into one "parcel," solely for purposes of resisting a particular claim. And under the majority's test, identifying the "parcel as a whole" in such cases will turn on the reasonableness of the regulation as applied to the claimant. The result is that the government's regulatory interests will come into play not once, but twice—first when identifying the relevant parcel, and again when determining whether the regulation has placed too great a public burden on that property.

Regulatory takings, however—by their very nature—pit the common good against the interests of a few. There is an inherent imbalance in that clash of interests. The widespread benefits of a regulation will often appear far weightier than the isolated losses suffered by individuals. And looking at the bigger picture, the overall societal good of an economic system grounded on private property will appear abstract when cast against a concrete regulatory problem. In the face of this imbalance, the Takings Clause "prevents the public from loading upon one individual more than his just share of the burdens of government," by considering the effect of a regulation on specific property rights as they are established at state law. But the majority's approach undermines that protection, defining property only after engaging in an ad hoc, case-specific consideration of individual and community interests. The result is that the government's goals shape the playing field before the contest over whether the challenged regulation goes "too far" even gets underway.

Put simply, today's decision knocks the definition of "private property" loose from its foundation on stable state law rules and throws it into the maelstrom of multiple factors that come into play at the second step of the takings analysis. The result: The majority's new framework compromises the Takings Clause as a barrier between individuals and the press of the public interest.

III

As I see it, the Wisconsin Court of Appeals was wrong to apply a takings-specific definition of the property at issue. Instead, the court should have asked whether, under general state law principles, Lots E and F are legally distinct parcels of land. I would therefore vacate the judgment below and remand for the court to identify the relevant property using ordinary principles of Wisconsin property law.

# Chapter 7

# Equal Protection

## C. Classifications Based on Race and National Origin

## 3. Proving the Existence of a Race or National Origin Classification

### a. Race and National Origin Classifications on the Face of the Law (casebook p. 761)

In *Pena-Rodriguez v. Colorado*, the Court considered how a court should respond to information that a juror made racist statements during jury deliberations.

PENA-RODRIGUEZ v. COLORADO
137 S. Ct. 788 (2017)

Justice KENNEDY delivered the opinion of the Court.

The jury is a central foundation of our justice system and our democracy. Whatever its imperfections in a particular case, the jury is a necessary check on governmental power. The jury, over the centuries, has been an inspired, trusted, and effective instrument for resolving factual disputes and determining ultimate questions of guilt or innocence in criminal cases. Over the long course its judgments find acceptance in the community, an acceptance essential to respect for the rule of law. The jury is a tangible implementation of the principle that the law comes from the people.

In the era of our Nation's founding, the right to a jury trial already had existed and evolved for centuries, through and alongside the common law. The jury was considered a fundamental safeguard of individual liberty. The right to a jury trial in criminal cases was part of the Constitution as first drawn, and it was restated in the Sixth Amendment. By operation of the Fourteenth Amendment, it is applicable to the States.

Like all human institutions, the jury system has its flaws, yet experience shows that fair and impartial verdicts can be reached if the jury follows the court's instructions and undertakes deliberations that are honest, candid, robust, and based on common sense. A general rule has evolved to give substantial protection to verdict finality and to assure jurors that, once their verdict has been entered, it will not later be called into question based on the comments or conclusions they expressed during deliberations. This principle, itself centuries old, is often referred to as the no-impeachment rule. The instant case presents the question whether there is an exception to the no-impeachment rule when, after the jury is discharged, a juror comes forward with compelling evidence that another juror made clear and explicit statements indicating that racial animus was a significant motivating factor in his or her vote to convict.

## I

State prosecutors in Colorado brought criminal charges against petitioner, Miguel Angel Peña-Rodriguez, based on the following allegations. In 2007, in the bathroom of a Colorado horse-racing facility, a man sexually assaulted two teenage sisters. The girls told their father and identified the man as an employee of the racetrack. The police located and arrested petitioner. Each girl separately identified petitioner as the man who had assaulted her.

The State charged petitioner with harassment, unlawful sexual contact, and attempted sexual assault on a child. Before the jury was empaneled, members of the venire were repeatedly asked whether they believed that they could be fair and impartial in the case. A written questionnaire asked if there was "anything about you that you feel would make it difficult for you to be a fair juror." The court repeated the question to the panel of prospective jurors and encouraged jurors to speak in private with the court if they had any concerns about their impartiality. Defense counsel likewise asked whether anyone felt that "this is simply not a good case" for them to be a fair juror. None of the empaneled jurors expressed any reservations based on racial or any other bias. And none asked to speak with the trial judge.

After a 3-day trial, the jury found petitioner guilty of unlawful sexual contact and harassment, but it failed to reach a verdict on the attempted sexual assault charge. Following the discharge of the jury, petitioner's counsel entered the jury room to discuss the trial with the jurors. As the room was emptying, two jurors remained to speak with counsel in private. They stated that, during deliberations, another juror had expressed anti-Hispanic bias toward petitioner and petitioner's alibi witness. Petitioner's counsel reported this to the court and, with the court's supervision, obtained sworn affidavits from the two jurors.

The affidavits by the two jurors described a number of biased statements made by another juror, identified as Juror H.C. According to the two jurors, H.C. told the other jurors that he "believed the defendant was guilty because, in [H.C.'s] experience as an ex-law enforcement officer, Mexican men had a bravado that caused them to believe they could do whatever they wanted with women." The jurors reported that H.C. stated his belief that Mexican men are physically controlling of women because of their sense of entitlement, and further stated, "'I think he did it because he's Mexican and Mexican men take whatever they want.'" According to the jurors, H.C. further explained that, in his experience, "nine times out of ten Mexican men were guilty of being aggressive toward women and young girls." Finally, the jurors recounted that Juror H.C. said that he did not find petitioner's alibi witness credible because, among other things, the witness was "'an illegal.'"

After reviewing the affidavits, the trial court acknowledged H.C.'s apparent bias. But the court denied petitioner's motion for a new trial, noting that "[t]he actual deliberations that occur among the jurors are protected from inquiry under [Colorado Rule of Evidence] 606(b)." Like its federal counterpart, Colorado's Rule 606(b) generally prohibits a juror from testifying as to any statement made during deliberations in a proceeding inquiring into the validity of the verdict. The Colorado Rule reads as follows:

> "(b) Inquiry into validity of verdict or indictment. Upon an inquiry into the validity of a verdict or indictment, a juror may not testify as to any matter or statement occurring during the course of the jury's deliberations or to the effect of anything upon his or any other juror's mind or emotions as influencing him to assent to or dissent from the verdict or indictment or concerning his mental processes in connection therewith. But a juror may testify about (1) whether extraneous prejudicial information was improperly brought to the jurors' attention, (2) whether any outside influence was improperly brought to bear upon any juror, or (3) whether there was a mistake in entering the verdict onto the verdict form. A juror's affidavit or evidence of any statement by the juror may not be received on a matter about which the juror would be precluded from testifying."

The verdict deemed final, petitioner was sentenced to two years' probation and was required to register as a sex offender.

Juror H.C.'s bias was based on petitioner's Hispanic identity, which the Court in prior cases has referred to as ethnicity, and that may be an instructive term here. Petitioner and respondent both refer to race, or to race and ethnicity, in this more expansive sense in their briefs to the Court. This opinion refers to the nature of the bias as racial in keeping with the primary terminology employed by the parties and used in our precedents.

## II

At common law jurors were forbidden to impeach their verdict, either by affidavit or live testimony. This rule originated in *Vaise v. Delaval* (K.B. 1785). There, Lord Mansfield excluded juror testimony that the jury had decided the case through a game of chance. The Mansfield rule, as it came to be known, prohibited jurors, after the verdict was entered, from testifying either about their subjective mental processes or about objective events that occurred during deliberations.

American courts adopted the Mansfield rule as a matter of common law, though not in every detail. The common-law development of the no-impeachment rule reached a milestone in 1975, when Congress adopted the Federal Rules of Evidence, including Rule 606(b). Congress endorsed a broad no-impeachment rule, with only limited exceptions. The version of the rule that Congress adopted was "no accident." This version of the no-impeachment rule has substantial merit. It promotes full and vigorous discussion by providing jurors with considerable assurance that after being discharged they will not be summoned to recount their deliberations, and they will not otherwise be harassed or annoyed by litigants seeking to challenge the verdict. The rule gives stability and finality to verdicts.

Some version of the no-impeachment rule is followed in every State and the District of Columbia. Variations make classification imprecise, but, as a general matter, it appears that 42 jurisdictions follow the Federal Rule.

## III

It must become the heritage of our Nation to rise above racial classifications that are so inconsistent with our commitment to the equal dignity of all persons. This imperative to purge racial prejudice from the administration of justice was given new force and direction by the ratification of the Civil War Amendments.

"[T]he central purpose of the Fourteenth Amendment was to eliminate racial discrimination emanating from official sources in the States." In the years before and after the ratification of the Fourteenth Amendment, it became clear that racial discrimination in the jury system posed a particular threat both to the promise of the Amendment and to the integrity of the jury trial. "Almost immediately after the Civil War, the South began a practice that would continue for many decades: All-white juries punished black defendants particularly harshly, while simultaneously refusing to punish violence by whites, including Ku Klux Klan members, against blacks and Republicans." To take one example, just in the years 1865 and 1866, all-white juries in Texas decided a total of 500 prosecutions of white defendants charged with killing African-Americans. All 500 were acquitted. The stark and unapologetic nature of race-motivated outcomes challenged the American belief that "the jury was a bulwark of liberty," and prompted Congress to pass legislation to integrate the jury system and to bar persons from eligibility for jury service if they had conspired to deny the civil rights of African-Americans. Members of Congress stressed that the legislation was necessary to preserve the right to a fair trial and to guarantee the equal protection of the laws.

The duty to confront racial animus in the justice system is not the legislature's alone. Time and again, this Court has been called upon to enforce the Constitution's guarantee against state-sponsored racial discrimination in the jury system. Beginning in 1880, the Court interpreted the Fourteenth Amendment to prohibit the exclusion of jurors on the basis of race. The Court has repeatedly struck down laws and practices that systematically exclude racial minorities from juries. To guard against discrimination in jury selection, the Court has ruled that no litigant may exclude a prospective juror on the basis of race. In an effort to ensure that individuals who sit on juries are free of racial bias, the Court has held that the Constitution at times demands that defendants be permitted to ask questions about racial bias during *voir dire*.

The unmistakable principle underlying these precedents is that discrimination on the basis of race, "odious in all aspects, is especially pernicious in the administration of justice." The jury is to be "a criminal defendant's fundamental 'protection of life and liberty against race or color prejudice.'" Permitting racial prejudice in the jury system damages "both the fact and the perception" of the jury's role as "a vital check against the wrongful exercise of power by the State."

## IV

This case lies at the intersection of the Court's decisions endorsing the no-impeachment rule and its decisions seeking to eliminate racial bias in the jury system. The two lines of precedent, however, need not conflict.

[R]acial bias, a familiar and recurring evil that, if left unaddressed, would risk systemic injury to the administration of justice. This Court's decisions demonstrate that racial bias implicates unique historical, constitutional, and institutional concerns. An effort to address the most grave and serious statements of racial bias is not an effort to perfect the jury but to ensure that our legal system remains capable of coming ever closer to the promise of equal treatment under the law that is so central to a functioning democracy.

Racial bias is distinct in a pragmatic sense as well. In past cases this Court has relied on other safeguards to protect the right to an impartial jury. Some of those safeguards, to be sure, can disclose racial bias. *Voir dire* at the outset of trial, observation of juror demeanor and conduct during trial, juror reports before the verdict, and nonjuror evidence after trial are important mechanisms for discovering bias. Yet their operation may be compromised, or they may prove insufficient. For instance, this Court has noted the dilemma faced by trial court judges and counsel in deciding whether to explore potential racial bias at *voir dire*. Generic questions about juror impartiality may not expose specific attitudes or biases that can poison jury deliberations. Yet more pointed questions "could well exacerbate whatever prejudice might exist without substantially aiding in exposing it."

The stigma that attends racial bias may make it difficult for a juror to report inappropriate statements during the course of juror deliberations. It is one thing to accuse a fellow juror of having a personal experience that improperly influences her consideration of the case. It is quite another to call her a bigot.

For the reasons explained above, the Court now holds that where a juror makes a clear statement that indicates he or she relied on racial stereotypes or animus to convict a criminal defendant, the Sixth Amendment requires that the no-impeachment rule give way in order to permit the trial court to consider the evidence of the juror's statement and any resulting denial of the jury trial guarantee.

Not every offhand comment indicating racial bias or hostility will justify setting aside the no-impeachment bar to allow further judicial inquiry. For the inquiry to proceed, there must be a showing that one or more jurors made statements exhibiting overt racial bias that cast serious doubt on the fairness and impartiality of the jury's deliberations and resulting verdict. To qualify, the statement must tend to show that racial animus was a significant motivating factor in the juror's vote to convict. Whether that threshold showing has been satisfied is a matter committed to the substantial discretion of the trial court in light of all the circumstances, including the content and timing of the alleged statements and the reliability of the proffered evidence.

The practical mechanics of acquiring and presenting such evidence will no doubt be shaped and guided by state rules of professional ethics and local court rules, both of which often limit counsel's post-trial contact with jurors. These limits seek to provide jurors some protection when they return to their daily affairs after the verdict has been entered. But while a juror can always tell counsel they do not wish to discuss the case, jurors in some instances may come forward of their own accord.

That is what happened here. In this case the alleged statements by a juror were egregious and unmistakable in their reliance on racial bias. Not only did juror H.C. deploy a dangerous racial stereotype to conclude petitioner was guilty and his alibi witness should not be believed, but he also encouraged other jurors to join him in convicting on that basis.

Petitioner's counsel did not seek out the two jurors' allegations of racial bias. Pursuant to Colorado's mandatory jury instruction, the trial court had set limits on juror contact and encouraged jurors to inform the court if anyone harassed them about their role in the case. Similar limits on juror contact can be found in other jurisdictions that recognize a racial-bias exception.

While the trial court concluded that Colorado's Rule 606(b) did not permit it even to consider the resulting affidavits, the Court's holding today removes that bar. When jurors disclose an instance of racial bias as serious as the one involved in this case, the law must not wholly disregard its occurrence.

The Court relies on the experiences of the 17 jurisdictions that have recognized a racial-bias exception to the no-impeachment rule — some for over half a century — with no signs of an increase in juror harassment or a loss of juror willingness to engage in searching and candid deliberations. The experience of these jurisdictions, and the experience of the courts going forward, will inform the proper exercise of trial judge discretion in these and related matters. This case does not ask, and the Court need not address, what procedures a trial court must follow when confronted with a motion for a new trial based on juror testimony of racial bias. The Court also does not decide the appropriate standard for determining when evidence of racial bias is sufficient to require that the verdict be set aside and a new trial be granted.

The Nation must continue to make strides to overcome race-based discrimination. The progress that has already been made underlies the Court's insistence that blatant racial prejudice is antithetical to the functioning of the jury system and must be confronted in egregious cases like this one despite the general bar of the no-impeachment rule. It is the mark of a maturing legal system that it seeks to understand and to implement the lessons of history. The Court now seeks to strengthen the broader principle that society can and must move forward by achieving the thoughtful, rational dialogue at the foundation of both the jury system and the free society that sustains our Constitution.

Justice THOMAS, dissenting.

The Court today holds that the Sixth Amendment requires the States to provide a criminal defendant the opportunity to impeach a jury's guilty verdict with juror testimony about a juror's alleged racial bias, notwithstanding a state procedural rule forbidding such testimony. I agree with Justice Alito that the Court's decision is incompatible with the text of the Amendment it purports to interpret and with our precedents. I write separately to explain that the Court's holding also cannot be squared with the original understanding of the Sixth or Fourteenth Amendments.

The Sixth Amendment's protection of the right, "[i]n all criminal prosecutions," to a "trial, by an impartial jury," is limited to the protections that existed at common law when the Amendment was ratified. The Sixth Amendment's specific guarantee of impartiality incorporates the common-law understanding of that term. The common law required a juror to have "freedome of mind" and to be "indifferent as hee stands unsworne." 1 E. Coke, First Part of the Institutes of the Laws of England § 234, p. 155a (16th ed. 1809).

The common-law right to a jury trial did not, however, guarantee a defendant the right to impeach a jury verdict with juror testimony about juror misconduct, including "a principal species of [juror] misbehaviour"—"notorious partiality." 3 Blackstone 388. Although partiality was a ground for setting aside a jury verdict, the English common-law rule at the time the Sixth Amendment was ratified did not allow jurors to supply evidence of that misconduct.

Perhaps good reasons exist to curtail or abandon the no-impeachment rule. Some States have done so, and others have not. Ultimately, that question is not for us to decide. It should be left to the political process described by Justice Alito. In its attempt to stimulate a "thoughtful, rational dialogue" on race relations, the Court today ends the political process and imposes a uniform, national rule. The Constitution does not require such a rule. Neither should we.

Justice ALITO with whom THE CHIEF JUSTICE and Justice THOMAS join, dissenting.

Our legal system has many rules that restrict the admission of evidence of statements made under circumstances in which confidentiality is thought to be essential. Statements made to an attorney in obtaining legal advice, statements to a treating physician, and statements made to a spouse or member of the clergy are familiar examples. Even if a criminal defendant whose constitutional rights are at stake has a critical need to obtain and introduce evidence of such statements, long-established rules stand in the way. The goal of avoiding interference with confidential communications of great value has long been thought to justify the loss of important evidence and the effect on our justice system that this loss entails.

The present case concerns a rule like those just mentioned, namely, the age-old rule against attempting to overturn or "impeach" a jury's verdict by offering statements made by jurors during the course of deliberations. For centuries, it has been the judgment of experienced judges, trial attorneys, scholars, and lawmakers that allowing jurors to testify after a trial about what took place in the jury room would undermine the system of trial by jury that is integral to our legal system.

Juries occupy a unique place in our justice system. The other participants in a trial — the presiding judge, the attorneys, the witnesses — function in an arena governed by strict rules of law. Their every word is recorded and may be closely scrutinized for missteps.

When jurors retire to deliberate, however, they enter a space that is not regulated in the same way. Jurors are ordinary people. They are expected to speak, debate, argue, and make decisions the way ordinary people do in their daily lives. Our Constitution places great value on this way of thinking, speaking, and deciding. The jury trial right protects parties in court cases from being judged by a special class of trained professionals who do not speak the language of ordinary people and may not understand or appreciate the way ordinary people live their lives. To protect that right, the door to the jury room has been locked, and the confidentiality of jury deliberations has been closely guarded.

Today, with the admirable intention of providing justice for one criminal defendant, the Court not only pries open the door; it rules that respecting the privacy of the jury room, as our legal system has done for centuries, violates the Constitution. This is a startling development, and although the Court tries to limit the degree of intrusion, it is doubtful that there are principled grounds for preventing the expansion of today's holding.

The Court justifies its decision on the ground that the nature of the confidential communication at issue in this particular case — a clear expression of what the Court terms racial bias[1] — is uniquely harmful to our criminal justice system. And the Court is surely correct that even a tincture of racial bias can inflict great damage on that system, which is dependent on the public's trust. But until today, the argument that the Court now finds convincing has not been thought to be sufficient to overcome confidentiality rules like the one at issue here.

Suppose that a prosecution witness gives devastating but false testimony against a defendant, and suppose that the witness's motivation is racial bias. Suppose that the witness admits this to his attorney, his spouse, and a member of the clergy. Suppose that the defendant, threatened with conviction for a serious crime and a lengthy term of imprisonment, seeks to compel the attorney, the spouse, or the member of the clergy to testify about the witness's admissions. Even though the constitutional rights of the defendant hang in the balance, the defendant's efforts to obtain the testimony would fail. The Court provides no good reason why the result in this case should not be the same.

## 5.   Racial Classification Benefiting Minorities

### Drawing Election Districts to Increase Minority Representation (casebook p. 878)

In two cases—*Bethune Hill v. Virginia State of Elections* and *Cooper v. Harris*—the Supreme Court confronted whether and when the government can use race in drawing election districts. *Cooper v. Harris* seems particularly important because of the footnote in Justice Kagan's opinion that the use of race must meet strict scrutiny even if it is being considered as a proxy for political party affiliation. In light of this, *it* is unclear whether and to what extent *Easley v. Cromartie* (casebook p. 880) remains good law.

### BETHUNE-HILL v. VIRGINIA STATE BOARD OF ELECTIONS
137 S. Ct. 788 (2017)

Justice KENNEDY delivered the opinion of the Court.

This case addresses whether the Virginia state legislature's consideration of race in drawing new lines for 12 state legislative districts violated the Equal Protection Clause of the Fourteenth Amendment. After the 2010 census, some redistricting was required to ensure proper numerical apportionment for the Virginia House of Delegates. It is undisputed that the boundary lines for the 12 districts at issue were drawn with a goal of ensuring that each district would have a black voting-age population (BVAP) of at least 55%.

Certain voters challenged the new districts as unconstitutional racial gerrymanders. The United States District Court for the Eastern District of Virginia, constituted as a three-judge district court, rejected the challenges as to each of the 12 districts. As to 11 of the districts, the District Court concluded that the voters had not shown, as this Court's precedent requires, "that race was the predominant factor motivating the legislature's decision to place a significant number of voters within or without a particular district." *Miller v. Johnson* (1995). The District Court held that race predominates only where there is an "'*actual* conflict between traditional redistricting criteria and race,'" so it confined the predominance analysis to the portions of the new lines that appeared to deviate from traditional criteria, and found no violation. As to the remaining district, District 75, the District Court found that race did predominate. It concluded, however, that the lines were constitutional because the legislature's use of race was narrowly tailored to a compelling state interest. In particular, the District Court determined that the legislature had "good reasons to believe" that a 55% racial target was necessary in District 75 to avoid diminishing the ability of black voters to elect their preferred candidates, which at the time would have violated § 5 of the Voting Rights Act of 1965.

This Court now affirms as to District 75 and vacates and remands as to the remaining 11 districts.

# I

After the 2010 census, the Virginia General Assembly set out to redraw the legislative districts for the State Senate and House of Delegates in time for the 2011 elections. In February 2011, the House Committee on Privileges and Elections adopted a resolution establishing criteria to guide the redistricting process. Among those criteria were traditional redistricting factors such as compactness, contiguity of territory, and respect for communities of interest. But above those traditional objectives, the committee gave priority to two other goals. First, in accordance with the principle of one person, one vote, the committee resolved that "[t]he population of each district shall be as nearly equal to the population of every other district as practicable," with any deviations falling "within plus-or-minus one percent." Second, the committee resolved that the new map must comply with the "protections against . . . unwarranted retrogression" contained in § 5 of the Voting Rights Act. At the time, § 5 required covered jurisdictions, including Virginia, to preclear any change to a voting standard, practice, or procedure by showing federal authorities that the change would not have the purpose or effect of "diminishing the ability of [members of a minority group] to elect their preferred candidates of choice." After the redistricting process here was completed, this Court held that the coverage formula in § 4(b) of the Voting Rights Act no longer may be used to require preclearance under § 5.

The committee's criteria presented potential problems for 12 House districts. Under § 5 as Congress amended it in 2005, "[a] plan leads to impermissible retrogression when, compared to the plan currently in effect (typically called a 'benchmark plan'), the new plan diminishes the number of districts in which minority groups can 'elect their preferred candidates of choice' (often called 'ability-to-elect' districts)." The parties agree that the 12 districts at issue here, where minorities had constituted a majority of the voting-age population for many past elections, qualified as "ability-to-elect" districts. Most of the districts were underpopulated, however, so any new plan required moving significant numbers of new voters into these districts in order to comply with the principle of one person, one vote. Under the benchmark plan, the districts had BVAPs ranging from 62.7% down to 46.3%. Three districts had BVAPs below 55%.

Seeking to maintain minority voters' ability to elect their preferred candidates in these districts while complying with the one-person, one-vote criterion, legislators concluded that each of the 12 districts "needed to contain a At trial, the parties disputed whether the 55% figure "was an aspiration or a target or a rule." But they did not dispute "the most important question—whether [the 55%] figure was used in drawing the Challenged Districts." The parties agreed, and the District Court found, "that the 55% BVAP figure was used in structuring the districts." In the enacted plan all 12 districts contained a BVAP greater than 55%.

## II

Against the factual and procedural background set out above, it is now appropriate to consider the controlling legal principles in this case. The Equal Protection Clause prohibits a State, without sufficient justification, from "separat[ing] its citizens into different voting districts on the basis of race." The harms that flow from racial sorting "include being personally subjected to a racial classification as well as being represented by a legislator who believes his primary obligation is to represent only the members of a particular racial group." At the same time, courts must "exercise extraordinary caution in adjudicating claims that a State has drawn district lines on the basis of race." "Electoral districting is a most difficult subject for legislatures," requiring a delicate balancing of competing considerations. And "redistricting differs from other kinds of state decisionmaking in that the legislature always is *aware* of race when it draws district lines, just as it is aware of . . . a variety of other demographic factors."

In light of these considerations, this Court has held that a plaintiff alleging racial gerrymandering bears the burden "to show, either through circumstantial evidence of a district's shape and demographics or more direct evidence going to legislative purpose, that race was the predominant factor motivating the legislature's decision to place a significant number of voters within or without a particular district." To satisfy this burden, the plaintiff "must prove that the legislature subordinated traditional race-neutral districting principles . . . to racial considerations." The challengers contend that, in finding that race did not predominate in 11 of the 12 districts, the District Court misapplied controlling law in two principal ways. This Court considers them in turn.

A

The challengers first argue that the District Court misunderstood the relevant precedents when it required the challengers to establish, as a prerequisite to showing racial predominance, an actual conflict between the enacted plan and traditional redistricting principles. The Court agrees with the challengers on this point.

A threshold requirement that the enacted plan must conflict with traditional principles might have been reconcilable with this Court's case law at an earlier time. In *Shaw I*, the Court recognized a claim of racial gerrymandering for the first time. Certain language in *Shaw I* can be read to support requiring a challenger who alleges racial gerrymandering to show an actual conflict with traditional principles. The opinion stated, for example, that strict scrutiny applies to "redistricting legislation that is so bizarre on its face that it is unexplainable on grounds other than race." The opinion also stated that "reapportionment is one area in which appearances do matter."

The Court's opinion in *Miller*, however, clarified the racial predominance inquiry. In particular, it rejected the argument that, "regardless of the legislature's purposes, a plaintiff must demonstrate that a district's shape is so bizarre that it is unexplainable other than on the basis of race." The Court held to the contrary in language central to the instant case: "Shape is relevant not because bizarreness is a necessary element of the constitutional wrong or a threshold requirement of proof, but because it may be persuasive circumstantial evidence that race for its own sake, and not other districting principles, was the legislature's dominant and controlling rationale." Parties therefore "may rely on evidence other than bizarreness to establish race-based districting," and may show predominance "either through circumstantial evidence of a district's shape and demographics or more direct evidence going to legislative purpose."

The Court addressed racial gerrymandering and traditional redistricting factors again in *Shaw v. Hunt* (1996) (*Shaw II*). The Court there rejected the view of one of the dissents that "strict scrutiny does not apply where a State 'respects' or 'complies with traditional districting principles.'" Race may predominate even when a reapportionment plan respects traditional principles, the Court explained, if "[r]ace was the criterion that, in the State's view, could not be compromised," and race-neutral considerations "came into play only after the race-based decision had been made."

The State's theory in this case is irreconcilable with *Miller* and *Shaw II*. The State insists, for example, that the harm from racial gerrymandering lies not in racial line-drawing *per se* but in grouping voters of the same race together when they otherwise lack shared interests. But "the constitutional violation" in racial gerrymandering cases stems from the "racial purpose of state action, not its stark manifestation." The Equal Protection Clause does not prohibit misshapen districts. It prohibits unjustified racial classifications.

The State contends further that race does not have a prohibited effect on a district's lines if the legislature could have drawn the same lines in accordance with traditional criteria. That argument parallels the District Court's reasoning that a reapportionment plan is not an express racial classification unless a racial purpose is apparent from the face of the plan based on the irregular nature of the lines themselves. This is incorrect. The racial predominance inquiry concerns the actual considerations that provided the essential basis for the lines drawn, not *post hoc* justifications the legislature in theory could have used but in reality did not.

Traditional redistricting principles, moreover, are numerous and malleable. The District Court here identified no fewer than 11 race-neutral redistricting factors a legislature could consider, some of which are "surprisingly ethereal" and "admi[t] of degrees." By deploying those factors in various combinations and permutations, a State could construct a plethora of potential maps that look consistent with traditional, race-neutral principles. But if race for its own sake is the overriding reason for choosing one map over others, race still may predominate.

For these reasons, a conflict or inconsistency between the enacted plan and traditional redistricting criteria is not a threshold requirement or a mandatory precondition in order for a challenger to establish a claim of racial gerrymandering. Of course, a conflict or inconsistency may be persuasive circumstantial evidence tending to show racial predomination, but there is no rule requiring challengers to present this kind of evidence in every case.

As a practical matter, in many cases, perhaps most cases, challengers will be unable to prove an unconstitutional racial gerrymander without evidence that the enacted plan conflicts with traditional redistricting criteria. In general, legislatures that engage in impermissible race-based redistricting will find it necessary to depart from traditional principles in order to do so. And, in the absence of a conflict with traditional principles, it may be difficult for challengers to find other evidence sufficient to show that race was the overriding factor causing neutral considerations to be cast aside. In fact, this Court to date has not affirmed a predominance finding, or remanded a case for a determination of predominance, without evidence that some district lines deviated from traditional principles. Yet the law responds to proper evidence and valid inferences in ever-changing circumstances, as it learns more about ways in which its commands are circumvented. So there may be cases where challengers will be able to establish racial predominance in the absence of an actual conflict by presenting direct evidence of the legislative purpose and intent or other compelling circumstantial evidence.

B

The challengers submit that the District Court erred further when it considered the legislature's racial motive only to the extent that the challengers identified deviations from traditional redistricting criteria that were attributable to race and not to some other factor. In the challengers' view, this approach foreclosed a holistic analysis of each district and led the District Court to give insufficient weight to the 55% BVAP target and other relevant evidence that race predominated. Again, this Court agrees.

As explained, showing a deviation from, or conflict with, traditional redistricting principles is not a necessary prerequisite to establishing racial predominance. But even where a challenger alleges a conflict, or succeeds in showing one, the court should not confine its analysis to the conflicting portions of the lines. That is because the basic unit of analysis for racial gerrymandering claims in general, and for the racial predominance inquiry in particular, is the district. Racial gerrymandering claims proceed "district-by-district." "We have consistently described a claim of racial gerrymandering as a claim that race was improperly used in the drawing of the boundaries of one or more *specific electoral districts*." And

*Miller*'s basic predominance test scrutinizes the legislature's motivation for placing "a significant number of voters within or without a particular district." Courts evaluating racial predominance therefore should not divorce any portion of the lines — whatever their relationship to traditional principles — from the rest of the district.

This is not to suggest that courts evaluating racial gerrymandering claims may not consider evidence pertaining to an area that is larger or smaller than the district at issue. The Court has recognized that "[v]oters, of course, can present statewide evidence in order to prove racial gerrymandering in a particular district." Districts share borders, after all, and a legislature may pursue a common redistricting policy toward multiple districts. Likewise, a legislature's race-based decisionmaking may be evident in a notable way in a particular part of a district. It follows that a court may consider evidence regarding certain portions of a district's lines, including portions that conflict with traditional redistricting principles.

The ultimate object of the inquiry, however, is the legislature's predominant motive for the design of the district as a whole. A court faced with a racial gerrymandering claim therefore must consider all of the lines of the district at issue; any explanation for a particular portion of the lines, moreover, must take account of the districtwide context. Concentrating on particular portions in isolation may obscure the significance of relevant districtwide evidence, such as stark splits in the racial composition of populations moved into and out of disparate parts of the district, or the use of an express racial target. A holistic analysis is necessary to give that kind of evidence its proper weight.

C

The challengers ask this Court not only to correct the District Court's racial predominance standard but also to apply that standard and conclude that race in fact did predominate in the 11 districts where the District Court held that it did not. For its part, the State asks the Court to hold that, even if race did predominate in these districts, the State's predominant use of race was narrowly tailored to the compelling interest in complying with § 5.

The Court declines these requests. "[O]urs is a court of final review and not first view." The District Court is best positioned to determine in the first instance the extent to which, under the proper standard, race directed the shape of these 11 districts. And if race did predominate, it is proper for the District Court to determine in the first instance whether strict scrutiny is satisfied. These matters are left for the District Court on remand.

III

The Court now turns to the arguments regarding District 75. Where a challenger succeeds in establishing racial predominance, the burden shifts to the State to "demonstrate that its districting legislation is narrowly tailored to achieve a compelling interest." The District Court here determined that the State's predominant use of race in District 75 was narrowly tailored to achieve compliance with § 5. The challengers contest the finding of narrow tailoring, but they do not dispute that compliance with § 5 was a compelling interest at the relevant time. As in previous cases, therefore, the Court assumes, without deciding, that the State's interest in complying with the Voting Rights Act was compelling.

Turning to narrow tailoring, the Court explained the contours of that requirement in *Alabama*. When a State justifies the predominant use of race in redistricting on the basis of the need to comply with the Voting Rights Act, "the narrow tailoring requirement insists only that the legislature have a strong basis in evidence in support of the (race-based) choice that it has made." That standard does not require the State to show that its action was "actually . . . necessary" to avoid a statutory violation, so that, but for its use of race, the State would have lost in court. Rather, the requisite strong basis in evidence exists when the legislature has "*good reasons* to believe" it must use race in order to satisfy the Voting Rights Act, "even if a court does not find that the actions were necessary for statutory compliance."

The Court now finds no error in the District Court's conclusion that the State had sufficient grounds to determine that the race-based calculus it employed in District 75 was necessary to avoid violating § 5. As explained, § 5 at the time barred Virginia from adopting any districting change that would "have the effect of diminishing the ability of [members of a minority group] to elect their preferred candidates of choice." Determining what minority population percentage will satisfy that standard is a difficult task requiring, in the view of the Department of Justice, a "functional analysis of the electoral behavior within the particular . . . election district."

Under the facts found by the District Court, the legislature performed that kind of functional analysis of District 75 when deciding upon the 55% BVAP target. Redrawing this district presented a difficult task, and the result reflected the good-faith efforts of Delegate Jones and his colleagues to achieve an informed bipartisan consensus. In light of Delegate Jones' careful assessment of local conditions and structures, the State had a strong basis in evidence to believe a 55% BVAP floor was required to avoid retrogression.

IV

The Court's holding in this case is controlled by precedent. The Court reaffirms the basic racial predominance analysis explained in *Miller* and *Shaw II*, and the basic narrow tailoring analysis explained in *Alabama*. The District Court's judgment as to District 75 is consistent with these principles. Applying these principles to the remaining 11 districts is entrusted to the District Court in the first instance.

Justice ALITO, concurring in part and concurring in the judgment.

I join the opinion of the Court insofar as it upholds the constitutionality of District 75. The districting plan at issue here was adopted prior to our decision in *Shelby County v. Holder* (2013), and therefore it is appropriate to apply the body of law in effect at that time. What is more, appellants have never contested the District Court's holding that compliance with § 5 of the Voting Rights Act was a compelling government interest for covered jurisdictions before our decision in *Shelby County*.

I concur in the judgment of the Court insofar as it vacates and remands the judgment below with respect to all the remaining districts. Unlike the Court, however, I would hold that all these districts must satisfy strict scrutiny. See *League of United Latin American Citizens v. Perry* (2006) (Scalia, J., concurring in judgment in part and dissenting in part) ("[W]hen a legislature intentionally creates a majority-minority district, race is necessarily its predominant motivation and strict scrutiny is therefore triggered").

Justice THOMAS, concurring in the judgment in part and dissenting in part.

Appellants contend that 12 of Virginia's state legislative districts are unconstitutional racial gerrymanders. The three-judge District Court rejected their challenge, holding that race was not the legislature's predominant motive in drawing 11 of the districts and that the remaining district survives strict scrutiny. I would reverse the District Court as to all 12 districts. I therefore concur in the judgment in part and dissent in part.

I

I concur in the Court's judgment reversing the District Court's decision to uphold 11 of the 12 districts at issue in this case—House Districts 63, 69, 70, 71, 74, 77, 80, 89, 90, 92, and 95. I do not agree, however, with the Court's decision to leave open the question whether race predominated in those districts and, thus, whether they are subject to strict scrutiny. Appellees (hereinafter State) concede that the legislature intentionally drew all 12 districts as majority-black districts. That concession, in my view, mandates strict scrutiny as to each district.

II

I disagree with the Court's judgment with respect to the remaining district, District 75. The majority affirms the District Court's holding that District 75 is subject to strict scrutiny. With this I agree, because, as with the other 11 districts, the State conceded that it intentionally drew District 75 as a majority-black district.

I disagree, however, with the majority's determination that District 75 satisfies strict scrutiny. This Court has held that a State may draw distinctions among its citizens based on race only when it "is pursuing a compelling state interest" and has chosen "narrowly tailored" means to accomplish that interest. The State asserts that it used race in drawing District 75 to further a "compelling interest in complying with Section 5 of the [Voting Rights Act of 1965]." And it argues that, based on its "good-faith functional analysis" of the district, it narrowly tailored its use of race to achieve that interest. In my view, the State has neither asserted a compelling state interest nor narrowly tailored its use of race.

A

As an initial matter, the majority errs by "assum[ing], without deciding, that the State's interest in complying with the Voting Rights Act was compelling." To be sure, this Court has previously assumed that a State has a compelling interest in complying with the Voting Rights Act. But it has done so only in cases in which it has not upheld the redistricting plan at issue. This Court has never, before today, assumed a compelling state interest while upholding a state redistricting plan. Indeed, I know of no other case, in any context, in which the Court has assumed away part of the State's burden to justify its intentional use of race. This should not be the first. I would hold that complying with § 5 of the Voting Rights Act is not a compelling interest.

"[C]ompliance with federal antidiscrimination laws cannot justify race-based districting where the challenged district was not reasonably necessary under a *constitutional* reading and application of those laws." Because, in my view, § 5 is unconstitutional, I would hold that a State does not have a compelling interest in complying with it.

B

Even if compliance with § 5 were a compelling interest, the State failed to narrowly tailor its use of race to further that interest. This Court has explained that "[a]ny preference based on racial or ethnic criteria must necessarily receive a most searching examination." This exacting scrutiny makes sense because "[d]iscrimination on the basis of race" is "odious in all aspects." Accordingly, a State's use of race must bear "'the most exact connection'" to the compelling state interest. In the context of redistricting, the redistricting map must, "at a minimum," actually "remedy the anticipated violation" or "achieve compliance" with the Voting Rights Act.

I have serious doubts about the Court's standard for narrow tailoring. [This] approach to narrow tailoring—deferring to a State's belief that it has good reasons to use race—is "strict" in name only. Applying the proper narrow-tailoring standard for state classifications based on race, I conclude that the State did not narrowly tailor its use of race to comply with § 5. As the majority recognizes, § 5 requires a state redistricting plan to maintain the black population's ability to elect the candidate of its choice in the district at issue—in other words, the State must "avoid retrogression" in the new district.

In reaching these conclusions, I recognize that this Court is at least as responsible as the state legislature for these racially gerrymandered districts. As explained above, this Court has repeatedly failed to decide whether compliance with the Voting Rights Act is a compelling governmental interest. Indeed, this Court has refused even to decide whether § 5 is constitutional, despite having twice taken cases to decide that question. As a result, the Court has left the State without clear guidance about its redistricting obligations under § 5.

This Court has put the State in a similar bind with respect to narrow tailoring. To comply with § 5, a State necessarily must make a deliberate and precise effort to sort its citizens on the basis of their race. But that result is fundamentally at odds with our "color-blind" Constitution, which "neither knows nor tolerates classes among citizens." That contradiction illustrates the perversity of the Court's jurisprudence in this area as well as the uncomfortable position in which the State might find itself.

Despite my sympathy for the State, I cannot ignore the Constitution's clear prohibition on state-sponsored race discrimination. "The Constitution abhors classifications based on race, not only because those classifications can harm favored races or are based on illegitimate motives, but also because every time the government places citizens on racial registers . . . , it demeans us all." This prohibition was "[p]urchased at the price of immeasurable human suffering," and it "reflects our Nation's understanding that such classifications ultimately have a destructive impact on the individual and our society." I respectfully dissent from the Court's judgment as to District 75.

***

COOPER v. HARRIS<br>137 S. Ct. 1455 (2017)

Justice KAGAN delivered the opinion of the Court.

The Constitution entrusts States with the job of designing congressional districts. But it also imposes an important constraint: A State may not use race as the predominant factor in drawing district lines unless it has a compelling reason. In this case, a three-judge District Court ruled that North Carolina officials violated that bar when they created two districts whose voting-age populations were majority black. Applying a deferential standard of review to the factual findings underlying that decision, we affirm.

## I

### A

The Equal Protection Clause of the Fourteenth Amendment limits racial gerrymanders in legislative districting plans. It prevents a State, in the absence of "sufficient justification," from "separating its citizens into different voting districts on the basis of race." When a voter sues state officials for drawing such race-based lines, our decisions call for a two-step analysis.

First, the plaintiff must prove that "race was the predominant factor motivating the legislature's decision to place a significant number of voters within or without a particular district." That entails demonstrating that the legislature "subordinated" other factors—compactness, respect for political subdivisions, partisan advantage, what have you—to "racial considerations." The plaintiff may make the required showing through "direct evidence" of legislative intent, "circumstantial evidence of a district's shape and demographics," or a mix of both.

Second, if racial considerations predominated over others, the design of the district must withstand strict scrutiny. The burden thus shifts to the State to prove that its race-based sorting of voters serves a "compelling interest" and is "narrowly tailored" to that end. This Court has long assumed that one compelling interest is complying with operative provisions of the Voting Rights Act of 1965 (VRA or Act). When a State invokes the VRA to justify race-based districting, it must show (to meet the "narrow tailoring" requirement) that it had "a strong basis in evidence" for concluding that the statute required its action. Or said otherwise, the State must establish that it had "good reasons" to think that it would transgress the Act if it did *not* draw race-based district lines. That "strong basis" (or "good reasons") standard gives States "breathing room" to adopt reasonable compliance measures that may prove, in perfect hindsight, not to have been needed.

A district court's assessment of a districting plan, in accordance with the two-step inquiry just described, warrants significant deference on appeal to this Court. We of course retain full power to correct a court's errors of law, at either stage of the analysis. But the court's findings of fact—most notably, as to whether racial considerations predominated in drawing district lines—are subject to review only for clear error. Under that standard, we may not reverse just because we "would have decided the [matter] differently." A finding that is "plausible" in light of the full record—even if another is equally or more so—must govern.


B

This case concerns North Carolina's most recent redrawing of two congressional districts, both of which have long included substantial populations of black voters. In its current incarnation, District 1 is anchored in the northeastern part of the State, with appendages stretching both south and west (the latter into Durham). District 12 begins in the south-central part of the State (where it takes in a large part of Charlotte) and then travels northeast, zig-zagging much of the way to the State's northern border. Both have quite the history before this Court.

Registered voters in the two districts (David Harris and Christine Bowser, here called "the plaintiffs") brought this suit against North Carolina officials (collectively, "the State" or "North Carolina"), complaining of impermissible racial gerrymanders. After a bench trial, a three-judge District Court held both districts unconstitutional. All the judges agreed that racial considerations predominated in the design of District 1. And in then applying strict scrutiny, all rejected the State's argument that it had a "strong basis" for thinking that the VRA compelled such a race-based drawing of District 1's lines. As for District 12, a majority of the panel held that "race predominated" over all other factors, including partisanship.

[II]

[W]e turn to the merits of this case, beginning (appropriately enough) with District 1. As noted above, the court below found that race furnished the predominant rationale for that district's redesign. And it held that the State's interest in complying with the VRA could not justify that consideration of race. We uphold both conclusions.

Uncontested evidence in the record shows that the State's mapmakers, in considering District 1, purposefully established a racial target: African-Americans should make up no less than a majority of the voting-age population. The result is a district with stark racial borders: Within the same counties, the portions that fall inside District 1 have black populations two to three times larger than the portions placed in neighboring districts. Faced with this body of evidence—showing an announced racial target that subordinated other districting criteria and produced boundaries amplifying divisions between blacks and whites—the District Court did not clearly err in finding that race predominated in drawing District 1. Indeed, as all three judges recognized, the court could hardly have concluded anything but.

The more substantial question is whether District 1 can survive the strict scrutiny applied to racial gerrymanders. As noted earlier, we have long assumed that complying with the VRA is a compelling interest. And we have held that race-based districting is narrowly tailored to that objective if a State had "good reasons" for thinking that the Act demanded such steps.

This Court identified, in *Thornburg v. Gingles*, three threshold conditions for proving vote dilution under § 2 of the VRA. First, a "minority group" must be "sufficiently large and geographically compact to constitute a majority" in some reasonably configured legislative district. Second, the minority group must be "politically cohesive." And third, a district's white majority must "vote [ ] sufficiently as a bloc" to usually "defeat the minority's preferred candidate." *Ibid*. Those three showings, we have explained, are needed to establish that "the minority [group] has the potential to elect a representative of its own choice" in a possible district, but that racially polarized voting prevents it from doing so in the district as actually drawn because it is "submerg[ed] in a larger white voting population." If a State has good reason to think that all the "*Gingles* preconditions" are met, then so too it has good reason to believe that § 2 requires drawing a majority-minority district. But if not, then not.

Here, electoral history provided no evidence that a § 2 plaintiff could demonstrate the third *Gingles* prerequisite—effective white bloc-voting.

For most of the twenty years prior to the new plan's adoption, African-Americans had made up less than a majority of District 1's voters . . . . So experience gave the State no reason to think that the VRA required it to ramp up District 1's BVAP.

Thus, North Carolina's belief that it was compelled to redraw District 1 (a successful crossover district) as a majority-minority district rested not on a "strong basis in evidence," but instead on a pure error of law. In sum: Although States enjoy leeway to take race-based actions reasonably judged necessary under a proper interpretation of the VRA, that latitude cannot rescue District 1. We by no means "insist that a state legislature, when redistricting, determine *precisely* what percent minority population [§ 2 of the VRA] demands." But neither will we approve a racial gerrymander whose necessity is supported by no evidence and whose *raison d'être* is a legal mistake. Accordingly, we uphold the District Court's conclusion that North Carolina's use of race as the predominant factor in designing District 1 does not withstand strict scrutiny.

[III]

We now look west to District 12, making its fifth(!) appearance before this Court. [T]he State altogether denied that racial considerations accounted for (or, indeed, played the slightest role in) District 12's redesign. According to the State's version of events, Senator Rucho, Representative Lewis, and Dr. Hofeller moved voters in and out of the district as part of a "strictly" political gerrymander, without regard to race. The mapmakers drew their lines, in other words, to "pack" District 12 with Democrats, not African-Americans. After hearing evidence supporting both parties' accounts, the District Court accepted the plaintiffs'.

Getting to the bottom of a dispute like this one poses special challenges for a trial court. In the more usual case alleging a racial gerrymander—where no one has raised a partisanship defense—the court can make real headway by exploring the challenged district's conformity to traditional districting principles, such as compactness and respect for county lines. But such evidence loses much of its value when the State asserts partisanship as a defense, because a bizarre shape—as of the new District 12—can arise from a "political motivation" as well as a racial one. And crucially, political and racial reasons are capable of yielding similar oddities in a district's boundaries. That is because, of course, "racial identification is highly correlated with political affiliation." As a result of those redistricting realities, a trial court has a formidable task: It must make "a sensitive inquiry" into all "circumstantial and direct evidence of intent" to assess whether the plaintiffs have managed to disentangle race from politics and prove that the former drove a district's lines.[7]

Our job is different—and generally easier. As described earlier, we review a district court's finding as to racial predominance only for clear error, except when the court made a legal mistake. Under that standard of review, we affirm the court's finding so long as it is "plausible"; we reverse only when "left with the definite and firm conviction that a mistake has been committed." And in deciding which side of that line to come down on, we give singular deference to a trial court's judgments about the credibility of witnesses. That is proper, we have explained, because the various cues that "bear so heavily on the listener's understanding of and belief in what is said" are lost on an appellate court later sifting through a paper record.

In light of those principles, we uphold the District Court's finding of racial predominance respecting District 12. The evidence offered at trial, including live witness testimony subject to credibility determinations, adequately supports the conclusion that race, not politics, accounted for the district's reconfiguration. And no error of law infected that judgment: Contrary to North Carolina's view, the District Court had no call to dismiss this challenge just because the plaintiffs did not proffer an alternative design for District 12 as circumstantial evidence of the legislature's intent.

The State mounts a final, legal rather than factual, attack on the District Court's finding of racial predominance. When race and politics are competing explanations of a district's lines, argues North Carolina, the party challenging the district must introduce a particular kind of circumstantial evidence: "an alternative [map] that achieves the legislature's political objectives while improving racial balance." That is true, the State says, irrespective of what other evidence is in the case—so even if the plaintiff offers powerful direct proof that the legislature adopted the map it did for racial reasons. Because the plaintiffs here (as all agree) did not present such a counter-map, North Carolina concludes that they cannot prevail. The dissent echoes that argument.

---

7. As earlier noted, that inquiry is satisfied when legislators have "place[d] a significant number of voters within or without" a district predominantly because of their race, regardless of their ultimate objective in taking that step. So, for example, if legislators use race as their predominant districting criterion with the end goal of advancing their partisan interests—perhaps thinking that a proposed district is more "sellable" as a race-based VRA compliance measure than as a political gerrymander and will accomplish much the same thing—their action still triggers strict scrutiny. In other words, the sorting of voters on the grounds of their race remains suspect even if race is meant to function as a proxy for other (including political) characteristics. [Footnote by Justice Kagan.]

We have no doubt that an alternative districting plan, of the kind North Carolina describes, can serve as key evidence in a race-versus-politics dispute. One, often highly persuasive way to disprove a State's contention that politics drove a district's lines is to show that the legislature had the capacity to accomplish all its partisan goals without moving so many members of a minority group into the district. If you were *really* sorting by political behavior instead of skin color (so the argument goes) you would have done—or, at least, could just as well have done—*this*. Such would-have, could-have, and (to round out the set) should-have arguments are a familiar means of undermining a claim that an action was based on a permissible, rather than a prohibited, ground.

But they are hardly the *only* means. Suppose that the plaintiff in a dispute like this one introduced scores of leaked emails from state officials instructing their mapmaker to pack as many black voters as possible into a district, or telling him to make sure its BVAP hit 75%. Based on such evidence, a court could find that racial rather than political factors predominated in a district's design, with or without an alternative map. And so too in cases lacking that kind of smoking gun, as long as the evidence offered satisfies the plaintiff's burden of proof. Similarly, it does not matter in this case, where the plaintiffs' introduction of mostly direct and some circumstantial evidence—documents issued in the redistricting process, testimony of government officials, expert analysis of demographic patterns—gave the District Court a sufficient basis, sans any map, to resolve the race-or-politics question.

Plaintiff's task, in other words, is simply to persuade the trial court—without any special evidentiary prerequisite—that race (not politics) was the "predominant consideration in deciding to place a significant number of voters within or without a particular district." That burden of proof, we have often held, is "demanding." And because that is so, a plaintiff will sometimes need an alternative map, as a practical matter, to make his case. But in no area of our equal protection law have we forced plaintiffs to submit one particular form of proof to prevail. Nor would it make sense to do so here. The Equal Protection Clause prohibits the unjustified drawing of district lines based on race. An alternative map is merely an evidentiary tool to show that such a substantive violation has occurred; neither its presence nor its absence can itself resolve a racial gerrymandering claim.

## V

Applying a clear error standard, we uphold the District Court's conclusions that racial considerations predominated in designing both District

1 and District 12. For District 12, that is all we must do, because North Carolina has made no attempt to justify race-based districting there. For District 1, we further uphold the District Court's decision that § 2 of the VRA gave North Carolina no good reason to reshuffle voters because of their race.

Justice THOMAS, concurring.

I join the opinion of the Court because it correctly applies our precedents under the Constitution and the Voting Rights Act of 1965 (VRA). I write briefly to explain the additional grounds on which I would affirm the three-judge District Court and to note my agreement, in particular, with the Court's clear-error analysis.

As to District 1, I think North Carolina's concession that it created the district as a majority-black district is by itself sufficient to trigger strict scrutiny. I also think that North Carolina cannot satisfy strict scrutiny based on its efforts to comply with § 2 of the VRA. In my view, § 2 does not apply to redistricting and therefore cannot justify a racial gerrymander.

As to District 12, I agree with the Court that the District Court did not clearly err when it determined that race was North Carolina's predominant motive in drawing the district. This is the same conclusion I reached when we last reviewed District 12. *Easley v. Cromartie* (2001) (*Cromartie II*) (dissenting opinion).

Justice ALITO, with whom THE CHIEF JUSTICE and Justice KENNEDY join, concurring in the judgment in part and dissenting in part.

A precedent of this Court should not be treated like a disposable household item — say, a paper plate or napkin — to be used once and then tossed in the trash. But that is what the Court does today in its decision regarding North Carolina's 12th Congressional District: The Court junks a rule adopted in a prior, remarkably similar challenge to this very same congressional district.

In *Easley v. Cromartie* (2001) (*Cromartie II*), the Court considered the constitutionality of the version of District 12 that was adopted in 1997. That district had the same basic shape as the district now before us, and the challengers argued that the legislature's predominant reason for adopting this configuration was race. The State responded that its motive was not race but politics. Its objective, the State insisted, was to create a district in which the Democratic candidate would win. Rejecting that explanation, a three-judge court found that the legislature's predominant motive was racial, specifically to pack African-Americans into District 12. But this Court held that this finding of fact was clearly erroneous.

A critical factor in our analysis was the failure of those challenging the district to come forward with an alternative redistricting map that served the legislature's political objective as well as the challenged version without producing the same racial effects. Noting that race and party affiliation in North Carolina were "highly correlated," we laid down this rule:

"In a case such as this one . . . the party attacking the legislatively drawn boundaries must show at the least that the legislature could have achieved its legitimate political objectives in alternative ways that are comparably consistent with traditional districting principles. That party must also show that those districting alternatives would have brought about significantly greater racial balance. Appellees failed to make any such showing here."

Now, District 12 is back before us. After the 2010 census, the North Carolina Legislature, with the Republicans in the majority, drew the present version of District 12. The challengers contend that this version violates equal protection because the predominant motive of the legislature was racial: to pack the district with African-American voters. The legislature responds that its objective was political: to pack the district with Democrats and thus to increase the chances of Republican candidates in neighboring districts.

You might think that the *Cromartie II* rule would be equally applicable in this case, which does not differ in any relevant particular, but the majority executes a stunning about-face. Now, the challengers' failure to produce an alternative map that meets the *Cromartie II* test is inconsequential. It simply "does not matter."

This is not the treatment of precedent that state legislatures have the right to expect from this Court. The failure to produce an alternative map doomed the challengers in *Cromartie II*, and the same should be true now. Partisan gerrymandering is always unsavory, but that is not the issue here. The issue is whether District 12 was drawn predominantly because of race. The record shows that it was not.

The alternative-map requirement deserves better. It is a logical response to the difficult problem of distinguishing between racial and political motivations when race and political party preference closely correlate. This is a problem with serious institutional and federalism implications. When a federal court says that race was a legislature's predominant purpose in drawing a district, it accuses the legislature of "offensive and demeaning" conduct. Indeed, we have said that racial gerrymanders "bea[r] an uncomfortable resemblance to political apartheid." That is a grave accusation to level against a state legislature.

In addition, "[f]ederal-court review of districting legislation represents a serious intrusion on the most vital of local functions" because "[i]t is well settled that reapportionment is primarily the duty and responsibility of the State." When a federal court finds that race predominated in the redistricting process, it inserts itself into that process. That is appropriate — indeed, constitutionally required — if the legislature truly did draw district boundaries on the basis of race. But if a court mistakes a political gerrymander for a racial gerrymander, it illegitimately invades a traditional domain of state authority, usurping the role of a State's elected representatives. This does violence to both the proper role of the Judiciary and the powers reserved to the States under the Constitution.

There is a final, often-unstated danger where race and politics correlate: that the federal courts will be transformed into weapons of political warfare. Unless courts "exercise extraordinary caution" in distinguishing race-based redistricting from politics-based redistricting, they will invite the losers in the redistricting process to seek to obtain in court what they could not achieve in the political arena. If the majority party draws districts to favor itself, the minority party can deny the majority its political victory by prevailing on a racial gerrymandering claim. Even if the minority party loses in court, it can exact a heavy price by using the judicial process to engage in political trench warfare for years on end.

The majority nevertheless absolves the challengers of their failure to submit an alternative map. It argues that an alternative map cannot be "the *only* means" of proving racial predominance, and it concludes from this that an alternative map "does not matter in this case." But even if there are cases in which a plaintiff could prove a racial gerrymandering claim without an alternative map, they would be exceptional ones in which the evidence of racial predominance is overwhelming. This most definitely is not one of those cases, and the plaintiffs' failure to produce an alternative map mandates reversal. Moreover, even in an exceptional case, the absence of such a map would still be strong evidence that a district's boundaries were determined by politics rather than race.

Even if we set aside the challengers' failure to submit an alternative map, the District Court's finding that race predominated in the drawing of District 12 is clearly erroneous. The State offered strong and coherent evidence that politics, not race, was the legislature's predominant aim, and the evidence supporting the District Court's contrary finding is weak and manifestly inadequate in light of the high evidentiary standard that our cases require challengers to meet in order to prove racial predominance.

# Chapter 8

# Fundamental Rights Under Due Process and Equal Protection

## C. Constitutional Protection for Family Autonomy

### 1. The Right to Marry (casebook p. 955)

In *Obergefell v. Hodges* (casebook p. 967), the Court held that gay and lesbian couples have the same right to marry as opposite sex couples. In *Pavan v. Smith*, the Court reversed — without briefs or oral arguments — an Arkansas Supreme Court decision preventing lesbian couples from listing both parents on the birth certificate. But three justices dissented.

PAVAN v. SMITH
137 S. Ct. 2075 (2017)

Per Curiam.

As this Court explained in *Obergefell v. Hodges* (2015), the Constitution entitles same-sex couples to civil marriage "on the same terms and conditions as opposite-sex couples." In the decision below, the Arkansas Supreme Court considered the effect of that holding on the State's rules governing the issuance of birth certificates. When a married woman gives birth in Arkansas, state law generally requires the name of the mother's male spouse to appear on the child's birth certificate — regardless of his biological relationship to the child. According to the court below, however, Arkansas need not extend that rule to similarly situated same-sex couples: The State need not, in other words, issue birth certificates including the female spouses of women who give birth in the State. Because that differential treatment infringes *Obergefell*'s commitment to provide same-sex couples "the constellation of benefits that the States have linked to marriage," we reverse the state court's judgment.

The petitioners here are two married same-sex couples who conceived children through anonymous sperm donation. Leigh and Jana Jacobs were married in Iowa in 2010, and Terrah and Marisa Pavan were married in New Hampshire in 2011. Leigh and Terrah each gave birth to a child in Arkansas in 2015. When it came time to secure birth certificates for the newborns, each couple filled out paperwork listing both spouses as parents—Leigh and Jana in one case, Terrah and Marisa in the other. Both times, however, the Arkansas Department of Health issued certificates bearing only the birth mother's name.

The department's decision rested on a provision of Arkansas law, Ark. Code § 20-18-401(2014), that specifies which individuals will appear as parents on a child's state-issued birth certificate. "For the purposes of birth registration," that statute says, "the mother is deemed to be the woman who gives birth to the child." And "[i]f the mother was married at the time of either conception or birth," the statute instructs that "the name of [her] husband shall be entered on the certificate as the father of the child." There are some limited exceptions to the latter rule—for example, another man may appear on the birth certificate if the "mother" and "husband" and "putative father" all file affidavits vouching for the putative father's paternity. But as all parties agree, the requirement that a married woman's husband appear on her child's birth certificate applies in cases where the couple conceived by means of artificial insemination with the help of an anonymous sperm donor.

The Jacobses and Pavans brought this suit in Arkansas state court against the director of the Arkansas Department of Health—seeking, among other things, a declaration that the State's birth-certificate law violates the Constitution. The trial court agreed, holding that the relevant portions of § 20-18-401 are inconsistent with *Obergefell* because they "categorically prohibi[t] every same-sex married couple . . . from enjoying the same spousal benefits which are available to every opposite-sex married couple." But a divided Arkansas Supreme Court reversed that judgment, concluding that the statute "pass[es] constitutional muster." In that court's view, "the statute centers on the relationship of the biological mother and the biological father to the child, not on the marital relationship of husband and wife," and so it "does not run afoul of *Obergefell*."

The Arkansas Supreme Court's decision, we conclude, denied married same-sex couples access to the "constellation of benefits that the Stat[e] ha[s] linked to marriage." As already explained, when a married woman in Arkansas conceives a child by means of artificial insemination, the State will—indeed, *must*—list the name of her male spouse on the child's birth certificate. And yet state law, as interpreted by the court below, allows

Arkansas officials in those very same circumstances to omit a married woman's female spouse from her child's birth certificate. As a result, same-sex parents in Arkansas lack the same right as opposite-sex parents to be listed on a child's birth certificate, a document often used for important transactions like making medical decisions for a child or enrolling a child in school.

*Obergefell* proscribes such disparate treatment. As we explained there, a State may not "exclude same-sex couples from civil marriage on the same terms and conditions as opposite-sex couples." Indeed, in listing those terms and conditions—the "rights, benefits, and responsibilities" to which same-sex couples, no less than opposite-sex couples, must have access—we expressly identified "birth and death certificates." That was no accident: Several of the plaintiffs in *Obergefell* challenged a State's refusal to recognize their same-sex spouses on their children's birth certificates. In considering those challenges, we held the relevant state laws unconstitutional to the extent they treated same-sex couples differently from opposite-sex couples. That holding applies with equal force to § 20-18-401.

Arkansas has thus chosen to make its birth certificates more than a mere marker of biological relationships: The State uses those certificates to give married parents a form of legal recognition that is not available to unmarried parents. Having made that choice, Arkansas may not, consistent with *Obergefell*, deny married same-sex couples that recognition.

Justice GORSUCH, with whom Justice THOMAS and Justice ALITO join, dissenting.

Summary reversal is usually reserved for cases where "the law is settled and stable, the facts are not in dispute, and the decision below is clearly in error." Respectfully, I don't believe this case meets that standard.

To be sure, *Obergefell* addressed the question whether a State must recognize same-sex marriages. But nothing in *Obergefell* spoke (let alone clearly) to the question whether § 20-18-401 of the Arkansas Code, or a state supreme court decision upholding it, must go. The statute in question establishes a set of rules designed to ensure that the biological parents of a child are listed on the child's birth certificate. Before the state supreme court, the State argued that rational reasons exist for a biology based birth registration regime, reasons that in no way offend *Obergefell*—like ensuring government officials can identify public health trends and helping individuals determine their biological lineage, citizenship, or susceptibility to genetic disorders. In an opinion that did not in any way seek to defy but rather earnestly engage *Obergefell*, the state supreme court agreed. And it is very hard to see what is wrong with this conclusion for, just as the state court recognized, nothing in *Obergefell* indicates that a birth registration regime based on biology, one no doubt with many analogues across the country and throughout history, offends the Constitution. To the contrary, to the extent they speak to the question at all, this Court's precedents suggest just the opposite conclusion. Neither does anything in today's opinion purport to identify any constitutional problem with a biology based birth registration regime. So whatever else we might do with this case, summary reversal would not exactly seem the obvious course.

Given all this, it seems far from clear what here warrants the strong medicine of summary reversal. Indeed, it is not even clear what the Court expects to happen on remand that hasn't happened already. The Court does not offer any remedial suggestion, and none leaps to mind. Perhaps the state supreme court could memorialize the State's concession on § 9-10-201, even though that law wasn't fairly challenged and such a chore is hardly the usual reward for seeking faithfully to apply, not evade, this Court's mandates.

# Chapter 9

# First Amendment: Freedom of Expression

## B. Free Speech Methodology

## 1. The Distinction Between Content-Based and Content-Neutral Laws (casebook p. 1244)

In *Matal v. Tam*, the Court considered whether it violated the First Amendment to deny a band the ability to register its name as a trademark because it was racially offensive. Notice all of the justices agree that this is unconstitutional because it is viewpoint discrimination.

### MATAL v. TAM
138 S. Ct. 1744 (2017)

Justice ALITO announced the judgment of the Court and delivered the opinion of the Court with respect to Parts I, II, and III-A, and an opinion with respect to Parts III-B, III-C, and IV, in which THE CHIEF JUSTICE, Justice THOMAS, and Justice BREYER join.

This case concerns a dance-rock band's application for federal trademark registration of the band's name, "The Slants." "Slants" is a derogatory term for persons of Asian descent, and members of the band are Asian-Americans. But the band members believe that by taking that slur as the name of their group, they will help to "reclaim" the term and drain its denigrating force.

The Patent and Trademark Office (PTO) denied the application based on a provision of federal law prohibiting the registration of trademarks that may "disparage . . . or bring . . . into contemp[t] or disrepute" any "persons, living or dead." We now hold that this provision violates the Free Speech Clause of the First Amendment. It offends a bedrock First Amendment principle: Speech may not be banned on the ground that it expresses ideas that offend.

## I

"The principle underlying trademark protection is that distinctive marks—words, names, symbols, and the like—can help distinguish a particular artisan's goods from those of others." A trademark "designate [s] the goods as the product of a particular trader" and "protect[s] his good will against the sale of another's product as his." It helps consumers identify goods and services that they wish to purchase, as well as those they want to avoid.

"[F]ederal law does not create trademarks." Trademarks and their precursors have ancient origins, and trademarks were protected at common law and in equity at the time of the founding of our country. The foundation of current federal trademark law is the Lanham Act, enacted in 1946. Under the Lanham Act, trademarks that are "used in commerce" may be placed on the "principal register," that is, they may be federally registered. There are now more than two million marks that have active federal certificates of registration. This system of federal registration helps to ensure that trademarks are fully protected and supports the free flow of commerce. "[N]ational protection of trademarks is desirable," we have explained, "because trademarks foster competition and the maintenance of quality by securing to the producer the benefits of good reputation."

Without federal registration, a valid trademark may still be used in commerce. And an unregistered trademark can be enforced against would-be infringers in several ways. Most important, even if a trademark is not federally registered, it may still be enforceable under § 43(a) of the Lanham Act, which creates a federal cause of action for trademark infringement. And an unregistered trademark can be enforced under state common law, or if it has been registered in a State, under that State's registration system.

Federal registration, however, "confers important legal rights and benefits on trademark owners who register their marks." Registration on the principal register (1) "serves as 'constructive notice of the registrant's claim of ownership' of the mark," (2) "is 'prima facie evidence of the validity of the registered mark and of the registration of the mark, of the owner's ownership of the mark, and of the owner's exclusive right to use the registered mark in commerce on or in connection with the goods or services specified in the certificate,'" and (3) can make a mark "'incontestable'" once a mark has been registered for five years. Registration also enables the trademark holder "to stop the importation into the United States of articles bearing an infringing mark."

The Lanham Act contains provisions that bar certain trademarks from the principal register. For example, a trademark cannot be registered if it is "merely descriptive or deceptively misdescriptive" of goods, or if it is so similar to an already registered trademark or trade name that it is "likely . . . to cause confusion, or to cause mistake, or to deceive." At issue in this case is one such provision, which we will call "the disparagement clause." This provision prohibits the registration of a trademark "which may disparage . . . persons, living or dead, institutions, beliefs, or national symbols, or bring them into contempt, or disrepute." § 1052(a). This clause appeared in the original Lanham Act and has remained the same to this day.

Simon Tam is the lead singer of "The Slants." He chose this moniker in order to "reclaim" and "take ownership" of stereotypes about people of Asian ethnicity. The group "draws inspiration for its lyrics from childhood slurs and mocking nursery rhymes" and has given its albums names such as "The Yellow Album" and "Slanted Eyes, Slanted Hearts."

Tam sought federal registration of "THE SLANTS," on the principal register, but an examining attorney at the PTO rejected the request, finding that "there is . . . a substantial composite of persons who find the term in the applied-for mark offensive." The examining attorney relied in part on the fact that "numerous dictionaries define 'slants' or 'slant-eyes' as a derogatory or offensive term." The examining attorney also relied on a finding that "the band's name has been found offensive numerous times"—citing a performance that was canceled because of the band's moniker and the fact that "several bloggers and commenters to articles on the band have indicated that they find the term and the applied-for mark offensive." *Id.*, at 29-30.

Tam contested the denial of registration before the examining attorney and before the PTO's Trademark Trial and Appeal Board (TTAB) but to no avail.

## II

[In Part II of the opinion the Court held that the statutory provision does prohibit trademarks that are disparaging to racial groups.]

## III

Because the disparagement clause applies to marks that disparage the members of a racial or ethnic group, we must decide whether the clause violates the Free Speech Clause of the First Amendment. And at the outset, we must consider three arguments that would either eliminate any First Amendment protection or result in highly permissive rational-basis review. Specifically, the Government contends (1) that trademarks are government speech, not private speech, (2) that trademarks are a form of government subsidy, and (3) that the constitutionality of the disparagement clause should be tested under a new "government-program" doctrine. We address each of these arguments below.

A

The First Amendment prohibits Congress and other government entities and actors from "abridging the freedom of speech"; the First Amendment does not say that Congress and other government entities must abridge their own ability to speak freely. And our cases recognize that "[t]he Free Speech Clause . . . does not regulate government speech." When a government entity embarks on a course of action, it necessarily takes a particular viewpoint and rejects others. The Free Speech Clause does not require government to maintain viewpoint neutrality when its officers and employees speak about that venture.

But while the government-speech doctrine is important—indeed, essential—it is a doctrine that is susceptible to dangerous misuse. If private speech could be passed off as government speech by simply affixing a government seal of approval, government could silence or muffle the expression of disfavored viewpoints. For this reason, we must exercise great caution before extending our government-speech precedents.

At issue here is the content of trademarks that are registered by the PTO, an arm of the Federal Government. The Federal Government does not dream up these marks, and it does not edit marks submitted for registration. Except as required by the statute involved here, an examiner may not reject a mark based on the viewpoint that it appears to express. Thus, unless that section is thought to apply, an examiner does not inquire whether any viewpoint conveyed by a mark is consistent with Government policy or whether any such viewpoint is consistent with that expressed by other marks already on the principal register. Instead, if the mark meets the Lanham Act's viewpoint-neutral requirements, registration is mandatory. And if an examiner finds that a mark is eligible for placement on the principal register, that decision is not reviewed by any higher official unless the registration is challenged.

In light of all this, it is far-fetched to suggest that the content of a registered mark is government speech. If the federal registration of a trademark makes the mark government speech, the Federal Government is babbling prodigiously and incoherently. It is saying many unseemly things. It is expressing contradictory views. It is unashamedly endorsing a vast array of commercial products and services.

None of our government speech cases even remotely supports the idea that registered trademarks are government speech.

[T]rademarks often have an expressive content. Companies spend huge amounts to create and publicize trademarks that convey a message. It is true that the necessary brevity of trademarks limits what they can say. But powerful messages can sometimes be conveyed in just a few words. Trademarks are private, not government, speech.

B

We next address the Government's argument that this case is governed by cases in which this Court has upheld the constitutionality of government programs that subsidized speech expressing a particular viewpoint. These cases implicate a notoriously tricky question of constitutional law. "[W]e have held that the Government 'may not deny a benefit to a person on a basis that infringes his constitutionally protected . . . freedom of speech even if he has no entitlement to that benefit.'" But at the same time, government is not required to subsidize activities that it does not wish to promote. Determining which of these principles applies in a particular case "is not always self-evident," but no difficult question is presented here.

Unlike the present case, the decisions on which the Government relies all involved cash subsidies or their equivalent. The federal registration of a trademark is nothing like the programs at issue in these cases. The PTO does not pay money to parties seeking registration of a mark. Quite the contrary is true: An applicant for registration must pay the PTO a filing fee of $225-$600. And to maintain federal registration, the holder of a mark must pay a fee of $300-$500 every 10 years.

The Government responds that registration provides valuable non-monetary benefits that "are directly traceable to the resources devoted by the federal government to examining, publishing, and issuing certificates of registration for those marks." But just about every government service requires the expenditure of government funds. This is true of services that benefit everyone, like police and fire protection, as well as services that are utilized by only some, *e.g.*, the adjudication of private lawsuits and the use of public parks and highways.

Trademark registration is not the only government registration scheme. For example, the Federal Government registers copyrights and patents. State governments and their subdivisions register the title to real property and security interests; they issue driver's licenses, motor vehicle registrations, and hunting, fishing, and boating licenses or permits.

C

Finally, the Government urges us to sustain the disparagement clause under a new doctrine that would apply to "government-program" cases. For the most part, this argument simply merges our government-speech cases and the previously discussed subsidy cases in an attempt to construct a broader doctrine that can be applied to the registration of trademarks. The only new element in this construct consists of two cases involving a public employer's collection of union dues from its employees. But those cases occupy a special area of First Amendment case law, and they are far removed from the registration of trademarks.

Potentially more analogous are cases in which a unit of government creates a limited public forum for private speech. When government creates such a forum, in either a literal or "metaphysical" sense, some content- and speaker-based restrictions may be allowed. However, even in such cases, what we have termed "viewpoint discrimination" is forbidden.

Our cases use the term "viewpoint" discrimination in a broad sense, and in that sense, the disparagement clause discriminates on the bases of "viewpoint." To be sure, the clause evenhandedly prohibits disparagement of all groups. It applies equally to marks that damn Democrats and Republicans, capitalists and socialists, and those arrayed on both sides of every possible issue. It denies registration to any mark that is offensive to a substantial percentage of the members of any group. But in the sense relevant here, that is viewpoint discrimination: Giving offense is a viewpoint.

We have said time and again that "the public expression of ideas may not be prohibited merely because the ideas are themselves offensive to some of their hearers." For this reason, the disparagement clause cannot be saved by analyzing it as a type of government program in which some content- and speaker-based restrictions are permitted.

IV

Having concluded that the disparagement clause cannot be sustained under our government-speech or subsidy cases or under the Government's proposed "government-program" doctrine, we must confront a dispute between the parties on the question whether trademarks are commercial speech and are thus subject to the relaxed scrutiny outlined in *Central Hudson Gas & Elec. Corp. v. Public Serv. Comm'n of N.Y.* (1980). The Government and *amici* supporting its position argue that all trademarks are commercial speech. They note that the central purposes of trademarks are commercial and that federal law regulates trademarks to promote fair and orderly interstate commerce. Tam and his *amici*, on the other hand, contend that many, if not all, trademarks have an expressive component. In other words, these trademarks do not simply identify the source of a product or service but go on to say something more, either about the product or service or some broader issue. The trademark in this case illustrates this point. The name "The Slants" not only identifies the band but expresses a view about social issues.

We need not resolve this debate between the parties because the disparagement clause cannot withstand even *Central Hudson* review. Under *Central Hudson*, a restriction of speech must serve "a substantial interest," and it must be "narrowly drawn." This means, among other things, that "[t]he regulatory technique may extend only as far as the interest it serves." The disparagement clause fails this requirement.

It is claimed that the disparagement clause serves two interests. The first is phrased in a variety of ways in the briefs. Echoing language in one of the opinions below, the Government asserts an interest in preventing "underrepresented groups" from being "bombarded with demeaning messages in commercial advertising.'" But no matter how the point is phrased, its unmistakable thrust is this: The Government has an interest in preventing speech expressing ideas that offend. And, as we have explained, that idea strikes at the heart of the First Amendment. Speech that demeans on the basis of race, ethnicity, gender, religion, age, disability, or any other similar ground is hateful; but the proudest boast of our free speech jurisprudence is that we protect the freedom to express "the thought that we hate." *United States v. Schwimmer* (1929) (Holmes, J., dissenting).

The second interest asserted is protecting the orderly flow of commerce. Commerce, we are told, is disrupted by trademarks that "involv[e] disparagement of race, gender, ethnicity, national origin, religion, sexual orientation, and similar demographic classification." A simple answer to this argument is that the disparagement clause is not "narrowly drawn" to drive out trademarks that support invidious discrimination. The clause reaches any trademark that disparages *any person, group, or institution.* It applies to trademarks like the following: "Down with racists," "Down with sexists," "Down with homophobes." It is not an anti-discrimination clause; it is a happy-talk clause. In this way, it goes much further than is necessary to serve the interest asserted.

The clause is far too broad in other ways as well. The clause protects every person living or dead as well as every institution. Is it conceivable that commerce would be disrupted by a trademark saying: "James Buchanan was a disastrous president" or "Slavery is an evil institution"?

There is also a deeper problem with the argument that commercial speech may be cleansed of any expression likely to cause offense. The commercial market is well stocked with merchandise that disparages prominent figures and groups, and the line between commercial and non-commercial speech is not always clear, as this case illustrates. If affixing the commercial label permits the suppression of any speech that may lead to political or social "volatility," free speech would be endangered.

For these reasons, we hold that the disparagement clause violates the Free Speech Clause of the First Amendment.

Justice KENNEDY, with whom Justice GINSBURG, Justice SOTOMAYOR, and Justice KAGAN join, concurring in part and concurring in the judgment.

As the Court is correct to hold, § 1052(a) constitutes viewpoint discrimination—a form of speech suppression so potent that it must be subject to rigorous constitutional scrutiny. The Government's action and the statute on which it is based cannot survive this scrutiny.

The Court is correct in its judgment, and I join Parts I, II, and III-A of its opinion. This separate writing explains in greater detail why the First Amendment's protections against viewpoint discrimination apply to the trademark here. It submits further that the viewpoint discrimination rationale renders unnecessary any extended treatment of other questions raised by the parties.

I

Those few categories of speech that the government can regulate or punish—for instance, fraud, defamation, or incitement—are well established within our constitutional tradition. Aside from these and a few other narrow exceptions, it is a fundamental principle of the First Amendment that the government may not punish or suppress speech based on disapproval of the ideas or perspectives the speech conveys.

The First Amendment guards against laws "targeted at specific subject matter," a form of speech suppression known as content based discrimination. This category includes a subtype of laws that go further, aimed at the suppression of "particular views . . . on a subject." A law found to discriminate based on viewpoint is an "egregious form of content discrimination," which is "presumptively unconstitutional."

At its most basic, the test for viewpoint discrimination is whether—within the relevant subject category—the government has singled out a subset of messages for disfavor based on the views expressed. In the instant case, the disparagement clause the Government now seeks to implement and enforce identifies the relevant subject as "persons, living or dead, institutions, beliefs, or national symbols." Within that category, an applicant may register a positive or benign mark but not a derogatory one. The law thus reflects the Government's disapproval of a subset of messages it finds offensive. This is the essence of viewpoint discrimination.

The Government disputes this conclusion. It argues, to begin with, that the law is viewpoint neutral because it applies in equal measure to any trademark that demeans or offends. This misses the point. A subject that is first defined by content and then regulated or censored by mandating only one sort of comment is not viewpoint neutral. To prohibit all sides from criticizing their opponents makes a law more viewpoint based, not less so. The logic of the Government's rule is that a law would be viewpoint neutral even if it provided that public officials could be praised but not condemned. The First Amendment's viewpoint neutrality principle protects more than the right to identify with a particular side. It protects the right to create and present arguments for particular positions in particular ways, as the speaker chooses. By mandating positivity, the law here might silence dissent and distort the marketplace of ideas.

The Government next suggests that the statute is viewpoint neutral because the disparagement clause applies to trademarks regardless of the applicant's personal views or reasons for using the mark. Instead, registration is denied based on the expected reaction of the applicant's audience. The Government may not insulate a law from charges of viewpoint discrimination by tying censorship to the reaction of the speaker's audience. The Court has suggested that viewpoint discrimination occurs when the government intends to suppress a speaker's beliefs, but viewpoint discrimination need not take that form in every instance. The danger of viewpoint discrimination is that the government is attempting to remove certain ideas or perspectives from a broader debate. That danger is all the greater if the ideas or perspectives are ones a particular audience might think offensive, at least at first hearing. An initial reaction may prompt further reflection, leading to a more reasoned, more tolerant position.

Indeed, a speech burden based on audience reactions is simply government hostility and intervention in a different guise. The speech is targeted, after all, based on the government's disapproval of the speaker's choice of message. And it is the government itself that is attempting in this case to decide whether the relevant audience would find the speech offensive. For reasons like these, the Court's cases have long prohibited the government from justifying a First Amendment burden by pointing to the offensiveness of the speech to be suppressed.

II

The parties dispute whether trademarks are commercial speech and whether trademark registration should be considered a federal subsidy. The former issue may turn on whether certain commercial concerns for the protection of trademarks might, as a general matter, be the basis for regulation. However that issue is resolved, the viewpoint based discrimination at issue here necessarily invokes heightened scrutiny. "Commercial speech is no exception," the Court has explained, to the principle that the First Amendment "requires heightened scrutiny whenever the government creates a regulation of speech because of disagreement with the message it conveys." Unlike content based discrimination, discrimination based on viewpoint, including a regulation that targets speech for its offensiveness, remains of serious concern in the commercial context.

A law that can be directed against speech found offensive to some portion of the public can be turned against minority and dissenting views to the detriment of all. The First Amendment does not entrust that power to the government's benevolence. Instead, our reliance must be on the substantial safeguards of free and open discussion in a democratic society. For these reasons, I join the Court's opinion in part and concur in the judgment.

## 2.   Vagueness and Overbreadth

### b.   *Overbreadth* (casebook p. 1285)

Although the Court did not explicitly use overbreadth analysis, in *Packingham v. North Carolina*, the Court concluded that a law preventing those convicted of sex crimes from being on social media was too broad and violated the First Amendment. Justice Kennedy's opinion may be particularly important for its discussion of the importance of protecting speech on the internet.

PACKINGHAM v. NORTH CAROLINA
137 S. Ct. 1730 (2018)

Justice KENNEDY delivered the opinion of the Court.

In 2008, North Carolina enacted a statute making it a felony for a registered sex offender to gain access to a number of websites, including commonplace social media websites like Facebook and Twitter. The question presented is whether that law is permissible under the First Amendment's

Free Speech Clause, applicable to the States under the Due Process Clause of the Fourteenth Amendment.

## I

North Carolina law makes it a felony for a registered sex offender "to access a commercial social networking Web site where the sex offender knows that the site permits minor children to become members or to create or maintain personal Web pages." A "commercial social networking Web site" is defined as a website that meets four criteria. First, it "[i]s operated by a person who derives revenue from membership fees, advertising, or other sources related to the operation of the Website." Second, it "[f]acilitates the social introduction between two or more persons for the purposes of friendship, meeting other persons, or information exchanges." Third, it "[a]llows users to create Web pages or personal profiles that contain information such as the name or nickname of the user, photographs placed on the personal Web page by the user, other personal information about the user, and links to other personal Web pages on the commercial social networking Web site of friends or associates of the user that may be accessed by other users or visitors to the Web site." And fourth, it "[p]rovides users or visitors . . . mechanisms to communicate with other users, such as a message board, chat room, electronic mail, or instant messenger."

The statute includes two express exemptions. The statutory bar does not extend to websites that "[p]rovid[e] only one of the following discrete services: photo-sharing, electronic mail, instant messenger, or chat room or message board platform." The law also does not encompass websites that have as their "primary purpose the facilitation of commercial transactions involving goods or services between [their] members or visitors."

According to sources cited to the Court, § 14-202.5 applies to about 20,000 people in North Carolina and the State has prosecuted over 1,000 people for violating it.

## B

In 2002, petitioner Lester Gerard Packingham — then a 21-year-old college student — had sex with a 13-year-old girl. He pleaded guilty to taking indecent liberties with a child. Because this crime qualifies as "an offense against a minor," petitioner was required to register as a sex offender — a status that can endure for 30 years or more. As a registered sex offender, petitioner was barred under § 14-202.5 from gaining access to commercial social networking sites.

In 2010, a state court dismissed a traffic ticket against petitioner. In response, he logged on to Facebook.com and posted the following statement on his personal profile:

"Man God is Good! How about I got so much favor they dismissed the ticket before court even started? No fine, no court cost, no nothing spent . . . Praise be to GOD, WOW! Thanks JESUS!"

At the time, a member of the Durham Police Department was investigating registered sex offenders who were thought to be violating § 14-202.5. The officer noticed that a "'J.R. Gerrard'" had posted the statement quoted above. By checking court records, the officer discovered that a traffic citation for petitioner had been dismissed around the time of the post. Evidence obtained by search warrant confirmed the officer's suspicions that petitioner was J.R. Gerrard.

Petitioner was indicted by a grand jury for violating § 14-202.5. The trial court denied his motion to dismiss the indictment on the grounds that the charge against him violated the First Amendment. Petitioner was ultimately convicted and given a suspended prison sentence. At no point during trial or sentencing did the State allege that petitioner contacted a minor — or committed any other illicit act — on the Internet.

## II

A fundamental principle of the First Amendment is that all persons have access to places where they can speak and listen, and then, after reflection, speak and listen once more. The Court has sought to protect the right to speak in this spatial context. A basic rule, for example, is that a street or a park is a quintessential forum for the exercise of First Amendment rights. Even in the modern era, these places are still essential venues for public gatherings to celebrate some views, to protest others, or simply to learn and inquire.

While in the past there may have been difficulty in identifying the most important places (in a spatial sense) for the exchange of views, today the answer is clear. It is cyberspace — the "vast democratic forums of the Internet" in general and social media in particular. Seven in ten American adults use at least one Internet social networking service. One of the most popular of these sites is Facebook, the site used by petitioner leading to his conviction in this case. According to sources cited to the Court in this case, Facebook has 1.79 billion active users. This is about three times the population of North America.

Social media offers "relatively unlimited, low-cost capacity for communication of all kinds." On Facebook, for example, users can debate religion and politics with their friends and neighbors or share vacation photos. On LinkedIn, users can look for work, advertise for employees, or review tips on entrepreneurship. And on Twitter, users can petition their elected representatives and otherwise engage with them in a direct manner. Indeed, Governors in all 50 States and almost every Member of Congress have set up accounts for this purpose. In short, social media users employ these websites to engage in a wide array of protected First Amendment activity on topics "as diverse as human thought."

The nature of a revolution in thought can be that, in its early stages, even its participants may be unaware of it. And when awareness comes, they still may be unable to know or foresee where its changes lead. So too here. While we now may be coming to the realization that the Cyber Age is a revolution of historic proportions, we cannot appreciate yet its full dimensions and vast potential to alter how we think, express ourselves, and define who we want to be. The forces and directions of the Internet are so new, so protean, and so far reaching that courts must be conscious that what they say today might be obsolete tomorrow.

This case is one of the first this Court has taken to address the relationship between the First Amendment and the modern Internet. As a result, the Court must exercise extreme caution before suggesting that the First Amendment provides scant protection for access to vast networks in that medium.

## III

This background informs the analysis of the North Carolina statute at issue. Even making the assumption that the statute is content neutral and thus subject to intermediate scrutiny, the provision cannot stand. In order to survive intermediate scrutiny, a law must be "narrowly tailored to serve a significant governmental interest."

For centuries now, inventions heralded as advances in human progress have been exploited by the criminal mind. New technologies, all too soon, can become instruments used to commit serious crimes. The railroad is one example, and the telephone another, So it will be with the Internet and social media.

There is also no doubt that, as this Court has recognized, "[t]he sexual abuse of a child is a most serious crime and an act repugnant to the moral instincts of a decent people." And it is clear that a legislature "may pass valid laws to protect children" and other victims of sexual assault "from abuse." The government, of course, need not simply stand by and allow these evils to occur. But the assertion of a valid governmental interest "cannot, in every context, be insulated from all constitutional protections."

It is necessary to make two assumptions to resolve this case. First, given the broad wording of the North Carolina statute at issue, it might well bar access not only to commonplace social media websites but also to websites as varied as Amazon.com, Washingtonpost.com, and Webmd. com. The Court need not decide the precise scope of the statute. It is enough to assume that the law applies (as the State concedes it does) to social networking sites "as commonly understood"—that is, websites like Facebook, LinkedIn, and Twitter.

Second, this opinion should not be interpreted as barring a State from enacting more specific laws than the one at issue. Specific criminal acts are not protected speech even if speech is the means for their commission. Though the issue is not before the Court, it can be assumed that the First Amendment permits a State to enact specific, narrowly tailored laws that prohibit a sex offender from engaging in conduct that often presages a sexual crime, like contacting a minor or using a website to gather information about a minor. Specific laws of that type must be the State's first resort to ward off the serious harm that sexual crimes inflict. (Of importance, the troubling fact that the law imposes severe restrictions on persons who already have served their sentence and are no longer subject to the supervision of the criminal justice system is also not an issue before the Court.)

Even with these assumptions about the scope of the law and the State's interest, the statute here enacts a prohibition unprecedented in the scope of First Amendment speech it burdens. Social media allows users to gain access to information and communicate with one another about it on any subject that might come to mind. By prohibiting sex offenders from using those websites, North Carolina with one broad stroke bars access to what for many are the principal sources for knowing current events, checking ads for employment, speaking and listening in the modern public square, and otherwise exploring the vast realms of human thought and knowledge. These websites can provide perhaps the most powerful mechanisms available to a private citizen to make his or her voice heard. They allow a person with an Internet connection to "become a town crier with a voice that resonates farther than it could from any soapbox."

In sum, to foreclose access to social media altogether is to prevent the user from engaging in the legitimate exercise of First Amendment rights. It is unsettling to suggest that only a limited set of websites can be used even by persons who have completed their sentences. Even convicted criminals—and in some instances especially convicted criminals—might receive legitimate benefits from these means for access to the world of ideas, in particular if they seek to reform and to pursue lawful and reward-ing lives.

## IV

The primary response from the State is that the law must be this broad to serve its preventative purpose of keeping convicted sex offenders away from vulnerable victims. The State has not, however, met its burden to show that this sweeping law is necessary or legitimate to serve that pur-pose. It is instructive that no case or holding of this Court has approved of a statute as broad in its reach.

It is well established that, as a general rule, the Government "may not suppress lawful speech as the means to suppress unlawful speech." That is what North Carolina has done here. Its law must be held invalid.

Justice ALITO, with whom THE CHIEF JUSTICE and Justice THOMAS join, concurring in the judgment.

The North Carolina statute at issue in this case was enacted to serve an interest of "surpassing importance"—but it has a staggering reach. It makes it a felony for a registered sex offender simply to visit a vast array of websites, including many that appear to provide no realistic opportunity for communications that could facilitate the abuse of children. Because of the law's extraordinary breadth, I agree with the Court that it violates the Free Speech Clause of the First Amendment.

I cannot join the opinion of the Court, however, because of its undisci-plined dicta. The Court is unable to resist musings that seem to equate the entirety of the internet with public streets and parks. And this language is bound to be interpreted by some to mean that the States are largely power-less to restrict even the most dangerous sexual predators from visiting any internet sites, including, for example, teenage dating sites and sites designed to permit minors to discuss personal problems with their peers. I am troubled by the implications of the Court's unnecessary rhetoric.

## I

As we have frequently noted, "[t]he prevention of sexual exploitation and abuse of children constitutes a government objective of surpassing impor-tance." "Sex offenders are a serious threat," and "the victims of sexual assault are most often juveniles." "[T]he . . . interest [of] safeguarding the physical and psychological well-being of a minor . . . is a compelling one," and "we have sustained legislation aimed at protecting the physical and emotional well-being of youth even when the laws have operated in the sensitive area of constitutionally protected rights." Repeat sex offenders pose an especially grave risk to children. "When convicted sex offenders reenter society, they are much more likely than any other type of offender to be rearrested for a new rape or sexual assault."

The State's interest in protecting children from recidivist sex offenders plainly applies to internet use. Several factors make the internet a powerful tool for the would-be child abuser. First, children often use the internet in a way that gives offenders easy access to their personal information—by, for example, communicating with strangers and allowing sites to disclose their location. Second, the internet provides previously unavailable ways of communicating with, stalking, and ultimately abusing children. An abuser can create a false profile that misrepresents the abuser's age and gender. The abuser can lure the minor into engaging in sexual conversations, sending explicit photos, or even meeting in person. And an abuser can use a child's location posts on the internet to determine the pattern of the child's day-to-day activities—and even the child's location at a given moment. Such uses of the internet are already well documented, both in research and in reported decisions.

Because protecting children from abuse is a compelling state interest and sex offenders can (and do) use the internet to engage in such abuse, it is legitimate and entirely reasonable for States to try to stop abuse from occurring before it happens.

It is not enough, however, that the law before us is designed to serve a compelling state interest; it also must not "burden substantially more speech than is necessary to further the government's legitimate interests." The North Carolina law fails this requirement.

A straightforward reading of the text of N.C. Gen. Stat. Ann. § 14-202.5 compels the conclusion that it prohibits sex offenders from accessing an enormous number of websites.

The fatal problem for § 14-202.5 is that its wide sweep precludes access to a large number of websites that are most unlikely to facilitate the commission of a sex crime against a child. A handful of examples illustrates this point. Take, for example, the popular retail website Amazon.com, which allows minors to use its services and meets all four requirements of § 14-202.5's definition of a commercial social networking website. Many news websites are also covered by this definition. For example, the Washington Post's website gives minors access and satisfies the four elements that define a commercial social networking website. Or consider WebMD—a website that contains health-related resources, from tools that help users find a doctor to information on preventative care and the symptoms associated with particular medical problems. WebMD, too, allows children on the site. And it exhibits the four hallmarks of a "commercial social networking" website.

As these examples illustrate, the North Carolina law has a very broad reach and covers websites that are ill suited for use in stalking or abusing children. The focus of the discussion on these sites — shopping, news, health — does not provide a convenient jumping off point for conversations that may lead to abuse. In addition, the social exchanges facilitated by these websites occur in the open, and this reduces the possibility of a child being secretly lured into an abusive situation. These websites also give sex offenders little opportunity to gather personal details about a child; the information that can be listed in a profile is limited, and the profiles are brief. What is more, none of these websites make it easy to determine a child's precise location at a given moment. For example, they do not permit photo streams (at most, a child could upload a single profile photograph), and they do not include up-to-the minute location services. Such websites would provide essentially no aid to a would-be child abuser.

Placing this set of websites categorically off limits from registered sex offenders prohibits them from receiving or engaging in speech that the First Amendment protects and does not appreciably advance the State's goal of protecting children from recidivist sex offenders. I am therefore compelled to conclude that, while the law before us addresses a critical problem, it sweeps far too broadly to satisfy the demands of the Free Speech Clause.

## II

While I thus agree with the Court that the particular law at issue in this case violates the First Amendment, I am troubled by the Court's loose rhetoric. After noting that "a street or a park is a quintessential forum for the exercise of First Amendment rights," the Court states that "cyberspace" and "social media in particular" are now "the most important places (in a spatial sense) for the exchange of views." But if the entirety of the internet or even just "social media" sites[16] are the 21st century equivalent of public streets and parks, then States may have little ability to restrict the sites that may be visited by even the most dangerous sex offenders. May a State preclude an adult previously convicted of molesting children from visiting a dating site for teenagers? Or a site where minors communicate with each other about personal problems? The Court should be more attentive to the implications of its rhetoric for, contrary to the Court's suggestion, there are important differences between cyberspace and the physical world.

I will mention a few that are relevant to internet use by sex offenders. First, it is easier for parents to monitor the physical locations that their children visit and the individuals with whom they speak in person than it is to monitor their internet use. Second, if a sex offender is seen approaching children or loitering in a place frequented by children, this conduct may be observed by parents, teachers, or others. Third, the internet offers an unprecedented degree of anonymity and easily permits a would-be molester to assume a false identity.

The Court is correct that we should be cautious in applying our free speech precedents to the internet. Cyberspace is different from the physical world, and if it is true, as the Court believes, that "we cannot appreciate yet" the "full dimensions and vast potential" of "the Cyber Age," we should proceed circumspectly, taking one step at a time. It is regrettable that the Court has not heeded its own admonition of caution.

## 4.    What Is an Infringement of Freedom of Speech?

### *Compelled Speech* (casebook p. 1324)

In October Term 2017, the Court decided two cases concerning compelled speech. Both found laws unconstitutional as impermissibly compelling speech. One, *National Institute of Family and Life Advocates v. Becerra*, declared unconstitutional a state law requiring disclosures by reproductive health care facilities. The other, *Janus v. American Federation*, is presented below in the discussion on compelled association. It, too, found the law unconstitutional as impermissible compelled speech.

NATIONAL FEDERATION OF FAMILY AND
LIFE ADVOCATES v. BECERRA
138 S. Ct. 2361 (2018)

Justice THOMAS delivered the opinion of the Court.

The California Reproductive Freedom, Accountability, Comprehensive Care, and Transparency Act (FACT Act) requires clinics that primarily serve pregnant women to provide certain notices. Licensed clinics must notify women that California provides free or low-cost services, including abortions, and give them a phone number to call. Unlicensed clinics must notify women that California has not licensed the clinics to provide

medical services. The question in this case is whether these notice requirements violate the First Amendment.

I

The California State Legislature enacted the FACT Act to regulate crisis pregnancy centers. Crisis pregnancy centers—according to a report
commissioned by the California State Assembly,—are "pro-life (largely
Christian belief-based) organizations that offer a limited range of free
pregnancy options, counseling, and other services to individuals that visit
a center." "[U]nfortunately," the author of the FACT Act stated, "there are
nearly 200 licensed and unlicensed" crisis pregnancy centers in California.
These centers "aim to discourage and prevent women from seeking abortions." The author of the FACT Act observed that crisis pregnancy centers
"are commonly affiliated with, or run by organizations whose stated goal"
is to oppose abortion—including "the National Institute of Family and
Life Advocates," one of the petitioners here. To address this perceived
problem, the FACT Act imposes two notice requirements on facilities that
provide pregnancy-related services—one for licensed facilities and one
for unlicensed facilities.

The first notice requirement applies to "licensed covered facilit[ies]." To
fall under the definition of "licensed covered facility," a clinic must be a
licensed primary care or specialty clinic or qualify as an intermittent clinic
under California law. A licensed covered facility also must have the "primary purpose" of "providing family planning or pregnancy-related services." And it must satisfy at least two of the following six requirements:

(1) The facility offers obstetric ultrasounds, obstetric sonograms, or prenatal care to
    pregnant women.
(2) The facility provides, or offers counseling about, contraception or contraceptive
    methods.
(3) The facility offers pregnancy testing or pregnancy diagnosis.
(4) The facility advertises or solicits patrons with offers to provide prenatal sonogra-
    phy, pregnancy tests, or pregnancy options counseling.
(5) The facility offers abortion services.
(6) The facility has staff or volunteers who collect health information from clients.

The FACT Act exempts several categories of clinics that would otherwise qualify as licensed covered facilities. Clinics operated by the United
States or a federal agency are excluded, as are clinics that are "enrolled
as a Medi-Cal provider" and participate in "the Family Planning, Access,
Care, and Treatment Program" (Family PACT program). To participate in

the Family PACT program, a clinic must provide "the full scope of family planning . . . services specified for the program," including sterilization and emergency contraceptive pills.

If a clinic is a licensed covered facility, the FACT Act requires it to disseminate a government-drafted notice on site. The notice states that "California has public programs that provide immediate free or low-cost access to comprehensive family planning services (including all FDA-approved methods of contraception), prenatal care, and abortion for eligible women. To determine whether you qualify, contact the county social services office at [insert the telephone number]." This notice must be posted in the waiting room, printed and distributed to all clients, or provided digitally at check-in. The notice must be in English and any additional languages identified by state law. In some counties, that means the notice must be spelled out in 13 different languages.

The stated purpose of the FACT Act, including its licensed notice requirement, is to "ensure that California residents make their personal reproductive health care decisions knowing their rights and the health care services available to them." The Legislature posited that "thousands of women remain unaware of the public programs available to provide them with contraception, health education and counseling, family planning, prenatal care, abortion, or delivery." Citing the "time sensitive" nature of pregnancy-related decisions, the Legislature concluded that requiring licensed facilities to inform patients themselves would be "[t]he most effective" way to convey this information.

The second notice requirement in the FACT Act applies to "unlicensed covered facilit[ies]." To fall under the definition of "unlicensed covered facility," a facility must not be licensed by the State, not have a licensed medical provider on staff or under contract, and have the "primary purpose" of "providing pregnancy-related services." An unlicensed covered facility also must satisfy at least two of the following four requirements:

(1) The facility offers obstetric ultrasounds, obstetric sonograms, or prenatal care to pregnant women.
(2) The facility offers pregnancy testing or pregnancy diagnosis.
(3) The facility advertises or solicits patrons with offers to provide prenatal sonography, pregnancy tests, or pregnancy options counseling.
(4) The facility has staff or volunteers who collect health information from clients.

Clinics operated by the United States and licensed primary care clinics enrolled in Medi-Cal and Family PACT are excluded.

Unlicensed covered facilities must provide a government-drafted notice stating that "[t]his facility is not licensed as a medical facility by the

State of California and has no licensed medical provider who provides or directly supervises the provision of services." Cal. Health & Safety Code Ann. This notice must be provided on site and in all advertising materials. Onsite, the notice must be posted "conspicuously" at the entrance of the facility and in at least one waiting area. It must be "at least 8.5 inches by 11 inches and written in no less than 48-point type." *Ibid.* In advertisements, the notice must be in the same size or larger font than the surrounding text, or otherwise set off in a way that draws attention to it. Like the licensed notice, the unlicensed notice must be in English and any additional languages specified by state law. Its stated purpose is to ensure "that pregnant women in California know when they are getting medical care from licensed professionals."

After the Governor of California signed the FACT Act, petitioners — a licensed pregnancy center, an unlicensed pregnancy center, and an organization composed of crisis pregnancy centers — filed this suit. Petitioners alleged that the licensed and unlicensed notices abridge the freedom of speech protected by the First Amendment. The District Court denied their motion for a preliminary injunction. The Court of Appeals for the Ninth Circuit affirmed. We reverse with respect to both notice requirements.

## II

We first address the licensed notice. The First Amendment, applicable to the States through the Fourteenth Amendment, prohibits laws that abridge the freedom of speech. When enforcing this prohibition, our precedents distinguish between content-based and content-neutral regulations of speech. Content-based regulations "target speech based on its communicative content." As a general matter, such laws "are presumptively unconstitutional and may be justified only if the government proves that they are narrowly tailored to serve compelling state interests." This stringent standard reflects the fundamental principle that governments have "'no power to restrict expression because of its message, its ideas, its subject matter, or its content.'"

The licensed notice is a content-based regulation of speech. By compelling individuals to speak a particular message, such notices "alte[r] the content of [their] speech." Here, for example, licensed clinics must provide a government-drafted script about the availability of state-sponsored services, as well as contact information for how to obtain them. One of those services is abortion — the very practice that petitioners are devoted to opposing. By requiring petitioners to inform women how they can obtain state-subsidized abortions — at the same time petitioners try to dissuade women from choosing that option—the licensed notice plainly "alters the content" of petitioners' speech.

Although the licensed notice is content based, the Ninth Circuit did not apply strict scrutiny because it concluded that the notice regulates "professional speech." Some Courts of Appeals have recognized "professional speech" as a separate category of speech that is subject to different rules. These courts define "professionals" as individuals who provide personalized services to clients and who are subject to "a generally applicable licensing and regulatory regime." "Professional speech" is then defined as any speech by these individuals that is based on "[their] expert knowledge and judgment," or that is "within the confines of [the] professional relationship." So defined, these courts except professional speech from the rule that content-based regulations of speech are subject to strict scrutiny.

But this Court has not recognized "professional speech" as a separate category of speech. Speech is not unprotected merely because it is uttered by "professionals." This Court has "been reluctant to mark off new categories of speech for diminished constitutional protection." And it has been especially reluctant to "exemp[t] a category of speech from the normal prohibition on content-based restrictions." This Court's precedents do not permit governments to impose content-based restrictions on speech without "'persuasive evidence . . . of a long (if heretofore unrecognized) tradition'" to that effect.

This Court's precedents do not recognize such a tradition for a category called "professional speech." This Court has afforded less protection for professional speech in two circumstances—neither of which turned on the fact that professionals were speaking. First, our precedents have applied more deferential review to some laws that require professionals to disclose factual, noncontroversial information in their "commercial speech." Second, under our precedents, States may regulate professional conduct, even though that conduct incidentally involves speech. But neither line of precedents is implicated here.

This Court's precedents have applied a lower level of scrutiny to laws that compel disclosures in certain contexts. Most obviously, the licensed notice is not limited to "purely factual and uncontroversial information about the terms under which . . . services will be available."

In addition, this Court has upheld regulations of professional conduct that incidentally burden speech. In *Planned Parenthood of Southeastern Pa. v. Casey*, for example, this Court upheld a law requiring physicians to obtain informed consent before they could perform an abortion. Pennsylvania law required physicians to inform their patients of "the nature of the procedure, the health risks of the abortion and childbirth, and the 'probable gestational age of the unborn child.'" The joint opinion in *Casey* rejected a free-speech challenge to this informed-consent requirement. It described the Pennsylvania law as "a requirement that a doctor give a woman certain information as part of obtaining her consent to an abortion," which "for constitutional purposes, [was] no different from a requirement that a doctor give certain specific information about any medical procedure." The joint opinion explained that the law regulated speech only "as part of the *practice* of medicine, subject to reasonable licensing and regulation by the State." Indeed, the requirement that a doctor obtain informed consent to perform an operation is "firmly entrenched in American tort law."

The licensed notice at issue here is not an informed-consent requirement or any other regulation of professional conduct. The notice does not facilitate informed consent to a medical procedure. In fact, it is not tied to a procedure at all. It applies to all interactions between a covered facility and its clients, regardless of whether a medical procedure is ever sought, offered, or performed. If a covered facility does provide medical procedures, the notice provides no information about the risks or benefits of those procedures. Tellingly, many facilities that provide the exact same services as covered facilities—such as general practice clinics,—are not required to provide the licensed notice. The licensed notice regulates speech as speech.

The dangers associated with content-based regulations of speech are also present in the context of professional speech. As with other kinds of speech, regulating the content of professionals' speech "pose[s] the inherent risk that the Government seeks not to advance a legitimate regulatory goal, but to suppress unpopular ideas or information." Take medicine, for example. "Doctors help patients make deeply personal decisions, and their candor is crucial." Throughout history, governments have "manipulat[ed] the content of doctor-patient discourse" to increase state power and suppress minorities. Further, when the government polices the content of professional speech, it can fail to "'preserve an uninhibited marketplace of ideas in which truth will ultimately prevail.'"

"Professional speech" is also a difficult category to define with precision. As defined by the courts of appeals, the professional-speech doctrine would cover a wide array of individuals—doctors, lawyers, nurses, physical therapists, truck drivers, bartenders, barbers, and many others. One court of appeals has even applied it to fortune tellers. All that is required to make something a "profession," according to these courts, is that it involves personalized services and requires a professional license from the State. But that gives the States unfettered power to reduce a group's First Amendment rights by simply imposing a licensing requirement.

States cannot choose the protection that speech receives under the First Amendment, as that would give them a powerful tool to impose "invidious discrimination of disfavored subjects."

In sum, neither California nor the Ninth Circuit has identified a persuasive reason for treating professional speech as a unique category that is exempt from ordinary First Amendment principles. We do not foreclose the possibility that some such reason exists. We need not do so because the licensed notice cannot survive even intermediate scrutiny. California asserts a single interest to justify the licensed notice: providing low-income women with information about state-sponsored services. Assuming that this is a substantial state interest, the licensed notice is not sufficiently drawn to achieve it.

If California's goal is to educate low-income women about the services it provides, then the licensed notice is "wildly underinclusive." The notice applies only to clinics that have a "primary purpose" of "providing family planning or pregnancy-related services" and that provide two of six categories of specific services. Other clinics that have another primary purpose, or that provide only one category of those services, also serve low-income women and could educate them about the State's services. According to the legislative record, California has "nearly 1,000 community clinics"—including "federally designated community health centers, migrant health centers, rural health centers, and frontier health centers"—that "serv[e] more than 5.6 million patients . . . annually through over 17 million patient encounters." But most of those clinics are excluded from the licensed notice requirement without explanation. Such "[u]nderinclusiveness raises serious doubts about whether the government is in fact pursuing the interest it invokes, rather than disfavoring a particular speaker or viewpoint." The FACT Act also excludes, without explanation, federal clinics and Family PACT providers from the licensed-notice requirement.

The FACT Act's exemption for these clinics, which serve many women who are pregnant or could become pregnant in the future, demonstrates the disconnect between its stated purpose and its actual scope. Yet "[p]recision . . . must be the touchstone" when it comes to regulations of speech, which "so closely touc[h] our most precious freedoms."

Further, California could inform low-income women about its services "without burdening a speaker with unwanted speech." Most obviously, it could inform the women itself with a public-information campaign. California could even post the information on public property near crisis pregnancy centers. California argues that it has already tried an advertising campaign, and that many women who are eligible for publicly-funded healthcare have not enrolled. But California has identified no evidence to that effect. And regardless, a "tepid response" does not prove that an advertising campaign is not a sufficient alternative. California cannot co-opt the licensed facilities to deliver its message for it. "[T]he First Amendment does not permit the State to sacrifice speech for efficiency."

In short, petitioners are likely to succeed on the merits of their challenge to the licensed notice. Contrary to the suggestion in the dissent, we do not question the legality of health and safety warnings long considered permissible, or purely factual and uncontroversial disclosures about commercial products.

III

We need not decide what type of state interest is sufficient to sustain a disclosure requirement like the unlicensed notice. California has not demonstrated any justification for the unlicensed notice that is more than "purely hypothetical." The only justification that the California Legislature put forward was ensuring that "pregnant women in California know when they are getting medical care from licensed professionals." At oral argument, however, California denied that the justification for the FACT Act was that women "go into [crisis pregnancy centers] and they don't realize what they are." Indeed, California points to nothing suggesting that pregnant women do not already know that the covered facilities are staffed by unlicensed medical professionals. The services that trigger the unlicensed notice — such as having "volunteers who collect health information from clients," "advertis[ing] . . . pregnancy options counseling," and offering over-the-counter "pregnancy testing," — do not require a medical license. And California already makes it a crime for individuals without a medical license to practice medicine. At this preliminary stage of the litigation, we agree that petitioners are likely to prevail on the question whether California has proved a justification for the unlicensed notice.[4]

Even if California had presented a nonhypothetical justification for the unlicensed notice, the FACT Act unduly burdens protected speech. The unlicensed notice imposes a government-scripted, speaker-based disclosure requirement that is wholly disconnected from California's informational interest. It requires covered facilities to post California's precise notice, no matter what the facilities say on site or in their advertisements. And it covers a curiously narrow subset of speakers. While the licensed notice applies to facilities that provide "family planning" services and "contraception or contraceptive methods," the California Legislature dropped these triggering conditions for the unlicensed notice. The unlicensed notice applies only to facilities that primarily provide "pregnancy-related" services. Thus, a facility that advertises and provides pregnancy tests is covered by the unlicensed notice, but a facility across the street that advertises and provides nonprescription contraceptives is excluded — even though the latter is no less likely to make women think it is licensed. This Court's precedents are deeply skeptical of laws that "distinguis [h] among different speakers, allowing speech by some but not others." Speaker-based laws run the risk that "the State has left unburdened those speakers whose messages are in accord with its own views."

The application of the unlicensed notice to advertisements demonstrates just how burdensome it is. The notice applies to all "print and digital advertising materials" by an unlicensed covered facility. These materials must include a government-drafted statement that "[t]his facility is not licensed as a medical facility by the State of California and has no licensed medical provider who provides or directly supervises the provision of services." An unlicensed facility must call attention to the notice, instead of its own message, by some method such as larger text or contrasting type or color. This scripted language must be posted in English and as many other languages as California chooses to require. As California conceded at oral argument, a billboard for an unlicensed facility that says "Choose Life" would have to surround that two-word statement with a 29-word statement from the government, in as many as 13 different languages. In this way, the unlicensed notice drowns out the facility's own message. More likely, the "detail required" by the unlicensed notice "effectively rules out" the possibility of having such a billboard in the first place. We express no view on the legality of a similar disclosure requirement that is better supported or less burdensome.

We hold that petitioners are likely to succeed on the merits of their claim that the FACT Act violates the First Amendment.

Justice KENNEDY, with whom THE CHIEF JUSTICE, Justice ALITO, and Justice GORSUCH join, concurring.

I join the Court's opinion in all respects. This separate writing seeks to underscore that the apparent viewpoint discrimination here is a matter of serious constitutional concern. The Court, in my view, is correct not to reach this question. It was not sufficiently developed, and the rationale for the Court's decision today suffices to resolve the case. And had the Court's analysis been confined to viewpoint discrimination, some legislators might have inferred that if the law were reenacted with a broader base and broader coverage it then would be upheld.

It does appear that viewpoint discrimination is inherent in the design and structure of this Act. This law is a paradigmatic example of the serious threat presented when government seeks to impose its own message in the place of individual speech, thought, and expression. For here the State requires primarily pro-life pregnancy centers to promote the State's own preferred message advertising abortions. This compels individuals to contradict their most deeply held beliefs, beliefs grounded in basic philosophical, ethical, or religious precepts, or all of these. And the history of the Act's passage and its underinclusive application suggest a real possibility that these individuals were targeted because of their beliefs.

The California Legislature included in its official history the congratulatory statement that the Act was part of California's legacy of "forward thinking." But it is not forward thinking to force individuals to "be an instrument for fostering public adherence to an ideological point of view [they] fin[d] unacceptable." It is forward thinking to begin by reading the First Amendment as ratified in 1791; to understand the history of authoritarian government as the Founders then knew it; to confirm that history since then shows how relentless authoritarian regimes are in their attempts to stifle free speech; and to carry those lessons onward as we seek to preserve and teach the necessity of freedom of speech for the generations to come. Governments must not be allowed to force persons to express a message contrary to their deepest convictions. Freedom of speech secures freedom of thought and belief. This law imperils those liberties.

Justice BREYER, with whom Justice GINSBURG, Justice SOTOMAYOR, and Justice KAGAN joins dissenting.

The petitioners ask us to consider whether two sections of a California statute violate the First Amendment. The first section requires licensed medical facilities (that provide women with assistance involving pregnancy or family planning) to tell those women where they might obtain help, including financial help, with comprehensive family planning services, prenatal care, and abortion. The second requires *un*licensed facilities offering somewhat similar services to make clear that they are unlicensed. In my view both statutory sections are likely constitutional, and I dissent from the Court's contrary conclusions.

I

Before turning to the specific law before us, I focus upon the general interpretation of the First Amendment that the majority says it applies. It applies heightened scrutiny to the Act because the Act, in its view, is "content based." "As a general matter," the majority concludes, such laws are "presumptively unconstitutional" and are subject to "stringent" review.

This constitutional approach threatens to create serious problems. Because much, perhaps most, human behavior takes place through speech and because much, perhaps most, law regulates that speech in terms of its content, the majority's approach at the least threatens considerable litigation over the constitutional validity of much, perhaps most, government regulation. Virtually every disclosure law could be considered "content based," for virtually every disclosure law requires individuals "to speak a particular message." Thus, the majority's view, if taken literally, could radically change prior law, perhaps placing much securities law or consumer protection law at constitutional risk, depending on how broadly its exceptions are interpreted.

The majority, at the end of Part II of its opinion, perhaps recognizing this problem, adds a general disclaimer. It says that it does not "question the legality of health and safety warnings long considered permissible, or purely factual and uncontroversial disclosures about commercial products." But this generally phrased disclaimer would seem more likely to invite litigation than to provide needed limitation and clarification. The majority, for example, does not explain why the Act here, which is justified in part by health and safety considerations, does not fall within its "health" category. Nor does the majority opinion offer any reasoned basis that might help apply its disclaimer for distinguishing lawful from unlawful disclosures. In the absence of a reasoned explanation of the disclaimer's meaning and rationale, the disclaimer is unlikely to withdraw the invitation to litigation that the majority's general broad "content-based" test issues. That test invites courts around the Nation to apply an unpredictable First Amendment to ordinary social and economic regulation, striking down disclosure laws that judges may disfavor, while upholding others, all without grounding their decisions in reasoned principle.

Precedent does not require a test such as the majority's. Rather, in saying the Act is not a longstanding health and safety law, the Court substitutes its own approach—without a defining standard—for an approach that was reasonably clear. Historically, the Court has been wary of claims that regulation of business activity, particularly health-related activity, violates the Constitution. Ever since this Court departed from the approach it set forth in *Lochner v. New York* (1905), ordinary economic and social legislation has been thought to raise little constitutional concern.

Even during the *Lochner* era, when this Court struck down numerous economic regulations concerning industry, this Court was careful to defer to state legislative judgments concerning the medical profession. The Court took the view that a State may condition the practice of medicine on any number of requirements, and physicians, in exchange for following those reasonable requirements, could receive a license to practice medicine from the State. Medical professionals do not, generally speaking, have a right to use the Constitution as a weapon allowing them rigorously to control the content of those reasonable conditions.

I, too, value this role that the First Amendment plays—in an appropriate case. But here, the majority enunciates a general test that reaches far beyond the area where this Court has examined laws closely in the service of those goals. And, in suggesting that heightened scrutiny applies to much economic and social legislation, the majority pays those First Amendment goals a serious disservice through dilution. Using the First Amendment to strike down economic and social laws that legislatures long would have thought themselves free to enact will, for the American public, obscure, not clarify, the true value of protecting freedom of speech.

Still, what about this specific case? The disclosure at issue here concerns speech related to abortion. It involves health, differing moral values, and differing points of view. Thus, rather than set forth broad, new, First Amendment principles, I believe that we should focus more directly upon precedent more closely related to the case at hand. This Court has more than once considered disclosure laws relating to reproductive health. Though those rules or holdings have changed over time, they should govern our disposition of this case.

In *Planned Parenthood of Southeastern Pa. v. Casey* (1992), the Court again considered a state law that required doctors to provide information to a woman deciding whether to proceed with an abortion. That law required the doctor to tell the woman about the nature of the abortion procedure, the health risks of abortion and of childbirth, the "'probable gestational age of the unborn child,'" and the availability of printed materials describing the fetus, medical assistance for childbirth, potential child support, and the agencies that would provide adoption services (or other alternatives to abortion). This time a joint opinion of the Court, in judging whether the State could impose these informational requirements, asked whether doing so imposed an "undue burden" upon women seeking an abortion. It held that it did not. Hence the statute was constitutional. The joint opinion stated that the statutory requirements amounted to "reasonable measure[s] to ensure an informed choice, one which might cause the woman to choose childbirth over abortion."

The joint opinion specifically discussed the First Amendment, the constitutional provision now directly before us. It concluded that the statute did not violate the First Amendment. It wrote: "All that is left of petitioners' argument is an asserted First Amendment right of a physician not to provide information about the risks of abortion, and childbirth, in a manner mandated by the State. To be sure, the physician's First Amendment rights not to speak are implicated, but only as part of the practice of medicine, subject to reasonable licensing and regulation by the State. We see no constitutional infirmity in the requirement that the physician provide the information mandated by the State here."

Thus, the Court considered the State's statutory requirements, including the requirement that the doctor must inform his patient about where she could learn how to have the newborn child adopted (if carried to term) and how she could find related financial assistance. To repeat the point, the Court then held that the State's requirements did *not* violate either the Constitution's protection of free speech or its protection of a woman's right to choose to have an abortion.

If a State can lawfully require a doctor to tell a woman seeking an abortion about adoption services, why should it not be able, as here, to require a medical counselor to tell a woman seeking prenatal care or other reproductive healthcare about childbirth and abortion services? As the question suggests, there is no convincing reason to distinguish between information about adoption and information about abortion in this context. After all, the rule of law embodies evenhandedness, and "what is sauce for the goose is normally sauce for the gander."

The majority also finds it "[t]ellin[g]" that general practice clinics — *i.e.*, paid clinics — are not required to provide the licensed notice. But the lack-of-information problem that the statute seeks to ameliorate is a problem that the State explains is commonly found among low-income women. That those with low income might lack the time to become fully informed and that this circumstance might prove disproportionately correlated with income is not intuitively surprising. Nor is it surprising that those with low income, whatever they choose in respect to pregnancy, might find information about financial assistance particularly useful. There is "nothing inherently suspect" about this distinction, which is not "based on the content of [the advocacy] each group offers," but upon the patients the group generally serves and the needs of that population.

Accordingly, the majority's reliance on cases that prohibit rather than require speech is misplaced. I agree that "'in the fields of medicine and public heath, . . . information can save lives,'" but the licensed disclosure *serves* that informational interest by requiring clinics to notify patients of the availability of state resources for family planning services, prenatal care, and abortion, which — unlike the majority's examples of normative statements, — is truthful and nonmisleading information. Abortion is a controversial topic and a source of normative debate, but the availability of state resources is not a normative statement or a fact of debatable truth. The disclosure includes information about resources available should a woman seek to continue her pregnancy or terminate it, and it expresses no official preference for one choice over the other. Similarly, the majority highlights an interest that often underlies our decisions in respect to speech prohibitions—the marketplace of ideas. But that marketplace is fostered, not hindered, by providing information to patients to enable them to make fully informed medical decisions in respect to their pregnancies.

Of course, one might take the majority's decision to mean that speech about abortion is special, that it involves in this case not only professional medical matters, but also views based on deeply held religious and moral beliefs about the nature of the practice. But assuming that is so, the law's insistence upon treating like cases alike should lead us to reject the petitioners' arguments that I have discussed. This insistence, the need for evenhandedness, should prove particularly weighty in a case involving abortion rights. That is because Americans hold strong, and differing, views about the matter. Some Americans believe that abortion involves the death of a live and innocent human being. Others believe that the ability to choose an abortion is "central to personal dignity and autonomy," and note that the failure to allow women to choose an abortion involves the deaths of innocent women. We have previously noted that we cannot try to adjudicate who is right and who is wrong in this moral debate. But we can do our best to interpret American constitutional law so that it applies fairly within a Nation whose citizens strongly hold these different points of view. That is one reason why it is particularly important to interpret the First Amendment so that it applies evenhandedly as between those who disagree so strongly. For this reason too a Constitution that allows States to insist that medical providers tell women about the possibility of adoption should also allow States similarly to insist that medical providers tell women about the possibility of abortion.

## II

The second statutory provision covers pregnancy-related facilities that provide women with certain medical-type services (such as obstetric ultrasounds or sonograms, pregnancy diagnosis, counseling about pregnancy options, or prenatal care), are not licensed as medical facilities by the State, and do not have a licensed medical provider on site. The statute says that such a facility must disclose that it is not "licensed as a medical facility." And it must make this disclosure in a posted notice and in advertising.

The majority does not question that the State's interest (ensuring that "pregnant women in California know when they are getting medical care from licensed professionals") is the type of informational interest that [prior decisions encompass]. There is no basis for finding the State's interest "hypothetical." The legislature heard that information-related delays in qualified healthcare negatively affect women seeking to terminate their pregnancies as well as women carrying their pregnancies to term, with delays in qualified prenatal care causing life-long health problems for infants. Even without such testimony, it is "self-evident" that patients might think they are receiving qualified medical care when they enter facilities that collect health information, perform obstetric ultrasounds or sonograms, diagnose pregnancy, and provide counseling about pregnancy options or other prenatal care. The State's conclusion to that effect is certainly reasonable.

Relatedly, the majority suggests that the Act is suspect because it covers some speakers but not others. There is no cause for such concern here. The Act does not, on its face, distinguish between facilities that favor pro-life and those that favor pro-choice points of view. Nor is there any convincing evidence before us or in the courts below that discrimination was the purpose or the effect of the statute. Notably, California does not single out pregnancy-related facilities for this type of disclosure requirement. And it is unremarkable that the State excluded the provision of family planning and contraceptive services as triggering conditions. After all, the State was seeking to ensure that "pregnant women in California know when they are getting medical care from licensed professionals," and pregnant women generally do not need contraceptive services.

Finally, the majority concludes that the Act is overly burdensome. But these and similar claims are claims that the statute could be applied unconstitutionally, not that it is unconstitutional on its face. As I understand the Act, it would require disclosure in no more than two languages—English and Spanish—in the vast majority of California's 58 counties. The exception is Los Angeles County, where, given the large number of different-language speaking groups, expression in many languages may prove necessary to communicate the message to those whom that message will help. Whether the requirement of 13 different languages goes too far and is unnecessarily burdensome in light of the need to secure the statutory objectives is a matter that concerns Los Angeles County alone, and it is a proper subject for a Los Angeles-based as applied challenge in light of whatever facts a plaintiff finds relevant. At most, such facts might show a need for fewer languages, not invalidation of the statute.

## C.  Types of Unprotected and Less Protected Speech

## 5.  Commercial Speech

### b.  What Is Commercial Speech? (p. 1478)

As *Sorrell v. IMS Health Care* (p. 1480) shows, the issue often arises as to when regulation of commercial transactions should be regarded as a regulation of commercial speech. That is the issue in *Expressions Hair Design v. Schneiderman.*

### EXPRESSIONS HAIR DESIGN v. SCHNEIDERMAN
137 S. Ct. 1144 (2017)

Chief Justice ROBERTS delivered the opinion of the Court.

Each time a customer pays for an item with a credit card, the merchant selling that item must pay a transaction fee to the credit card issuer. Some merchants balk at paying the fees and want to discourage the use of credit cards, or at least pass on the fees to customers who use them. One method of achieving those ends is through differential pricing — charging credit card users more than customers using cash. Merchants who wish to employ differential pricing may do so in two ways relevant here: impose a surcharge for the use of a credit card, or offer a discount for the use of cash. In N.Y. Gen. Bus. Law § 518, New York has banned the former practice. The question presented is whether § 518 regulates merchants' speech and — if so — whether the statute violates the First Amendment. We conclude that § 518 does regulate speech and remand for the Court of Appeals to determine in the first instance whether that regulation is unconstitutional.

I

When credit cards were first introduced, contracts between card issuers and merchants barred merchants from charging credit card users higher prices than cash customers. Congress put a partial stop to this practice in the 1974 amendments to the Truth in Lending Act (TILA). The amendments prohibited card issuers from contractually preventing merchants from giving discounts to customers who paid in cash. The law, however, said nothing about surcharges for the use of credit.

Two years later, Congress refined its dissimilar treatment of discounts and surcharges. First, the 1976 version of TILA barred merchants from imposing surcharges on customers who use credit cards. Second, Congress added definitions of the two terms. A discount was "a reduction made from the regular price," while a surcharge was "any means of increasing the regular price to a cardholder which is not imposed upon customers paying by cash, check, or similar means."

In 1981, Congress further delineated the distinction between discounts and surcharges by defining "regular price." Where a merchant "tagged or posted" a single price, the regular price was that single price. If no price was tagged or posted, or if a merchant employed a two-tag approach—posting one price for credit and another for cash—the regular price was whatever was charged to credit card users. Because a surcharge was defined as an increase from the regular price, there could be no credit card surcharge where the regular price was the same as the amount charged to customers using credit cards. The effect of all this was that a merchant could violate the surcharge ban only by posting a single price and charging credit card users more than that posted price.

The federal surcharge ban was short lived. Congress allowed it to expire in 1984 and has not renewed the ban since. The provision preventing credit card issuers from contractually barring discounts for cash, however, remained in place. With the lapse of the federal surcharge ban, several States, New York among them, immediately enacted their own surcharge bans. Passed in 1984, N.Y. Gen. Bus. Law § 518 adopted the operative language of the federal ban verbatim, providing that "[n]o seller in any sales transaction may impose a surcharge on a holder who elects to use a credit card in lieu of payment by cash, check, or similar means." Unlike the federal ban, the New York legislation included no definition of "surcharge."

In addition to these state legislative bans, credit card companies—though barred from prohibiting discounts for cash—included provisions in their contracts prohibiting merchants from imposing surcharges for credit card use. For most of its history, the New York law was essentially coextensive with these contractual prohibitions. In recent years, however, merchants have brought antitrust challenges to contractual no-surcharge provisions. Those suits have created uncertainty about the legal validity of such contractual surcharge bans. The result is that otherwise redundant legislative surcharge bans like § 518 have increasingly gained importance, and increasingly come under scrutiny.

Petitioners, five New York businesses and their owners, wish to impose surcharges on customers who use credit cards. Each time one of their customers pays with a credit card, these merchants must pay some transaction fee to the company that issued the credit card. The fee is generally two to three percent of the purchase price. Those fees add up, and the merchants allege that they pay tens of thousands of dollars every year to credit card companies. Rather than increase prices across the board to absorb those costs, the merchants want to pass the fees along only to their customers who choose to use credit cards. They also want to make clear that they are not the bad guys—that the credit card companies, not the merchants, are responsible for the higher prices. The merchants believe that surcharges for credit are more effective than discounts for cash in accomplishing these goals.

In 2013, after several major credit card issuers agreed to drop their contractual surcharge prohibitions, the merchants filed suit against the New York Attorney General and three New York District Attorneys to challenge § 518—the only remaining obstacle to their charging surcharges for credit card use. As relevant here, they argued that the law violated the First Amendment by regulating how they communicated their prices, and that it was unconstitutionally vague because liability under the law "turn[ed] on the blurry difference" between surcharges and discounts.

The District Court ruled in favor of the merchants. It read the statute as "draw[ing a] line between prohibited 'surcharges' and permissible 'discounts' based on words and labels, rather than economic realities." The court concluded that the law therefore regulated speech, and violated the First Amendment under this Court's commercial speech doctrine. In addition, because the law turned on the "virtually incomprehensible distinction between what a vendor can and cannot tell its customers," the District Court found that the law was unconstitutionally vague.

The Court of Appeals for the Second Circuit vacated the judgment of the District Court with instructions to dismiss the merchants' claims. It began by considering single-sticker pricing, where merchants post one price and would like to charge more to customers who pay by credit card. All the law did in this context, the Court of Appeals explained, was regulate a relationship between two prices—the sticker price and the price charged to a credit card user—by requiring that the two prices be equal. Relying on our precedent holding that price regulation alone regulates conduct, not speech, the Court of Appeals concluded that § 518 did not violate the First Amendment.

II

As a preliminary matter, we note that petitioners present us with a limited challenge. Observing that the merchants were not always particularly clear about the scope of their suit, the Court of Appeals deemed them to be bringing a facial attack on § 518 as well as a challenge to the application of the statute to two particular pricing regimes: single-sticker pricing and two-sticker pricing. Before us, however, the merchants have disclaimed a facial challenge, assuring us that theirs is an as-applied challenge only.

There remains the question of what precise application of the law they seek to challenge. Although the merchants have presented a wide array of hypothetical pricing regimes, they have expressly identified only one pricing scheme that they seek to employ: posting a cash price and an additional credit card surcharge, expressed either as a percentage surcharge or a "dollars-and-cents" additional amount. Under this pricing approach, petitioner Expressions Hair Design might, for example, post a sign outside its salon reading "Haircuts $10 (we add a 3% surcharge if you pay by credit card)." Or, petitioner Brooklyn Farmacy & Soda Fountain might list one of the sundaes on its menu as costing "$10 (with a $0.30 surcharge for credit card users)." We take petitioners at their word and limit our review to the question whether § 518 is unconstitutional as applied to this particular pricing practice.

## III

The next question is whether § 518 prohibits the pricing regime petitioners wish to employ. The Court of Appeals concluded that it does. The court read "surcharge" in § 518 to mean "an additional amount above the seller's regular price," and found it "basically self-evident" how § 518 applies to sellers who post a single sticker price: "the sticker price is the 'regular' price, so sellers may not charge credit-card customers an additional amount above the sticker price that is not also charged to cash customers." Under this interpretation, signs of the kind that the merchants wish to post—"$10, with a $0.30 surcharge for credit card users"—violate § 518 because they identify one sticker price—$10—and indicate that credit card users are charged more than that amount.

"We generally accord great deference to the interpretation and application of state law by the courts of appeals." This deference is warranted to "render unnecessary review of their decisions in this respect" and because lower federal courts "are better schooled in and more able to interpret the laws of their respective States." "[W]e surely have the authority to differ with the lower federal courts as to the meaning of a state statute," and have done so in instances where the lower court's construction was "clearly wrong" or "plain error." But that is not the case here. Section 518 does not define "surcharge," but the Court of Appeals looked to the ordinary meaning of the term: "a charge in excess of the usual or normal amount." Where a seller posts a single sticker price, it is reasonable to treat that sticker price as the "usual or normal amount" and conclude, as the court below did, that a merchant imposes a surcharge when he charges a credit card user more than that sticker price. In short, we cannot dismiss the Court of Appeals' interpretation of § 518 as "clearly wrong." Accordingly, consistent with our customary practice, we follow that interpretation.

## IV

Having concluded that § 518 bars the pricing regime petitioners wish to employ, we turn to their constitutional arguments: that the law unconstitutionally regulates speech and is impermissibly vague.

The Court of Appeals concluded that § 518 posed no First Amendment problem because the law regulated conduct, not speech. In reaching this conclusion, the Court of Appeals began with the premise that price controls regulate conduct alone. Section 518 regulates the relationship between "(1) the seller's sticker price and (2) the price the seller charges to credit card customers," requiring that these two amounts be equal. 808 F.3d, at 131. A law regulating the relationship between two prices regulates speech no more than a law regulating a single price. The Court of Appeals concluded that § 518 was therefore simply a conduct regulation.

But § 518 is not like a typical price regulation. Such a regulation—for example, a law requiring all New York delis to charge $10 for their sandwiches—would simply regulate the amount that a store could collect. In other words, it would regulate the sandwich seller's conduct. To be sure, in order to actually collect that money, a store would likely have to put "$10" on its menus or have its employees tell customers that price. Those written or oral communications would be speech, and the law—by determining the amount charged—would indirectly dictate the content of that speech. But the law's effect on speech would be only incidental to its primary effect on conduct, and "it has never been deemed an abridgment of freedom of speech or press to make a course of conduct illegal merely because the conduct was in part initiated, evidenced, or carried out by means of language, either spoken, written, or printed."

Section 518 is different. The law tells merchants nothing about the amount they are allowed to collect from a cash or credit card payer. Sellers are free to charge $10 for cash and $9.70, $10, $10.30, or any other amount for credit. What the law does regulate is how sellers may communicate their prices. A merchant who wants to charge $10 for cash and $10.30 for credit may not convey that price any way he pleases. He is not free to say "$10, with a 3% credit card surcharge" or "$10, plus $0.30 for credit" because both of those displays identify a single sticker price—$10—that is less than the amount credit card users will be charged. Instead, if the merchant wishes to post a single sticker price, he must display $10.30 as his sticker price. Accordingly, while we agree with the Court of Appeals that § 518 regulates a relationship between a sticker price and the price charged to credit card users, we cannot accept its conclusion that § 518 is nothing more than a mine-run price regulation. In regulating the communication of prices rather than prices themselves, § 518 regulates speech.

Because it concluded otherwise, the Court of Appeals had no occasion to conduct a further inquiry into whether § 518, as a speech regulation, survived First Amendment scrutiny. On that question, the parties dispute whether § 518 is a valid commercial speech regulation under *Central Hudson Gas & Elec. Corp. v. Public Serv. Comm'n of N.Y.* (1980), and whether the law can be upheld as a valid disclosure requirement. "[W]e are a court of review, not of first view." Accordingly, we decline to consider those questions in the first instance. Instead, we remand for the Court of Appeals to analyze § 518 as a speech regulation.

Justice BREYER, concurring in the judgment.

I agree with the Court that New York's statute regulates speech. But that is because virtually all government regulation affects speech. Human relations take place through speech. And human relations include community activities of all kinds—commercial and otherwise.

When the government seeks to regulate those activities, it is often wiser not to try to distinguish between "speech" and "conduct." Instead, we can, and normally do, simply ask whether, or how, a challenged statute, rule, or regulation affects an interest that the First Amendment protects. If, for example, a challenged government regulation negatively affects the processes through which political discourse or public opinion is formed or expressed (interests close to the First Amendment's protective core), courts normally scrutinize that regulation with great care.

If the challenged regulation restricts the "informational function" provided by truthful commercial speech, courts will apply a "lesser" (but still elevated) form of scrutiny. If, however, a challenged regulation simply requires a commercial speaker to disclose "purely factual and uncontroversial information," courts will apply a more permissive standard of review. Because that kind of regulation normally has only a "minimal" effect on First Amendment interests, it normally need only be "reasonably related to the State's interest in preventing deception of consumers." Courts apply a similarly permissive standard of review to "regulatory legislation affecting ordinary commercial transactions." *United States v. Carolene Products Co.* (1938). Since that legislation normally does not significantly affect the interests that the First Amendment protects, we normally look only for assurance that the legislation "rests upon some rational basis."

I repeat these well-known general standards or judicial approaches both because I believe that determining the proper approach is typically more important than trying to distinguish "speech" from "conduct," and because the parties here differ as to which approach applies. That difference reflects the fact that it is not clear just what New York's law does. On its face, the law seems simply to tell merchants that they cannot charge higher prices to credit-card users. If so, then it is an ordinary piece of commercial legislation subject to "rational basis" review. It may, however, make more sense to interpret the statute as working like the expired federal law that it replaced. If so, it would require a merchant, who posts prices and who wants to charge a higher credit-card price, simply to disclose that credit-card price. In that case, though affecting the merchant's "speech," it would not hinder the transmission of information to the public; the merchant would remain free to say whatever it wanted so long as it also revealed its credit-card price to customers. Accordingly, the law would still receive a deferential form of review.

Nonetheless, petitioners suggest that the statute does more. Because the statute's operation is unclear and because its interpretation is a matter of state law, I agree with the majority that we should remand the case to the Second Circuit. I also agree with Justice Sotomayor that on remand, it may well be helpful for the Second Circuit to ask the New York Court of Appeals to clarify the nature of the obligations the statute imposes.

Justice SOTOMAYOR, with whom Justice ALITO joins, concurring in the judgment.

The Court addresses only one part of one half of petitioners' First Amendment challenge to the New York statute at issue here. This quarter-loaf outcome is worse than none. I would vacate the judgment below and remand with directions to certify the case to the New York Court of Appeals for a definitive interpretation of the statute that would permit the full resolution of petitioners' claims.

## D.  *What Places Are Available for Speech?*

## 1.  Government Properties and Speech

### *f.  Nonpublic Forums* (casebook p. 1628)

In *Burson v. Freeman* (1992) (casebook p. 1597), the Supreme Court upheld a Tennessee law that prohibited distribution of campaign literature within 100 feet of a polling place. But in *Minnesota Voters Alliance v. Mansky*, 138 S. Ct. 1876 (2018), the Court declared unconstitutional a Minnesota law that prohibits individuals, including voters, from wearing a "political badge, political button, or other political insignia" inside a polling place on Election Day. The Court explicitly said that the inside of polling places "qualifies as a nonpublic forum. It is, at least on Election Day, government-controlled property set aside for the sole purpose of voting." The Court said that the restriction on speech had to be reasonable and viewpoint neutral. The Court said that the Minnesota law was unconstitutional because the meaning of "political" is too ambiguous and uncertain. Chief Justice Roberts writing for the Court explained: "the statute prohibits wearing a 'political badge, political button, or other political insignia.' It does not define the term 'political.' And the word can be expansive. It can encompass anything 'of or relating to government, a government, or the conduct of governmental affairs,' Webster's Third New International Dictionary 1755 (2002), or anything '[o]f, relating to, or dealing with the structure or affairs of government, politics, or the state,' American Heritage Dictionary 1401 (3d ed. 1996). Under a literal reading of those definitions, a button or T-shirt merely imploring others to "Vote!" could qualify." The Court concluded: "But we do hold that if a State wishes to set its polling places apart as areas free of partisan discord, it must employ a more discernible approach than the one Minnesota has offered here."

## E.  *Freedom of Association*

## 3.  Compelled Association (casebook p. 1674)

In *Abood v. Detroit Board of Education* (casebook p. 1674), the Court held that no one can be forced to join a public employees' union, but that non-union members can be required to pay the share of the dues that go to support the collective bargaining activities of the union. In *Janus v. American Federation* (2018), the Court expressly overruled *Abood*.

## JANUS v. AMERICAN FEDERATION OF STATE, COUNTY, AND MUNICIPAL EMPLOYEES, COUNCIL 31
### 138 S. Ct. 2448 (2018)

Justice ALITO delivered the opinion of the Court.

Under Illinois law, public employees are forced to subsidize a union, even if they choose not to join and strongly object to the positions the union takes in collective bargaining and related activities. We conclude that this arrangement violates the free speech rights of nonmembers by compelling them to subsidize private speech on matters of substantial public concern.

We upheld a similar law in *Abood v. Detroit Bd. of Ed.* (1977), and we recognize the importance of following precedent unless there are strong reasons for not doing so. But there are very strong reasons in this case. Fundamental free speech rights are at stake. *Abood* was poorly reasoned. It has led to practical problems and abuse. It is inconsistent with other First Amendment cases and has been undermined by more recent decisions. Developments since *Abood* was handed down have shed new light on the issue of agency fees, and no reliance interests on the part of public-sector unions are sufficient to justify the perpetuation of the free speech violations that *Abood* has countenanced for the past 41 years. *Abood* is therefore overruled.

I

Under the Illinois Public Labor Relations Act (IPLRA), employees of the State and its political subdivisions are permitted to unionize. If a majority of the employees in a bargaining unit vote to be represented by a union, that union is designated as the exclusive representative of all the employees. Employees in the unit are not obligated to join the union selected by their co-workers, but whether they join or not, that union is deemed to be their sole permitted representative.

Once a union is so designated, it is vested with broad authority. Only the union may negotiate with the employer on matters relating to "pay, wages, hours [,] and other conditions of employment." And this authority extends to the negotiation of what the IPLRA calls "policy matters," such as merit pay, the size of the work force, layoffs, privatization, promotion methods, and non-discrimination policies.

Designating a union as the employees' exclusive representative substantially restricts the rights of individual employees. Among other things, this designation means that individual employees may not be represented by any agent other than the designated union; nor may individual employees negotiate directly with their employer. Protection of the employees' interests is placed in the hands of the union, and therefore the union is required by law to provide fair representation for all employees in the unit, members and nonmembers alike.

Employees who decline to join the union are not assessed full union dues but must instead pay what is generally called an "agency fee," which amounts to a percentage of the union dues. Under *Abood*, nonmembers may be charged for the portion of union dues attributable to activities that are "germane to [the union's] duties as collective-bargaining representative," but nonmembers may not be required to fund the union's political and ideological projects. bor-law parlance, the outlays in the first category are known as "chargeable" expenditures, while those in the latter are labeled "nonchargeable."

Illinois law does not specify in detail which expenditures are chargeable and which are not. The IPLRA provides that an agency fee may compensate a union for the costs incurred in "the collective bargaining process, contract administration[,] and pursuing matters affecting wages, hours [,] and conditions of employment." Excluded from the agency-fee calculation are union expenditures "related to the election or support of any candidate for political office."

As illustrated by the record in this case, unions charge nonmembers, not just for the cost of collective bargaining *per se*, but also for many other supposedly connected activities. Here, the nonmembers were told that they had to pay for "[l]obbying," "[s]ocial and recreational activities," "advertising," "[m]embership meetings and conventions," and "litigation," as well as other unspecified "[s]ervices" that "may ultimately inure to the benefit of the members of the local bargaining unit." The total chargeable amount for nonmembers was 78.06% of full union dues.

Petitioner Mark Janus is employed by the Illinois Department of Healthcare and Family Services as a child support specialist. The employees in his unit are among the 35,000 public employees in Illinois who are represented by respondent American Federation of State, County, and Municipal Employees, Council 31 (Union). Janus refused to join the Union because he opposes "many of the public policy positions that [it] advocates," including the positions it takes in collective bargaining. Janus believes that the Union's "behavior in bargaining does not appreciate the current fiscal crises in Illinois and does not reflect his best interests or the interests of Illinois citizens." Therefore, if he had the choice, he "would not pay any fees or otherwise subsidize [the Union]." Under his unit's collective-bargaining agreement, however, he was required to pay an agency fee of $44.58 per month,—which would amount to about $535 per year.

[II]

We first consider whether *Abood*'s holding is consistent with standard First Amendment principles. We have held time and again that freedom of speech "includes both the right to speak freely and the right to refrain from speaking at all." The right to eschew association for expressive purposes is likewise protected. As Justice Jackson memorably put it: "If there is any fixed star in our constitutional constellation, it is that no official, high or petty, can prescribe what shall be orthodox in politics, nationalism, religion, or other matters of opinion or *force citizens to confess by word or act their faith therein.*"

Compelling individuals to mouth support for views they find objectionable violates that cardinal constitutional command, and in most contexts, any such effort would be universally condemned. Suppose, for example, that the State of Illinois required all residents to sign a document expressing support for a particular set of positions on controversial public issues—say, the platform of one of the major political parties. No one, we trust, would seriously argue that the First Amendment permits this.

Perhaps because such compulsion so plainly violates the Constitution, most of our free speech cases have involved restrictions on what can be said, rather than laws compelling speech. But measures compelling speech are at least as threatening.

Whenever the Federal Government or a State prevents individuals from saying what they think on important matters or compels them to voice ideas with which they disagree, it undermines these ends. When speech is compelled, however, additional damage is done. In that situation, individuals are coerced into betraying their convictions. Forcing free and independent individuals to endorse ideas they find objectionable is always demeaning, and for this reason, one of our landmark free speech cases said that a law commanding "involuntary affirmation" of objected-to beliefs would require "even more immediate and urgent grounds" than a law demanding silence.

Compelling a person to *subsidize* the speech of other private speakers raises similar First Amendment concerns. As Jefferson famously put it, "to compel a man to furnish contributions of money for the propagation of opinions which he disbelieves and abhor[s] is sinful and tyrannical." We have therefore recognized that a "'significant impingement on First Amendment rights'" occurs when public employees are required to provide financial support for a union that "takes many positions during collective bargaining that have powerful political and civic consequences."

Because the compelled subsidization of private speech seriously impinges on First Amendment rights, it cannot be casually allowed.

[P]etitioner in the present case contends that the Illinois law at issue should be subjected to "strict scrutiny." The dissent, on the other hand, proposes that we apply what amounts to rational-basis review, that is, that we ask only whether a government employer could reasonably believe that the exaction of agency fees serves its interests. This form of minimal scrutiny is foreign to our free-speech jurisprudence, and we reject it here. At the same time, we again find it unnecessary to decide the issue of strict scrutiny because the Illinois scheme cannot survive under even the more permissive standard.

In *Abood*, the main defense of the agency-fee arrangement was that it served the State's interest in "labor peace." By "labor peace," the *Abood* Court meant avoidance of the conflict and disruption that it envisioned would occur if the employees in a unit were represented by more than one union. In such a situation, the Court predicted, "inter-union rivalries" would foster "dissension within the work force," and the employer could face "conflicting demands from different unions." Confusion would ensue if the employer entered into and attempted to "enforce two or more agreements specifying different terms and conditions of employment." And a settlement with one union would be "subject to attack from [a] rival labor organizatio[n."

We assume that "labor peace," in this sense of the term, is a compelling state interest, but *Abood* cited no evidence that the pandemonium it imagined would result if agency fees were not allowed, and it is now clear that *Abood*'s fears were unfounded. The *Abood* Court assumed that designation of a union as the exclusive representative of all the employees in a unit and the exaction of agency fees are inextricably linked, but that is simply not true.

Whatever may have been the case 41 years ago when *Abood* was handed down, it is now undeniable that "labor peace" can readily be achieved "through means significantly less restrictive of associational freedoms" than the assessment of agency fees.

In addition to the promotion of "labor peace," *Abood* cited "the risk of 'free riders'" as justification for agency fees. Respondents and some of their *amici* endorse this reasoning, contending that agency fees are needed to prevent nonmembers from enjoying the benefits of union representation without shouldering the costs.

Petitioner strenuously objects to this free-rider label. He argues that he is not a free rider on a bus headed for a destination that he wishes to reach but is more like a person shanghaied for an unwanted voyage.

Whichever description fits the majority of public employees who would not subsidize a union if given the option, avoiding free riders is not a compelling interest. As we have noted, "free-rider arguments . . . are generally insufficient to overcome First Amendment objections." To hold otherwise across the board would have startling consequences. Many private groups speak out with the objective of obtaining government action that will have the effect of benefiting nonmembers. May all those who are thought to benefit from such efforts be compelled to subsidize this speech?

Suppose that a particular group lobbies or speaks out on behalf of what it thinks are the needs of senior citizens or veterans or physicians, to take just a few examples. Could the government require that all seniors, veterans, or doctors pay for that service even if they object? It has never been thought that this is permissible. "[P]rivate speech often furthers the interests of nonspeakers," but "that does not alone empower the state to compel the speech to be paid for." . In simple terms, the First Amendment does not permit the government to compel a person to pay for another party's speech just because the government thinks that the speech furthers the interests of the person who does not want to pay.

In any event, whatever unwanted burden is imposed by the representation of nonmembers in disciplinary matters can be eliminated "through means significantly less restrictive of associational freedoms" than the imposition of agency fees. Individual nonmembers could be required to pay for that service or could be denied union representation altogether. Thus, agency fees cannot be sustained on the ground that unions would otherwise be unwilling to represent nonmembers.

In sum, we do not see any reason to treat the free-rider interest any differently in the agency-fee context than in any other First Amendment context. We therefore hold that agency fees cannot be upheld on free-rider grounds.

[III]

Implicitly acknowledging the weakness of *Abood*'s own reasoning, proponents of agency fees have come forward with alternative justifications for the decision, and we now address these arguments.

The most surprising of these new arguments is the Union respondent's originalist defense of *Abood*. According to this argument, *Abood* was correctly decided because the First Amendment was not originally understood to provide *any* protection for the free speech rights of public employees.

As an initial matter, we doubt that the Union—or its members—actually want us to hold that public employees have "*no* [free speech] rights.*" It is particularly discordant to find this argument in a brief that trumpets the importance of *stare decisis*. See Brief for Union Taking away free speech protection for public employees would mean overturning decades of landmark precedent. In short, the Union has offered no basis for concluding that *Abood* is supported by the original understanding of the First Amendment.

The principal defense of *Abood* advanced by respondents and the dissent is based on our decision in *Pickering* [v. *Board of Education* (1968)], which held that a school district violated the First Amendment by firing a teacher for writing a letter critical of the school administration. Under *Pickering* and later cases in the same line, employee speech is largely unprotected if it is part of what the employee is paid to do, see *Garcetti v. Ceballos* (2006), or if it involved a matter of only private concern. On the other hand, when a public employee speaks as a citizen on a matter of public concern, the employee's speech is protected unless "'the interest of the state, as an employer, in promoting the efficiency of the public services it performs through its employees' outweighs 'the interests of the [employee], as a citizen, in commenting upon matters of public concern.'" *Abood* was not based on *Pickering*. The *Abood* majority cited the case exactly once—in a footnote—and then merely to acknowledge that "there may be limits on the extent to which an employee in a sensitive or policymaking position may freely criticize his superiors and the policies they espouse." We see no good reason, at this late date, to try to shoehorn *Abood* into the *Pickering* framework.

Even if we were to apply some form of *Pickering*, Illinois' agency-fee arrangement would not survive. Respondents begin by suggesting that union speech in collective-bargaining and grievance proceedings should be treated like the employee speech in *Garcetti*, *i.e.*, as speech "pursuant to [an employee's] official duties." Many employees, in both the public and private sectors, are paid to write or speak for the purpose of furthering the interests of their employers. There are laws that protect public employees from being compelled to say things that they reasonably believe to be untrue or improper, but in general when public employees are performing their job duties, their speech may be controlled by their employer. Trying to fit union speech into this framework, respondents now suggest that the union speech funded by agency fees forms part of the official duties of the union officers who engage in the speech.

This argument distorts collective bargaining and grievance adjustment beyond recognition. When an employee engages in speech that is part of the employee's job duties, the employee's words are really the words of the employer. The employee is effectively the employer's spokesperson. But when a union negotiates with the employer or represents employees in disciplinary proceedings, the union speaks for the *employees*, not the employer. Otherwise, the employer would be negotiating with itself and disputing its own actions. That is not what anybody understands to be happening.

What is more, if the union's speech is really the employer's speech, then the employer could dictate what the union says. Unions, we trust, would be appalled by such a suggestion. For these reasons, *Garcetti* is totally inapposite here.

Although the dissent would accept without any serious independent evaluation the State's assertion that the absence of agency fees would cripple public-sector unions and thus impair the efficiency of government operations, ample experience, as we have noted, shows that this is questionable. It is also not disputed that the State may require that a union serve as exclusive bargaining agent for its employees—itself a significant impingement on associational freedoms that would not be tolerated in other contexts. We simply draw the line at allowing the government to go further still and require all employees to support the union irrespective of whether they share its views. Nothing in the *Pickering* line of cases requires us to uphold every speech restriction the government imposes as an employer.

[V]

For the reasons given above, we conclude that public-sector agency-shop arrangements violate the First Amendment, and *Abood* erred in concluding otherwise. There remains the question whether *stare decisis* nonetheless counsels against overruling *Abood*. It does not.

The doctrine "is at its weakest when we interpret the Constitution because our interpretation can be altered only by constitutional amendment or by overruling our prior decisions." And *stare decisis* applies with perhaps least force of all to decisions that wrongly denied First Amendment rights: "This Court has not hesitated to overrule decisions offensive to the First Amendment (a fixed star in our constitutional constellation, if there is one)."

Our cases identify factors that should be taken into account in deciding whether to overrule a past decision. Five of these are most important here: the quality of *Abood*'s reasoning, the workability of the rule it established, its consistency with other related decisions, developments since the decision was handed down, and reliance on the decision.

An important factor in determining whether a precedent should be overruled is the quality of its reasoning. "*Abood* failed to appreciate the conceptual difficulty of distinguishing in public-sector cases between union expenditures that are made for collective-bargaining purposes and those that are made to achieve political ends." Likewise, "*Abood* does not seem to have anticipated the magnitude of the practical administrative problems that would result in attempting to classify public-sector union expenditures as either 'chargeable' . . . or nonchargeable." Nor did *Abood* "foresee the practical problems that would face objecting nonmembers."

In sum, *Abood* was not well reasoned.

Another relevant consideration in the *stare decisis* calculus is the workability of the precedent in question, and that factor also weighs against *Abood*. *Abood*'s line between chargeable and nonchargeable union expenditures has proved to be impossible to draw with precision.

Respondents agree that *Abood*'s chargeable-nonchargeable line suffers from "a vagueness problem," that it sometimes "allows what it shouldn't allow," and that "a firm[er] line c[ould] be drawn." This concession only underscores the reality that *Abood* has proved unworkable: Not even the parties defending agency fees support the line that it has taken this Court over 40 years to draw.

Developments since *Abood*, both factual and legal, have also "eroded" the decision's "underpinnings" and left it an outlier among our First Amendment cases. *Abood* is also an "anomaly" in our First Amendment jurisprudence., as we recognized in *Harris* and *Knox*.

*Abood* particularly sticks out when viewed against our cases holding that public employees generally may not be required to support a political party. It is an odd feature of our First Amendment cases that political patronage has been deemed largely unconstitutional, while forced subsidization of union speech (which has no such pedigree) has been largely permitted.

In some cases, reliance provides a strong reason for adhering to established law, and this is the factor that is stressed most strongly by respondents, their *amici*, and the dissent. They contend that collective-bargaining agreements now in effect were negotiated with agency fees in mind and that unions may have given up other benefits in exchange for provisions granting them such fees. In this case, however, reliance does not carry decisive weight.

For one thing, it would be unconscionable to permit free speech rights to be abridged in perpetuity in order to preserve contract provisions that will expire on their own in a few years' time. "The fact that [public-sector unions] may view [agency fees] as an entitlement does not establish the sort of reliance interest that could outweigh the countervailing interest that [nonmembers] share in having their constitutional rights fully protected." For another, *Abood* does not provide "a clear or easily applicable standard, so arguments for reliance based on its clarity are misplaced." This is especially so because public-sector unions have been on notice for years regarding this Court's misgivings about *Abood*.

In short, the uncertain status of *Abood*, the lack of clarity it provides, the short-term nature of collective-bargaining agreements, and the ability of unions to protect themselves if an agency-fee provision was crucial to its bargain all work to undermine the force of reliance as a factor supporting *Abood*.

We recognize that the loss of payments from nonmembers may cause unions to experience unpleasant transition costs in the short term, and may require unions to make adjustments in order to attract and retain members. But we must weigh these disadvantages against the considerable windfall that unions have received under *Abood* for the past 41 years. It is hard to estimate how many billions of dollars have been taken from nonmembers and transferred to public-sector unions in violation of the First Amendment. Those unconstitutional exactions cannot be allowed to continue indefinitely.

[VI]

For these reasons, States and public-sector unions may no longer extract agency fees from nonconsenting employees. Under Illinois law, if a public-sector collective-bargaining agreement includes an agency-fee provision and the union certifies to the employer the amount of the fee, that amount is automatically deducted from the nonmember's wages. No form of employee consent is required.

This procedure violates the First Amendment and cannot continue. Neither an agency fee nor any other payment to the union may be deducted from a nonmember's wages, nor may any other attempt be made to collect such a payment, unless the employee affirmatively consents to pay. By agreeing to pay, nonmembers are waiving their First Amendment rights, and such a waiver cannot be presumed. Rather, to be effective, the waiver must be freely given and shown by "clear and compelling" evidence. Unless employees clearly and affirmatively consent before any money is taken from them, this standard cannot be met.

*Abood* was wrongly decided and is now overruled.

Justice KAGAN, with whom Justice GINSBURG, Justice BREYER, and Justice SOTOMAYOR join, dissenting.

For over 40 years, *Abood v. Detroit Bd. of Ed.* (1977), struck a stable balance between public employees' First Amendment rights and government entities' interests in running their workforces as they thought proper. Under that decision, a government entity could require public employees to pay a fair share of the cost that a union incurs when negotiating on their behalf over terms of employment. But no part of that fair-share payment could go to any of the union's political or ideological activities.

That holding fit comfortably with this Court's general framework for evaluating claims that a condition of public employment violates the First Amendment. The Court's decisions have long made plain that government entities have substantial latitude to regulate their employees' speech—especially about terms of employment—in the interest of operating their workplaces effectively. *Abood* allowed governments to do just that. While protecting public employees' expression about non-workplace matters, the decision enabled a government to advance important managerial interests—by ensuring the presence of an exclusive employee representative to bargain with. Far from an "anomaly," the *Abood* regime was a paradigmatic example of how the government can regulate speech in its capacity as an employer.

Not any longer. Its decision will have large-scale consequences. Public employee unions will lose a secure source of financial support. State and local governments that thought fair-share provisions furthered their interests will need to find new ways of managing their workforces. Across the country, the relationships of public employees and employers will alter in both predictable and wholly unexpected ways.

Rarely if ever has the Court overruled a decision—let alone one of this import—with so little regard for the usual principles of *stare decisis*. There are no special justifications for reversing *Abood*. It has proved workable. No recent developments have eroded its underpinnings. And it is deeply entrenched, in both the law and the real world. More than 20 States have statutory schemes built on the decision. Those laws underpin thousands of ongoing contracts involving millions of employees. Reliance interests do not come any stronger than those surrounding *Abood*. And likewise, judicial disruption does not get any greater than what the Court does today. I respectfully dissent.

## [I]

Unlike the majority, I see nothing "questionable" about *Abood*'s analysis. The decision's account of why some government entities have a strong interest in agency fees (now often called fair-share fees) is fundamentally sound. And the balance *Abood* struck between public employers' interests and public employees' expression is right at home in First Amendment doctrine.

In many cases over many decades, this Court has addressed how the First Amendment applies when the government, acting not as sovereign but as employer, limits its workers' speech. Those decisions have granted substantial latitude to the government, in recognition of its significant interests in managing its workforce so as to best serve the public. *Abood* fit neatly with that caselaw, in both reasoning and result. Indeed, its reversal today creates a significant anomaly — an exception, applying to union fees alone, from the usual rules governing public employees' speech.

In striking the proper balance between employee speech rights and managerial interests, the Court has long applied a test originating in *Pickering v. Board of Ed. of Township High School Dist. 205, Will Cty.* (1968). *Abood* coheres with that framework. *Abood* and *Pickering* raised variants of the same basic issue: the extent of the government's authority to make employment decisions affecting expression. And in both, the Court struck the same basic balance, enabling the government to curb speech when — but only when — the regulation was designed to protect its managerial interests.

The key point about *Abood* is that it fit naturally with this Court's consistent teaching about the permissibility of regulating public employees' speech. The Court allows a government entity to regulate that expression in aid of managing its workforce to effectively provide public services. That is just what a government aims to do when it enforces a fair-share agreement. And so, the key point about today's decision is that it creates an unjustified hole in the law, applicable to union fees alone. This case is *sui generis* among those addressing public employee speech — and will almost surely remain so.

## [II]

But the worse part of today's opinion is where the majority subverts all known principles of *stare decisis*. The majority makes plain, in the first

33 pages of its decision, that it believes *Abood* was wrong.[4] But even if that were true (which it is not), it is not enough. "Respecting *stare decisis* means sticking to some wrong decisions." Any departure from settled precedent (so the Court has often stated) demands a "special justification—over and above the belief that the precedent was wrongly decided." And the majority does not have anything close. To the contrary: all that is "special" in this case—especially the massive reliance interests at stake—demands retaining *Abood*, beyond even the normal precedent.

And *Abood* is not just any precedent: It is embedded in the law (not to mention, as I'll later address, in the world) in a way not many decisions are. Over four decades, this Court has cited *Abood* favorably many times, and has affirmed and applied its central distinction between the costs of collective bargaining (which the government can charge to all employees) and those of political activities (which it cannot).

The majority is likewise wrong to invoke "workability" as a reason for overruling *Abood*. Does *Abood* require drawing a line? Yes, between a union's collective-bargaining activities and its political activities. Is that line perfectly and pristinely "precis[e]," as the majority demands? Well, not quite that—but as exercises of constitutional linedrawing go, *Abood* stands well above average. In the 40 years since *Abood*, this Court has had to resolve only a handful of cases raising questions about the distinction. To my knowledge, the circuit courts are not divided on any classification issue; neither are they issuing distress signals of the kind that sometimes prompt the Court to reverse a decision. And that tranquility is unsurprising: There may be some gray areas (there always are), but in the mine run of cases, everyone knows the difference between politicking and collective bargaining.

And in any event, one *stare decisis* factor—reliance—dominates all others here and demands keeping *Abood*. *Stare decisis*, this Court has held, "has added force when the legislature, in the public sphere, and citizens, in the private realm, have acted in reliance on a previous decision." That is because overruling a decision would then "require an extensive legislative response" or "dislodge settled rights and expectations." Both will happen here: The Court today wreaks havoc on entrenched legislative and contractual arrangements.

Over 20 States have by now enacted statutes authorizing fair-share provisions. To be precise, 22 States, the District of Columbia, and Puerto Rico—plus another two States for police and firefighter unions. Many of those States have multiple statutory provisions, with variations for different categories of public employees. Every one of them will now need to come up with new ways—elaborated in new statutes—to structure relations between government employers and their workers. Still more, thousands of current contracts covering millions of workers provide for agency fees. Usually, this Court recognizes that "[c]onsiderations in favor of *stare decisis* are at their acme in cases involving property and contract rights." Not today. The majority undoes bargains reached all over the country. It prevents the parties from fulfilling other commitments they have made based on those agreements. It forces the parties—immediately—to renegotiate once-settled terms and create new tradeoffs. It does so knowing that many of the parties will have to revise (or redo) multiple contracts simultaneously. It does so knowing that those renegotiations will occur in an environment of legal uncertainty, as state governments scramble to enact new labor legislation. It does so with no real clue of what will happen next—of how its action will alter public-sector labor relations. It does so even though the government services affected—policing, firefighting, teaching, transportation, sanitation (and more)—affect the quality of life of tens of millions of Americans.

[III]

There is no sugarcoating today's opinion. The majority overthrows a decision entrenched in this Nation's law—and in its economic life—for over 40 years. As a result, it prevents the American people, acting through their state and local officials, from making important choices about workplace governance. And it does so by weaponizing the First Amendment, in a way that unleashes judges, now and in the future, to intervene in economic and regulatory policy.

The majority has overruled *Abood* for no exceptional or special reason, but because it never liked the decision. It has overruled *Abood* because it wanted to.

Because, that is, it wanted to pick the winning side in what should be—and until now, has been—an energetic policy debate. Some state and local governments (and the constituents they serve) think that stable unions promote healthy labor relations and thereby improve the provision of services to the public. Other state and local governments (and their constituents) think, to the contrary, that strong unions impose excessive costs and impair those services. Americans have debated the pros and cons for many decades—in large part, by deciding whether to use fair-share arrangements. Yesterday, 22 States were on one side, 28 on the other (ignoring a couple of in-betweeners). Today, that healthy—that democratic—debate ends. The majority has adjudged who should prevail.

And maybe most alarming, the majority has chosen the winners by turning the First Amendment into a sword, and using it against workaday economic and regulatory policy. And it threatens not to be the last. Speech is everywhere—a part of every human activity (employment, health care, securities trading, you name it). For that reason, almost all economic and regulatory policy affects or touches speech. So the majority's road runs long. And at every stop are black-robed rulers overriding citizens' choices. The First Amendment was meant for better things. It was meant not to undermine but to protect democratic governance—including over the role of public-sector unions.

# Chapter 10

# *The First Amendment: Religion*

## B. *The Free Exercise Clause*

### 2. The Current Test (p. 1732)

The Supreme Court has held that the government violates free exercise of religion when it acts with hostility to religion. In *Masterpiece Cakeshop v. Colorado Civil Rights Commission*, the Court found hostility to religion when the Colorado Civil Rights Commission ruled against a baker who refused to design and bake a case to celebrate the wedding of a same-sex couple. The Court left unresolved whether it violates free exercise of religion or freedom of speech to hold a baker—or other business—liable for refusal to serve a same-sex couple.

MASTERPIECE CAKE SHOP, LTD. v.
COLORADO CIVIL RIGHTS COMMISSION
138 S. Ct. 1719 (2018)

Justice KENNEDY delivered the opinion of the Court.

In 2012 a same-sex couple visited Masterpiece Cakeshop, a bakery in Colorado, to make inquiries about ordering a cake for their wedding reception. The shop's owner told the couple that he would not create a cake for their wedding because of his religious opposition to same-sex marriages—marriages the State of Colorado itself did not recognize at that time. The couple filed a charge with the Colorado Civil Rights Commission alleging discrimination on the basis of sexual orientation in violation of the Colorado Anti-Discrimination Act.

The Commission determined that the shop's actions violated the Act and ruled in the couple's favor. The Colorado state courts affirmed the ruling and its enforcement order, and this Court now must decide whether the Commission's order violated the Constitution.

The case presents difficult questions as to the proper reconciliation of at least two principles. The first is the authority of a State and its governmental entities to protect the rights and dignity of gay persons who are, or wish to be, married but who face discrimination when they seek goods or services. The second is the right of all persons to exercise fundamental freedoms under the First Amendment, as applied to the States through the Fourteenth Amendment.

The freedoms asserted here are both the freedom of speech and the free exercise of religion. The free speech aspect of this case is difficult, for few persons who have seen a beautiful wedding cake might have thought of its creation as an exercise of protected speech. This is an instructive example, however, of the proposition that the application of constitutional freedoms in new contexts can deepen our understanding of their meaning.

One of the difficulties in this case is that the parties disagree as to the extent of the baker's refusal to provide service. If a baker refused to design a special cake with words or images celebrating the marriage — for instance, a cake showing words with religious meaning — that might be different from a refusal to sell any cake at all. In defining whether a baker's creation can be protected, these details might make a difference.

The same difficulties arise in determining whether a baker has a valid free exercise claim. A baker's refusal to attend the wedding to ensure that the cake is cut the right way, or a refusal to put certain religious words or decorations on the cake, or even a refusal to sell a cake that has been baked for the public generally but includes certain religious words or symbols on it are just three examples of possibilities that seem all but endless.

Whatever the confluence of speech and free exercise principles might be in some cases, the Colorado Civil Rights Commission's consideration of this case was inconsistent with the State's obligation of religious neutrality. The reason and motive for the baker's refusal were based on his sincere religious beliefs and convictions. The Court's precedents make clear that the baker, in his capacity as the owner of a business serving the public, might have his right to the free exercise of religion limited by generally applicable laws. Still, the delicate question of when the free exercise of his religion must yield to an otherwise valid exercise of state power needed to be determined in an adjudication in which religious hostility on the part of the State itself would not be a factor in the balance the State sought to reach. That requirement, however, was not met here. When the Colorado Civil Rights Commission considered this case, it did not do so with the religious neutrality that the Constitution requires.

Given all these considerations, it is proper to hold that whatever the outcome of some future controversy involving facts similar to these, the

Commission's actions here violated the Free Exercise Clause; and its order must be set aside.

## I

Masterpiece Cakeshop, Ltd., is a bakery in Lakewood, Colorado, a suburb of Denver. The shop offers a variety of baked goods, ranging from everyday cookies and brownies to elaborate custom-designed cakes for birthday parties, weddings, and other events.

Jack Phillips is an expert baker who has owned and operated the shop for 24 years. Phillips is a devout Christian. He has explained that his "main goal in life is to be obedient to" Jesus Christ and Christ's "teachings in all aspects of his life." And he seeks to "honor God through his work at Masterpiece Cakeshop." One of Phillips' religious beliefs is that "God's intention for marriage from the beginning of history is that it is and should be the union of one man and one woman." To Phillips, creating a wedding cake for a same-sex wedding would be equivalent to participating in a celebration that is contrary to his own most deeply held beliefs.

Phillips met Charlie Craig and Dave Mullins when they entered his shop in the summer of 2012. Craig and Mullins were planning to marry. At that time, Colorado did not recognize same-sex marriages, so the couple planned to wed legally in Massachusetts and afterwards to host a reception for their family and friends in Denver. To prepare for their celebration, Craig and Mullins visited the shop and told Phillips that they were interested in ordering a cake for "our wedding." They did not mention the design of the cake they envisioned.

Phillips informed the couple that he does not "create" wedding cakes for same-sex weddings. He explained, "I'll make your birthday cakes, shower cakes, sell you cookies and brownies, I just don't make cakes for same sex weddings." The couple left the shop without further discussion.

The following day, Craig's mother, who had accompanied the couple to the cakeshop and been present for their interaction with Phillips, telephoned to ask Phillips why he had declined to serve her son. Phillips explained that he does not create wedding cakes for same-sex weddings because of his religious opposition to same-sex marriage, and also because Colorado (at that time) did not recognize same-sex marriages. He later explained his belief that "to create a wedding cake for an event that celebrates something that directly goes against the teachings of the Bible, would have been a personal endorsement and participation in the ceremony and relationship that they were entering into."

Today, the Colorado Anti-Discrimination Act (CADA) carries forward the state's tradition of prohibiting discrimination in places of public accommodation. Amended in 2007 and 2008 to prohibit discrimination on the basis of sexual orientation as well as other protected characteristics, CADA in relevant part provides as follows:

> It is a discriminatory practice and unlawful for a person, directly or indirectly, to refuse, withhold from, or deny to an individual or a group, because of disability, race, creed, color, sex, sexual orientation, marital status, national origin, or ancestry, the full and equal enjoyment of the goods, services, facilities, privileges, advantages, or accommodations of a place of public accommodation.

The Act defines "public accommodation" broadly to include any "place of business engaged in any sales to the public and any place offering services . . . to the public," but excludes "a church, synagogue, mosque, or other place that is principally used for religious purposes."

Craig and Mullins filed a discrimination complaint against Masterpiece Cakeshop and Phillips in September 2012, shortly after the couple's visit to the shop. App. 31. The complaint alleged that Craig and Mullins had been denied "full and equal service" at the bakery because of their sexual orientation, and that it was Phillips' "standard business practice" not to provide cakes for same-sex weddings.

The Civil Rights Division opened an investigation. The investigator found that "on multiple occasions," Phillips "turned away potential customers on the basis of their sexual orientation, stating that he could not create a cake for a same-sex wedding ceremony or reception" because his religious beliefs prohibited it and because the potential customers "were doing something illegal" at that time. The investigation found that Phillips had declined to sell custom wedding cakes to about six other same-sex couples on this basis. The investigator also recounted that, according to affidavits submitted by Craig and Mullins, Phillips' shop had refused to sell cupcakes to a lesbian couple for their commitment celebration because the shop "had a policy of not selling baked goods to same-sex couples for this type of event." Based on these findings, the Division found probable cause that Phillips violated CADA and referred the case to the Civil Rights Commission.

The Commission found it proper to conduct a formal hearing, and it sent the case to a State ALJ. Finding no dispute as to material facts, the ALJ entertained cross-motions for summary judgment and ruled in the couple's favor. The ALJ first rejected Phillips' argument that declining to make or create a wedding cake for Craig and Mullins did not violate Colorado law. It was undisputed that the shop is subject to state public accommodations laws. And the ALJ determined that Phillips' actions constituted prohibited discrimination on the basis of sexual orientation, not simply opposition to same-sex marriage as Phillips contended.

The Commission affirmed the ALJ's decision in full. The Commission ordered Phillips to "cease and desist from discriminating against . . . same-sex couples by refusing to sell them wedding cakes or any product [they] would sell to heterosexual couples." It also ordered additional remedial measures, including "comprehensive staff training on the Public Accommodations section" of CADA "and changes to any and all company policies to comply with . . . this Order." The Commission additionally required Phillips to prepare "quarterly compliance reports" for a period of two years documenting "the number of patrons denied service" and why, along with "a statement describing the remedial actions taken."

Phillips appealed to the Colorado Court of Appeals, which affirmed the Commission's legal determinations and remedial order.

## II

Our society has come to the recognition that gay persons and gay couples cannot be treated as social outcasts or as inferior in dignity and worth. For that reason the laws and the Constitution can, and in some instances must, protect them in the exercise of their civil rights. The exercise of their freedom on terms equal to others must be given great weight and respect by the courts. At the same time, the religious and philosophical objections to gay marriage are protected views and in some instances protected forms of expression. As this Court observed in *Obergefell v. Hodges* (2015), "[t]he First Amendment ensures that religious organizations and persons are given proper protection as they seek to teach the principles that are so fulfilling and so central to their lives and faiths." Nevertheless, while those religious and philosophical objections are protected, it is a general rule that such objections do not allow business owners and other actors in the economy and in society to deny protected persons equal access to goods and services under a neutral and generally applicable public accommodations law.

When it comes to weddings, it can be assumed that a member of the clergy who objects to gay marriage on moral and religious grounds could not be compelled to perform the ceremony without denial of his or her right to the free exercise of religion. This refusal would be well understood in our constitutional order as an exercise of religion, an exercise that gay persons could recognize and accept without serious diminishment to their own dignity and worth. Yet if that exception were not confined, then a long list of persons who provide goods and services for marriages and weddings might refuse to do so for gay persons, thus resulting in a community-wide stigma inconsistent with the history and dynamics of civil rights laws that ensure equal access to goods, services, and public accommodations.

It is unexceptional that Colorado law can protect gay persons, just as it can protect other classes of individuals, in acquiring whatever products and services they choose on the same terms and conditions as are offered to other members of the public. And there are no doubt innumerable goods and services that no one could argue implicate the First Amendment. Petitioners conceded, moreover, that if a baker refused to sell any goods or any cakes for gay weddings, that would be a different matter and the State would have a strong case under this Court's precedents that this would be a denial of goods and services that went beyond any protected rights of a baker who offers goods and services to the general public and is subject to a neutrally applied and generally applicable public accommodations law.

Phillips claims, however, that a narrower issue is presented. He argues that he had to use his artistic skills to make an expressive statement, a wedding endorsement in his own voice and of his own creation. As Phillips would see the case, this contention has a significant First Amendment speech component and implicates his deep and sincere religious beliefs. In this context the baker likely found it difficult to find a line where the customers' rights to goods and services became a demand for him to exercise the right of his own personal expression for their message, a message he could not express in a way consistent with his religious beliefs.

Phillips' dilemma was particularly understandable given the background of legal principles and administration of the law in Colorado at that time. His decision and his actions leading to the refusal of service all occurred in the year 2012. At that point, Colorado did not recognize the validity of gay marriages performed in its own State. Since the State itself did not allow those marriages to be performed in Colorado, there is some force to the argument that the baker was not unreasonable in deeming it lawful to decline to take an action that he understood to be an expression of support for their validity when that expression was contrary to his sincerely held religious beliefs, at least insofar as his refusal was limited to refusing to create and express a message in support of gay marriage, even one planned to take place in another State.

At the time, state law also afforded storekeepers some latitude to decline to create specific messages the storekeeper considered offensive. Indeed, while enforcement proceedings against Phillips were ongoing, the Colorado Civil Rights Division itself endorsed this proposition in cases involving other bakers' creation of cakes, concluding on at least three occasions that a baker acted lawfully in declining to create cakes with decorations that demeaned gay persons or gay marriages.

[A]ny decision in favor of the baker would have to be sufficiently constrained, lest all purveyors of goods and services who object to gay marriages for moral and religious reasons in effect be allowed to put up signs saying "no goods or services will be sold if they will be used for gay marriages," something that would impose a serious stigma on gay persons. But, nonetheless, Phillips was entitled to the neutral and respectful consideration of his claims in all the circumstances of the case.

The neutral and respectful consideration to which Phillips was entitled was compromised here, however. The Civil Rights Commission's treatment of his case has some elements of a clear and impermissible hostility toward the sincere religious beliefs that motivated his objection.

That hostility surfaced at the Commission's formal, public hearings, as shown by the record. On May 30, 2014, the seven-member Commission convened publicly to consider Phillips' case. At several points during its meeting, commissioners endorsed the view that religious beliefs cannot legitimately be carried into the public sphere or commercial domain, implying that religious beliefs and persons are less than fully welcome in Colorado's business community. One commissioner suggested that Phillips can believe "what he wants to believe," but cannot act on his religious beliefs "if he decides to do business in the state." A few moments later, the commissioner restated the same position: "[I]f a businessman wants to do business in the state and he's got an issue with the—the law's impacting his personal belief system, he needs to look at being able to compromise." Standing alone, these statements are susceptible of different interpretations. On the one hand, they might mean simply that a business cannot refuse to provide services based on sexual orientation, regardless of the proprietor's personal views. On the other hand, they might be seen as inappropriate and dismissive comments showing lack of due consideration for Phillips' free exercise rights and the dilemma he faced. In view of the comments that followed, the latter seems the more likely.

On July 25, 2014, the Commission met again. This meeting, too, was conducted in public and on the record. On this occasion another commissioner made specific reference to the previous meeting's discussion but said far more to disparage Phillips' beliefs. The commissioner stated:

"I would also like to reiterate what we said in the hearing or the last meeting. Freedom of religion and religion has been used to justify all kinds of discrimination throughout history, whether it be slavery, whether it be the holocaust, whether it be—I mean, we—we can list hundreds of situations where freedom of religion has been used to justify discrimination. And to me it is one of the most despicable pieces of rhetoric that people can use to—to use their religion to hurt others."

To describe a man's faith as "one of the most despicable pieces of rhetoric that people can use" is to disparage his religion in at least two distinct ways: by describing it as despicable, and also by characterizing it as merely rhetorical—something insubstantial and even insincere. The commissioner even went so far as to compare Phillips' invocation of his sincerely held religious beliefs to defenses of slavery and the Holocaust. This sentiment is inappropriate for a Commission charged with the solemn responsibility of fair and neutral enforcement of Colorado's antidiscrimination law—a law that protects against discrimination on the basis of religion as well as sexual orientation.

The record shows no objection to these comments from other commissioners. And the later state-court ruling reviewing the Commission's decision did not mention those comments, much less express concern with their content. Nor were the comments by the commissioners disavowed in the briefs filed in this Court. For these reasons, the Court cannot avoid the conclusion that these statements cast doubt on the fairness and impartiality of the Commission's adjudication of Phillips' case. Members of the Court have disagreed on the question whether statements made by lawmakers may properly be taken into account in determining whether a law intentionally discriminates on the basis of religion. In this case, however, the remarks were made in a very different context—by an adjudicatory body deciding a particular case.

Another indication of hostility is the difference in treatment between Phillips' case and the cases of other bakers who objected to a requested cake on the basis of conscience and prevailed before the Commission. As noted above, on at least three other occasions the Civil Rights Division considered the refusal of bakers to create cakes with images that conveyed disapproval of same-sex marriage, along with religious text. Each time, the Division found that the baker acted lawfully in refusing service. It made these determinations because, in the words of the Division, the requested cake included "wording and images [the baker] deemed derogatory," featured "language and images [the baker] deemed hateful," or displayed a message the baker "deemed as discriminatory.

The treatment of the conscience-based objections at issue in these three cases contrasts with the Commission's treatment of Phillips' objection. The Commission ruled against Phillips in part on the theory that any message the requested wedding cake would carry would be attributed to the customer, not to the baker. Yet the Division did not address this point in any of the other cases with respect to the cakes depicting anti-gay marriage symbolism. Additionally, the Division found no violation of CADA in the other cases in part because each bakery was willing to sell other products, including those depicting Christian themes, to the prospective customers. But the Commission dismissed Phillips' willingness to sell "birthday cakes, shower cakes, [and] cookies and brownies," to gay and lesbian customers as irrelevant. The treatment of the other cases and Phillips' case could reasonably be interpreted as being inconsistent as to the question of whether speech is involved, quite apart from whether the cases should ultimately be distinguished. In short, the Commission's consideration of Phillips' religious objection did not accord with its treatment of these other objections.

For the reasons just described, the Commission's treatment of Phillips' case violated the State's duty under the First Amendment not to base laws or regulations on hostility to a religion or religious viewpoint. In view of these factors the record here demonstrates that the Commission's consideration of Phillips' case was neither tolerant nor respectful of Phillips' religious beliefs. The Commission gave "every appearance," of adjudicating Phillips' religious objection based on a negative normative "evaluation of the particular justification" for his objection and the religious grounds for it. It hardly requires restating that government has no role in deciding or even suggesting whether the religious ground for Phillips' conscience-based objection is legitimate or illegitimate. On these facts, the Court must draw the inference that Phillips' religious objection was not considered with the neutrality that the Free Exercise Clause requires.

While the issues here are difficult to resolve, it must be concluded that the State's interest could have been weighed against Phillips' sincere religious objections in a way consistent with the requisite religious neutrality that must be strictly observed. The official expressions of hostility to religion in some of the commissioners' comments — comments that were not disavowed at the Commission or by the State at any point in the proceedings that led to affirmance of the order — were inconsistent with what the Free Exercise Clause requires. The Commission's disparate consideration of Phillips' case compared to the cases of the other bakers suggests the same. For these reasons, the order must be set aside.

## III

The Commission's hostility was inconsistent with the First Amendment's guarantee that our laws be applied in a manner that is neutral toward religion. Phillips was entitled to a neutral decisionmaker who would give full and fair consideration to his religious objection as he sought to assert it in all of the circumstances in which this case was presented, considered, and decided. However later cases raising these or similar concerns are resolved in the future, for these reasons the rulings of the Commission and of the state court that enforced the Commission's order must be invalidated.

The outcome of cases like this in other circumstances must await further elaboration in the courts, all in the context of recognizing that these disputes must be resolved with tolerance, without undue disrespect to sincere religious beliefs, and without subjecting gay persons to indignities when they seek goods and services in an open market.

Justice KAGAN, with whom Justice BREYER joins, concurring.

"[I]t is a general rule that [religious and philosophical] objections do not allow business owners and other actors in the economy and in society to deny protected persons equal access to goods and services under a neutral and generally applicable public accommodations law." But in upholding that principle, state actors cannot show hostility to religious views; rather, they must give those views "neutral and respectful consideration." I join the Court's opinion in full because I believe the Colorado Civil Rights Commission did not satisfy that obligation. I write separately to elaborate on one of the bases for the Court's holding.

The Court partly relies on the "disparate consideration of Phillips' case compared to the cases of [three] other bakers" who "objected to a requested cake on the basis of conscience." What makes the state agencies' consideration yet more disquieting is that a proper basis for distinguishing the cases was available—in fact, was obvious. The Colorado Anti-Discrimination Act (CADA) makes it unlawful for a place of public accommodation to deny "the full and equal enjoyment" of goods and services to individuals based on certain characteristics, including sexual orientation and creed. The three bakers in the Jack cases did not violate that law. Jack requested them to make a cake (one denigrating gay people and same-sex marriage) that they would not have made for any customer. In refusing that request, the bakers did not single out Jack because of his religion, but instead treated him in the same way they would have treated anyone else—just as CADA requires. By contrast, the same-sex couple in this case requested a wedding cake that Phillips would have made for an opposite-sex couple. In refusing that request, Phillips contravened CADA's demand that customers receive "the full and equal enjoyment" of public accommodations irrespective of their sexual orientation.

The different outcomes in the Jack cases and the Phillips case could thus have been justified by a plain reading and neutral application of Colorado law—untainted by any bias against a religious belief.[*]

Justice GORSUCH, with whom Justice ALITO joins, concurring.

In *Employment Div., Dept. of Human Resources of Ore. v. Smith*, this Court held that a neutral and generally applicable law will usually survive a constitutional free exercise challenge. *Smith* remains controversial in many quarters. But we know this with certainty: when the government fails to act neutrally toward the free exercise of religion, it tends to run into trouble. Then the government can prevail only if it satisfies strict scrutiny, showing that its restrictions on religion both serve a compelling interest and are narrowly tailored.

Today's decision respects these principles. As the Court explains, the Colorado Civil Rights Commission failed to act neutrally toward Jack Phillips's religious faith. Maybe most notably, the Commission allowed three other bakers to refuse a customer's request that would have required them to violate their secular commitments. Yet it denied the same accommodation to Mr. Phillips when he refused a customer's request that would have required him to violate his religious beliefs. As the Court also explains, the only reason the Commission seemed to supply for its discrimination was that it found Mr. Phillips's religious beliefs "offensive." That kind of judgmental dismissal of a sincerely held religious belief is, of course, antithetical to the First Amendment and cannot begin to satisfy strict scrutiny. The Constitution protects not just popular religious exercises from the condemnation of civil authorities. It protects them all.

The only wrinkle is this. In the face of so much evidence suggesting hostility toward Mr. Phillips's sincerely held religious beliefs, two of our colleagues have written separately to suggest that the Commission acted neutrally toward his faith when it treated him differently from the other bakers—or that it could have easily done so consistent with the First Amendment.

Justice THOMAS, with whom Justice GORSUCH joins, concurring in part and concurring in the judgment.

I agree that the Colorado Civil Rights Commission (Commission) violated Jack Phillips' right to freely exercise his religion. While Phillips rightly prevails on his free-exercise claim, I write separately to address his free-speech claim. The Court does not address this claim because it has some uncertainties about the record.

The conduct that the Colorado Court of Appeals ascribed to Phillips—creating and designing custom wedding cakes—is expressive. Phillips considers himself an artist. The logo for Masterpiece Cakeshop is an artist's paint palette with a paintbrush and baker's whisk. Behind the counter Phillips has a picture that depicts him as an artist painting on a canvas. Phillips takes exceptional care with each cake that he creates—sketching the design out on paper, choosing the color scheme, creating the frosting and decorations, baking and sculpting the cake, decorating it, and delivering it to the wedding. Examples of his creations can be seen on Masterpiece's website.

Phillips is an active participant in the wedding celebration. He sits down with each couple for a consultation before he creates their custom wedding cake. He discusses their preferences, their personalities, and the details of their wedding to ensure that each cake reflects the couple who ordered it. In addition to creating and delivering the cake—a focal point of the wedding celebration—Phillips sometimes stays and interacts with the guests at the wedding. And the guests often recognize his creations and seek his bakery out afterward. Phillips also sees the inherent symbolism in wedding cakes. To him, a wedding cake inherently communicates that "a wedding has occurred, a marriage has begun, and the couple should be celebrated."

Wedding cakes do, in fact, communicate this message. A tradition from Victorian England that made its way to America after the Civil War, "[w]edding cakes are so packed with symbolism that it is hard to know where to begin." If an average person walked into a room and saw a white, multi-tiered cake, he would immediately know that he had stumbled upon a wedding. The cake is "so standardised and inevitable a part of getting married that few ever think to question it." Almost no wedding, no matter how spartan, is missing the cake.

Accordingly, Phillips' creation of custom wedding cakes is expressive. The use of his artistic talents to create a well-recognized symbol that celebrates the beginning of a marriage clearly communicates a message—certainly more so than nude dancing, or flying a plain red flag. By forcing Phillips to create custom wedding cakes for same-sex weddings, Colorado's public-accommodations law "alter[s] the expressive content" of his message. Forcing Phillips to make custom wedding cakes for same-sex marriages requires him to, at the very least, acknowledge that same-sex weddings are "weddings" and suggest that they should be celebrated—the precise message he believes his faith forbids. The First Amendment prohibits Colorado from requiring Phillips to "bear witness to [these] fact[s]," or to "affir[m] . . . a belief with which [he] disagrees."

In *Obergefell*, I warned that the Court's decision would "inevitabl[y] . . . come into conflict" with religious liberty, "as individuals . . . are confronted with demands to participate in and endorse civil marriages between same-sex couples." This case proves that the conflict has already emerged. Because the Court's decision vindicates Phillips' right to free exercise, it seems that religious liberty has lived to fight another day. But, in future cases, the freedom of speech could be essential to preventing *Obergefell* from being used to "stamp out every vestige of dissent" and "vilify Americans who are unwilling to assent to the new orthodoxy."

Justice GINSBURG, with whom Justice SOTOMAYOR joins, dissenting.

There is much in the Court's opinion with which I agree. "[I]t is a general rule that [religious and philosophical] objections do not allow business owners and other actors in the economy and in society to deny protected persons equal access to goods and services under a neutral and generally applicable public accommodations law." "Colorado law can protect gay persons, just as it can protect other classes of individuals, in acquiring whatever products and services they choose on the same terms and conditions as are offered to other members of the public." "[P]urveyors of goods and services who object to gay marriages for moral and religious reasons [may not] put up signs saying 'no goods or services will be sold if they will be used for gay marriages.'" Gay persons may be spared from "indignities when they seek goods and services in an open market." I strongly disagree, however, with the Court's conclusion that Craig and Mullins should lose this case. All of the above-quoted statements point in the opposite direction.

The Court concludes that "Phillips' religious objection was not considered with the neutrality that the Free Exercise Clause requires." This conclusion rests on evidence said to show the Colorado Civil Rights Commission's (Commission) hostility to religion. Hostility is discernible, the Court maintains, from the asserted "disparate consideration of Phillips' case compared to the cases of" three other bakers who refused to make cakes requested by William Jack. The Court also finds hostility in statements made at two public hearings on Phillips' appeal to the Commission. The different outcomes the Court features do not evidence hostility to religion of the kind we have previously held to signal a free-exercise violation, nor do the comments by one or two members of one of the four decisionmaking entities considering this case justify reversing the judgment below.

The Court concludes that "the Commission's consideration of Phillips' religious objection did not accord with its treatment of [the other bakers'] objections." But the cases the Court aligns are hardly comparable. The bakers would have refused to make a cake with Jack's requested message for any customer, regardless of his or her religion. And the bakers visited by Jack would have sold him any baked goods they would have sold anyone else. The bakeries' refusal to make Jack cakes of a kind they would not make for any customer scarcely resembles Phillips' refusal to serve Craig and Mullins: Phillips would *not* sell to Craig and Mullins, for no reason other than their sexual orientation, a cake of the kind he regularly sold to others. When a couple contacts a bakery for a wedding cake, the product they are seeking is a cake celebrating *their* wedding—not a cake celebrating heterosexual weddings or same-sex weddings—and that is the service Craig and Mullins were denied. Colorado, the Court does not gainsay, prohibits precisely the discrimination Craig and Mullins encountered. Jack, on the other hand, suffered no service refusal on the basis of his religion or any other protected characteristic. He was treated as any other customer would have been treated—no better, no worse.

The fact that Phillips might sell other cakes and cookies to gay and lesbian customers[4] was irrelevant to the issue Craig and Mullins' case presented. What matters is that Phillips would not provide a good or service to a same-sex couple that he would provide to a heterosexual couple. In contrast, the other bakeries' sale of other goods to Christian customers was relevant: It shows that there were no goods the bakeries would sell to a non-Christian customer that they would refuse to sell to a Christian customer.

Statements made at the Commission's public hearings on Phillips' case provide no firmer support for the Court's holding today. Whatever one may think of the statements in historical context, I see no reason why the comments of one or two Commissioners should be taken to overcome Phillips' refusal to sell a wedding cake to Craig and Mullins. The proceedings involved several layers of independent decisionmaking, of which the Commission was but one. First, the Division had to find probable cause that Phillips violated CADA. Second, the ALJ entertained the parties' cross-motions for summary judgment. Third, the Commission heard Phillips' appeal. Fourth, after the Commission's ruling, the Colorado Court of Appeals considered the case *de novo*. What prejudice infected the determinations of the adjudicators in the case before and after the Commission? The Court does not say. Phillips' case is thus far removed from the only precedent upon which the Court relies, *Church of Lukumi Babalu Aye, Inc. v. Hialeah* (1993), where the government action that violated a principle of religious neutrality implicated a sole decisionmaking body, the city council.

# 1.  Is the Denial of Funding for Religious Education a Violation of Free Exercise of Religion? (casebook p. 1756)

### TRINITY LUTHERAN CHURCH OF COLUMBIA, MISSOURI v. PAULEY
137 S. Ct. 2012 (2017)

Chief Justice ROBERTS delivered the opinion of the Court, except as to footnote 3.

The Missouri Department of Natural Resources offers state grants to help public and private schools, nonprofit daycare centers, and other nonprofit entities purchase rubber playground surfaces made from recycled tires. Trinity Lutheran Church applied for such a grant for its preschool and daycare center and would have received one, but for the fact that Trinity Lutheran is a church. The Department had a policy of categorically disqualifying churches and other religious organizations from receiving grants under its playground resurfacing program. The question presented is whether the Department's policy violated the rights of Trinity Lutheran under the Free Exercise Clause of the First Amendment.

I

A

The Trinity Lutheran Church Child Learning Center is a preschool and daycare center open throughout the year to serve working families in Boone County, Missouri, and the surrounding area. Established as a nonprofit organization in 1980, the Center merged with Trinity Lutheran Church in 1985 and operates under its auspices on church property. The Center admits students of any religion, and enrollment stands at about 90 children ranging from age two to five.

The Center includes a playground that is equipped with the basic playground essentials: slides, swings, jungle gyms, monkey bars, and sandboxes. Almost the entire surface beneath and surrounding the play equipment is coarse pea gravel. Youngsters, of course, often fall on the playground or tumble from the equipment. And when they do, the gravel can be unforgiving.

In 2012, the Center sought to replace a large portion of the pea gravel with a pour-in-place rubber surface by participating in Missouri's Scrap Tire Program. Run by the State's Department of Natural Resources to reduce the number of used tires destined for landfills and dump sites, the program offers reimbursement grants to qualifying nonprofit organizations that purchase playground surfaces made from recycled tires. It is funded through a fee imposed on the sale of new tires in the State.

Due to limited resources, the Department cannot offer grants to all applicants and so awards them on a competitive basis to those scoring highest based on several criteria, such as the poverty level of the population in the surrounding area and the applicant's plan to promote recycling. When the Center applied, the Department had a strict and express policy of denying grants to any applicant owned or controlled by a church, sect, or other religious entity. That policy, in the Department's view, was compelled by Article I, Section 7 of the Missouri Constitution, which provides: "That no money shall ever be taken from the public treasury, directly or indirectly, in aid of any church, sect or denomination of religion, or in aid of any priest, preacher, minister or teacher thereof, as such; and that no preference shall be given to nor any discrimination made against any church, sect or creed of religion, or any form of religious faith or worship."

The Center ranked fifth among the 44 applicants in the 2012 Scrap Tire Program. But despite its high score, the Center was deemed categorically ineligible to receive a grant. In a letter rejecting the Center's application, the program director explained that, under Article I, Section 7 of the Missouri Constitution, the Department could not provide financial assistance directly to a church.

The Department ultimately awarded 14 grants as part of the 2012 program. Because the Center was operated by Trinity Lutheran Church, it did not receive a grant.

B

Trinity Lutheran sued the Director of the Department in Federal District Court. The Church alleged that the Department's failure to approve the Center's application, pursuant to its policy of denying grants to religiously affiliated applicants, violates the Free Exercise Clause of the First Amendment. Trinity Lutheran sought declaratory and injunctive relief prohibiting the Department from discriminating against the Church on that basis in future grant applications.

The District Court granted the Department's motion to dismiss. The Free Exercise Clause, the District Court stated, prohibits the government from outlawing or restricting the exercise of a religious practice; it generally does not prohibit withholding an affirmative benefit on account of religion. The District Court likened the Department's denial of the scrap tire grant to the situation this Court encountered in *Locke v. Davey* (2004). In that case, we upheld against a free exercise challenge the State of Washington's decision not to fund degrees in devotional theology as part of a state scholarship program. Finding the present case "nearly indistinguishable from *Locke,*" the District Court held that the Free Exercise Clause did not require the State to make funds available under the Scrap Tire Program to religious institutions like Trinity Lutheran. The Court of Appeals for the Eighth Circuit affirmed.

## II

The First Amendment provides, in part, that "Congress shall make no law respecting an establishment of religion, or prohibiting the free exercise thereof." The parties agree that the Establishment Clause of that Amendment does not prevent Missouri from including Trinity Lutheran in the Scrap Tire Program. That does not, however, answer the question under the Free Exercise Clause, because we have recognized that there is "play in the joints" between what the Establishment Clause permits and the Free Exercise Clause compels.

The Free Exercise Clause "protect[s] religious observers against unequal treatment" and subjects to the strictest scrutiny laws that target the religious for "special disabilities" based on their "religious status." Applying that basic principle, this Court has repeatedly confirmed that denying a generally available benefit solely on account of religious identity imposes a penalty on the free exercise of religion that can be justified only by a state interest "of the highest order."

In *Everson v. Board of Education of Ewing* (1947), for example, we upheld against an Establishment Clause challenge a New Jersey law enabling a local school district to reimburse parents for the public transportation costs of sending their children to public and private schools, including parochial schools. In the course of ruling that the Establishment Clause allowed New Jersey to extend that public benefit to all its citizens regardless of their religious belief, we explained that a State "cannot hamper its citizens in the free exercise of their own religion. Consequently, it cannot exclude individual Catholics, Lutherans, Mohammedans, Baptists, Jews, Methodists, Non-believers, Presbyterians, or the members of any other faith, *because of their faith, or lack of it,* from receiving the benefits of public welfare legislation."

## III

### A

The Department's policy expressly discriminates against otherwise eligible recipients by disqualifying them from a public benefit solely because of their religious character. If the cases just described make one thing clear, it is that such a policy imposes a penalty on the free exercise of religion that triggers the most exacting scrutiny. This conclusion is unremarkable in light of our prior decisions.

The Department contends that merely declining to extend funds to Trinity Lutheran does not *prohibit* the Church from engaging in any religious conduct or otherwise exercising its religious rights. Here the Department has simply declined to allocate to Trinity Lutheran a subsidy the State had no obligation to provide in the first place. That decision does not meaningfully burden the Church's free exercise rights. And absent any such burden, the argument continues, the Department is free to heed the State's antiestablishment objection to providing funds directly to a church.

It is true the Department has not criminalized the way Trinity Lutheran worships or told the Church that it cannot subscribe to a certain view of the Gospel. But, as the Department itself acknowledges, the Free Exercise Clause protects against "indirect coercion or penalties on the free exercise of religion, not just outright prohibitions." As the Court put it more than 50 years ago, "[i]t is too late in the day to doubt that the liberties of religion and expression may be infringed by the denial of or placing of conditions upon a benefit or privilege."

Trinity Lutheran is not claiming any entitlement to a subsidy. It instead asserts a right to participate in a government benefit program without having to disavow its religious character. The "imposition of such a condition upon even a gratuitous benefit inevitably deter[s] or discourage[s] the exercise of First Amendment rights." The express discrimination against religious exercise here is not the denial of a grant, but rather the refusal to allow the Church — solely because it is a church — to compete with secular organizations for a grant. Trinity Lutheran is a member of the community too, and the State's decision to exclude it for purposes of this public program must withstand the strictest scrutiny.

B

The Department attempts to get out from under the weight of our precedents by arguing that the free exercise question in this case is instead controlled by our decision in *Locke v. Davey*. It is not. In *Locke*, the State of Washington created a scholarship program to assist high-achieving students with the costs of postsecondary education. The scholarships were paid out of the State's general fund, and eligibility was based on criteria such as an applicant's score on college admission tests and family income. While scholarship recipients were free to use the money at accredited religious and non-religious schools alike, they were not permitted to use the funds to pursue a devotional theology degree — one "devotional in nature or designed to induce religious faith." Davey was selected for a scholarship but was denied the funds when he refused to certify that he would not use them toward a devotional degree. He sued, arguing that the State's refusal to allow its scholarship money to go toward such degrees violated his free exercise rights.

At the outset the Court made clear that *Locke* was not like the case now before us.

Washington's restriction on the use of its scholarship funds was different. According to the Court, the State had "merely chosen not to fund a distinct category of instruction." Davey was not denied a scholarship because of who he *was*; he was denied a scholarship because of what he proposed *to do* — use the funds to prepare for the ministry. Here there is no question that Trinity Lutheran was denied a grant simply because of what it is — a church.

The Court in *Locke* also stated that Washington's choice was in keeping with the State's antiestablishment interest in not using taxpayer funds to pay for the training of clergy; in fact, the Court could "think of few areas in which a State's antiestablishment interests come more into play." The claimant in *Locke* sought funding for an "essentially religious endeavor . . . akin to a religious calling as well as an academic pursuit," and opposition to such funding "to support church leaders" lay at the historic core of the Religion Clauses. Here nothing of the sort can be said about a program to use recycled tires to resurface playgrounds.

Relying on *Locke*, the Department nonetheless emphasizes Missouri's similar constitutional tradition of not furnishing taxpayer money directly to churches. But *Locke* took account of Washington's antiestablishment interest only after determining, as noted, that the scholarship program did not "require students to choose between their religious beliefs and receiving a government benefit." As the Court put it, Washington's scholarship program went "a long way toward including religion in its benefits." Students in the program were free to use their scholarships at "pervasively religious schools." Davey could use his scholarship to pursue a secular degree at one institution while studying devotional theology at another. He could also use his scholarship money to attend a religious college and take devotional theology courses there. The only thing he could not do was use the scholarship to pursue a degree in that subject.

In this case, there is no dispute that Trinity Lutheran *is* put to the choice between being a church and receiving a government benefit. The rule is simple: No churches need apply.[3]

## C

The State in this case expressly requires Trinity Lutheran to renounce its religious character in order to participate in an otherwise generally available public benefit program, for which it is fully qualified. Our cases make clear that such a condition imposes a penalty on the free exercise of religion that must be subjected to the "most rigorous" scrutiny.

Under that stringent standard, only a state interest "of the highest order" can justify the Department's discriminatory policy. Yet the Department offers nothing more than Missouri's policy preference for skating as far as possible from religious establishment concerns. In the face of the clear infringement on free exercise before us, that interest cannot qualify as compelling. As we said when considering Missouri's same policy preference on a prior occasion, "the state interest asserted here — in achieving greater separation of church and State than is already ensured under the Establishment Clause of the Federal Constitution — is limited by the Free Exercise Clause."

The State has pursued its preferred policy to the point of expressly denying a qualified religious entity a public benefit solely because of its religious character. Under our precedents, that goes too far. The Department's policy violates the Free Exercise Clause.

Nearly 200 years ago, a legislator urged the Maryland Assembly to adopt a bill that would end the State's disqualification of Jews from public office: "If, on account of my religious faith, I am subjected to disqualifications, from which others are free, . . . I cannot but consider myself a persecuted man. . . . An odious exclusion from any of the benefits common to the rest of my fellow-citizens, is a persecution, differing only in degree, but of a nature equally unjustifiable with that, whose instruments are chains and torture."

The Missouri Department of Natural Resources has not subjected anyone to chains or torture on account of religion. And the result of the State's policy is nothing so dramatic as the denial of political office. The

---

3. This case involves express discrimination based on religious identity with respect to playground resurfacing. We do not address religious uses of funding or other forms of discrimination. [Footnote by the Court.]

consequence is, in all likelihood, a few extra scraped knees. But the exclusion of Trinity Lutheran from a public benefit for which it is otherwise qualified, solely because it is a church, is odious to our Constitution all the same, and cannot stand.

Justice THOMAS, with whom Justice GORSUCH joins, concurring in part.

This Court's endorsement in *Locke* of even a "mil[d] kind" of discrimination against religion remains troubling. But because the Court today appropriately construes *Locke* narrowly, and because no party has asked us to reconsider it, I join nearly all of the Court's opinion. I do not, however, join footnote 3, for the reasons expressed by Justice Gorsuch.

Justice GORSUCH, with whom Justice THOMAS joins, concurring in part.

Missouri's law bars Trinity Lutheran from participating in a public benefits program only because it is a church. I agree this violates the First Amendment and I am pleased to join nearly all of the Court's opinion. I offer only two modest qualifications.

First, the Court leaves open the possibility a useful distinction might be drawn between laws that discriminate on the basis of religious *status* and religious *use*. Respectfully, I harbor doubts about the stability of such a line. Does a religious man say grace before dinner? Or does a man begin his meal in a religious manner? Is it a religious group that built the playground? Or did a group build the playground so it might be used to advance a religious mission? The distinction blurs in much the same way the line between acts and omissions can blur when stared at too long, leaving us to ask (for example) whether the man who drowns by awaiting the incoming tide does so by act (coming upon the sea) or omission (allowing the sea to come upon him). Often enough the same facts can be described both ways.

Neither do I see why the First Amendment's Free Exercise Clause should care. After all, that Clause guarantees the free *exercise* of religion, not just the right to inward belief (or status). And this Court has long explained that government may not "devise mechanisms, overt or disguised, designed to persecute or oppress a religion or its practices." Generally the government may not force people to choose between participation in a public program and their right to free exercise of religion. I don't see why it should matter whether we describe that benefit, say, as closed to Lutherans (status) or closed to people who do Lutheran things (use). It is free exercise either way. For these reasons, reliance on the status-use distinction does not suffice for me to distinguish.

Second and for similar reasons, I am unable to join the footnoted observation that "[t]his case involves express discrimination based on religious identity with respect to playground resurfacing." Of course the footnote is entirely correct, but I worry that some might mistakenly read it to suggest that only "playground resurfacing" cases, or only those with some association with children's safety or health, or perhaps some other social good we find sufficiently worthy, are governed by the legal rules recounted in and faithfully applied by the Court's opinion. Such a reading would be unreasonable for our cases are "governed by general principles, rather than ad hoc improvisations." And the general principles here do not permit discrimination against religious exercise — whether on the playground or anywhere else.

Justice BREYER concurring in the judgment.

I agree with much of what the Court says and with its result. But I find relevant, and would emphasize, the particular nature of the "public benefit" here at issue. The Court stated in *Everson* that "cutting off church schools from" such "general government services as ordinary police and fire protection . . . is obviously not the purpose of the Here, the State would cut Trinity Lutheran off from participation in a general program designed to secure or to improve the health and safety of children. I see no significant difference. The fact that the program at issue ultimately funds only a limited number of projects cannot itself justify a religious distinction. Nor is there any administrative or other reason to treat church schools differently. The sole reason advanced that explains the difference is faith. And it is that last-mentioned fact that calls the Free Exercise Clause into play. We need not go further. Public benefits come in many shapes and sizes. I would leave the application of the Free Exercise Clause to other kinds of public benefits for another day.

Justice SOTOMAYOR, with whom Justice GINSBURG joins, dissenting.

To hear the Court tell it, this is a simple case about recycling tires to resurface a playground. The stakes are higher. This case is about nothing less than the relationship between religious institutions and the civil government—that is, between church and state. The Court today profoundly changes that relationship by holding, for the first time, that the Constitution requires the government to provide public funds directly to a church. Its decision slights both our precedents and our history, and its reasoning weakens this country's longstanding commitment to a separation of church and state beneficial to both.

## I

Founded in 1922, Trinity Lutheran Church (Church) "operates . . . for the express purpose of carrying out the commission of . . . Jesus Christ as directed to His church on earth." The Church uses "preaching, teaching, worship, witness, service, and fellowship according to the Word of God" to carry out its mission "to 'make disciples.'" The Church's religious beliefs include its desire to "associat[e] with the [Trinity Church Child] Learning Center." The Learning Center serves as "a ministry of the Church and incorporates daily religion and developmentally appropriate activities into . . . [its] program." In this way, "[t]hrough the Learning Center, the Church teaches a Christian world view to children of members of the Church, as well as children of non-member residents" of the area. These activities represent the Church's "sincere religious belief . . . to use [the Learning Center] to teach the Gospel to children of its members, as well to bring the Gospel message to non-members."

## II

Properly understood then, this is a case about whether Missouri can decline to fund improvements to the facilities the Church uses to practice and spread its religious views. This Court has repeatedly warned that funding of exactly this kind—payments from the government to a house of worship—would cross the line drawn by the Establishment Clause. So it is surprising that the Court mentions the Establishment Clause only to note the parties' agreement that it "does not prevent Missouri from including Trinity Lutheran in the Scrap Tire Program." Constitutional questions are decided by this Court, not the parties' concessions. The Establishment Clause does not allow Missouri to grant the Church's funding request because the Church uses the Learning Center, including its playground, in conjunction with its religious mission. The Court's silence on this front signals either its misunderstanding of the facts of this case or a startling departure from our precedents.

The government may not directly fund religious exercise. Nowhere is this rule more clearly implicated than when funds flow directly from the public treasury to a house of worship. A house of worship exists to foster and further religious exercise. When a government funds a house of worship, it underwrites this religious exercise.

This case is no different. The Church seeks state funds to improve the Learning Center's facilities, which, by the Church's own avowed description, are used to assist the spiritual growth of the children of its members and to spread the Church's faith to the children of nonmembers. The Church's playground surface—like a Sunday School room's walls or the sanctuary's pews—are integrated with and integral to its religious mission. The conclusion that the funding the Church seeks would impermissibly advance religion is inescapable.

True, this Court has found some direct government funding of religious institutions to be consistent with the Establishment Clause. But the funding in those cases came with assurances that public funds would not be used for religious activity, despite the religious nature of the institution. The Church has not and cannot provide such assurances here. The Church has a religious mission, one that it pursues through the Learning Center. The playground surface cannot be confined to secular use any more than lumber used to frame the Church's walls, glass stained and used to form its windows, or nails used to build its altar.

The Court may simply disagree with this account of the facts and think that the Church does not put its playground to religious use. If so, its mistake is limited to this case. But if it agrees that the State's funding would further religious activity and sees no Establishment Clause problem, then it must be implicitly applying a rule other than the one agreed to in our precedents.

When the Court last addressed direct funding of religious institutions, in *Mitchell*, it adhered to the rule that the Establishment Clause prohibits the direct funding of religious activities.

Today's opinion suggests the Court has made the leap the *Mitchell* plurality could not. For if it agrees that the funding here will finance religious activities, then only a rule that considers that fact irrelevant could support a conclusion of constitutionality. It has no basis in the history to which the Court has repeatedly turned to inform its understanding of the Establishment Clause. It permits direct subsidies for religious indoctrination, with all the attendant concerns that led to the Establishment Clause. And it favors certain religious groups, those with a belief system that allows them to compete for public dollars and those well-organized and well-funded enough to do so successfully.

Such a break with precedent would mark a radical mistake. The Establishment Clause protects both religion and government from the dangers that result when the two become entwined, "*not* by providing every religion with an *equal opportunity* (say, to secure state funding or to pray in the public schools), but by drawing fairly clear lines of *separation* between church and state—at least where the heartland of religious belief, such as primary religious [worship], is at issue."

III

Even assuming the absence of an Establishment Clause violation and proceeding on the Court's preferred front—the Free Exercise Clause—the Court errs. It claims that the government may not draw lines based on an entity's religious "status." But we have repeatedly said that it can. When confronted with government action that draws such a line, we have carefully considered whether the interests embodied in the Religion Clauses justify that line. The question here is thus whether those interests support the line drawn in Missouri's Article I, § 7, separating the State's treasury from those of houses of worship. They unquestionably do.

The Establishment Clause prohibits laws "respecting an establishment of religion" and the Free Exercise Clause prohibits laws "prohibiting the free exercise thereof." "[I]f expanded to a logical extreme," these prohibitions "would tend to clash with the other." Even in the absence of a violation of one of the Religion Clauses, the interaction of government and religion can raise concerns that sound in both Clauses. For that reason, the government may sometimes act to accommodate those concerns, even when not required to do so by the Free Exercise Clause, without violating the Establishment Clause. And the government may sometimes act to accommodate those concerns, even when not required to do so by the Establishment Clause, without violating the Free Exercise Clause. "[T]here is room for play in the joints productive of a benevolent neutrality which will permit religious exercise to exist without sponsorship and without interference." This space between the two Clauses gives government some room to recognize the unique status of religious entities and to single them out on that basis for exclusion from otherwise generally applicable laws.

Invoking this principle, this Court has held that the government may sometimes relieve religious entities from the requirements of government programs. A State need not, for example, require nonprofit houses of worship to pay property taxes. Nor must a State require nonprofit religious entities to abstain from making employment decisions on the basis of religion. But the government may not invoke the space between the Religion Clauses in a manner that "devolve[s] into an unlawful fostering of religion."

Missouri has decided that the unique status of houses of worship requires a special rule when it comes to public funds. Its Constitution reflects that choice and provides:

"That no money shall ever be taken from the public treasury, directly or indirectly, in aid of any church, sect, or denomination of religion, or in aid of any priest, preacher, minister or teacher thereof, as such; and that no preference shall be given to nor any discrimination made against any church, sect or creed of religion, or any form of religious faith or worship." Art. I, § 7.

Missouri's decision, which has deep roots in our Nation's history, reflects a reasonable and constitutional judgment.

This Court has consistently looked to history for guidance when applying the Constitution's Religion Clauses. Those Clauses guard against a return to the past, and so that past properly informs their meaning. This case is no different.

Those who fought to end the public funding of religion based their opposition on a powerful set of arguments, all stemming from the basic premise that the practice harmed both civil government and religion. The civil government, they maintained, could claim no authority over religious belief. For them, support for religion compelled by the State marked an overstep of authority that would only lead to more. Equally troubling, it risked divisiveness by giving religions reason to compete for the State's beneficence. Faith, they believed, was a personal matter, entirely between an individual and his god. Religion was best served when sects reached out on the basis of their tenets alone, unsullied by outside forces, allowing adherents to come to their faith voluntarily. Over and over, these arguments gained acceptance and led to the end of state laws exacting payment for the support of religion.

In *Locke*, this Court expressed an understanding of, and respect for, this history.

The same is true of this case, about directing taxpayer funds to houses of worship. Like the use of public dollars for ministers at issue in *Locke*, turning over public funds to houses of worship implicates serious anti-establishment and free exercise interests. The history just discussed fully supports this conclusion. As states disestablished, they repealed laws allowing taxation to support religion because the practice threatened other forms of government support for, involved some government control over, and weakened supporters' control of religion. Common sense also supports this conclusion. Recall that a state may not fund religious activities without violating the Establishment Clause. A state can reasonably use status as a "house of worship" as a stand-in for "religious activities." Inside a house of worship, dividing the religious from the secular would require intrusive line-drawing by government, and monitoring those lines would entangle government with the house of worship's activities. And so while not every activity a house of worship undertakes will be inseparably linked to religious activity, "the likelihood that many are makes a categorical rule a suitable means to avoid chilling the exercise of religion."

Finally, and of course, such funding implicates the free exercise rights of taxpayers by denying them the chance to decide for themselves whether and how to fund religion. If there is any "'room for play in the joints' between" the Religion Clauses, it is here.

As was true in *Locke*, a prophylactic rule against the use of public funds for houses of worship is a permissible accommodation of these weighty interests. The rule has a historical pedigree identical to that of the provision in Today, thirty-eight States have a counterpart to Missouri's Article I, § 7. The provisions, as a general matter, date back to or before these States' original Constitutions. That so many States have for so long drawn a line that prohibits public funding for houses of worship, based on principles rooted in this Nation's understanding of how best to foster religious liberty, supports the conclusion that public funding of houses of worship "is of a different ilk."

Missouri has recognized the simple truth that, even absent an Establishment Clause violation, the transfer of public funds to houses of worship raises concerns that sit exactly between the Religion Clauses. To avoid those concerns, and only those concerns, it has prohibited such funding. In doing so, it made the same choice made by the earliest States centuries ago and many other States in the years since. The Constitution permits this choice.

In the Court's view, none of this matters. It focuses on one aspect of Missouri's Article I, § 7, to the exclusion of all else: that it denies funding to a house of worship, here the Church, "simply because of what it [i]s — a church."

Start where the Court stays silent. Its opinion does not acknowledge that our precedents have expressly approved of a government's choice to draw lines based on an entity's religious status. Those cases did not deploy strict scrutiny to create a presumption of unconstitutionality, as the Court does today. Instead, they asked whether the government had offered a strong enough reason to justify drawing a line based on that status.

The Court takes two steps to avoid these precedents. First, it recasts *Locke* as a case about a restriction that prohibited the would-be minister from "us[ing] the funds to prepare for the ministry." A faithful reading of *Locke* gives it a broader reach. *Locke* stands for the reasonable proposition that the government may, but need not, choose not to fund certain religious entities (there, ministers) where doing so raises "historic and substantial" establishment and free exercise concerns.

Second, it suggests that this case is different because it involves "discrimination" in the form of the denial of access to a possible benefit. But in this area of law, a decision to treat entities differently based on distinctions that the Religion Clauses make relevant does not amount to discrimination. To understand why, keep in mind that "the Court has unambiguously concluded that the individual freedom of conscience protected by the First Amendment embraces the right to select any religious faith or none at all." If the denial of a benefit others may receive is discrimination that violates the Free Exercise Clause, then the accommodations of religious entities we have approved would violate the free exercise rights of nonreligious entities. We have, with good reason, rejected that idea and instead focused on whether the government has provided a good enough reason, based in the values the Religion Clauses protect, for its decision.

The Court offers no real reason for rejecting the balancing approach in our precedents in favor of strict scrutiny, beyond its references to discrimination. The Court's desire to avoid what it views as discrimination is understandable. But in this context, the description is particularly inappropriate. A State's decision not to fund houses of worship does not disfavor religion; rather, it represents a valid choice to remain secular in the face of serious establishment and free exercise concerns. That does not make the State "atheistic or antireligious." The Court's conclusion "that the only alternative to governmental support of religion is governmental hostility to it represents a giant step backward in our Religion Clause jurisprudence."

At bottom, the Court creates the following rule today: The government may draw lines on the basis of religious status to grant a benefit to religious persons or entities but it may not draw lines on that basis when doing so would further the interests the Religion Clauses protect in other ways. Nothing supports this lopsided outcome. Not the Religion Clauses, as they protect establishment and free exercise interests in the same constitutional breath, neither privileged over the other. Not precedent, since we have repeatedly explained that the Clauses protect not religion but "the individual's freedom of conscience," — that which allows him to choose religion, reject it, or remain undecided. And not reason, because as this case shows, the same interests served by lifting government-imposed burdens on certain religious entities may sometimes be equally served by denying government-provided benefits to certain religious entities.[14] Today's decision discounts centuries of history and jeopardizes the government's ability to remain secular.

---

14. In the end, the soundness of today's decision may matter less than what it might enable tomorrow. The principle it establishes can be manipulated to call for a similar fate for lines drawn on the basis of religious use. It is enough for today to explain why the Court's decision is wrong. The error of the concurrences' hoped-for decisions can be left for tomorrow. [Footnote by Justice Sotomayor.]

IV

The Court today dismantles a core protection for religious freedom provided in these Clauses. It holds not just that a government may support houses of worship with taxpayer funds, but that—at least in this case and perhaps in others, it must do so whenever it decides to create a funding program. History shows that the Religion Clauses separate the public treasury from religious coffers as one measure to secure the kind of freedom of conscience that benefits both religion and government. If this separation means anything, it means that the government cannot, or at the very least need not, tax its citizens and turn that money over to houses of worship. The Court today blinds itself to the outcome this history requires and leads us instead to a place where separation of church and state is a constitutional slogan, not a constitutional commitment.

CPSIA information can be obtained
at www.ICGtesting.com
Printed in the USA
FSHW021204181218